# Drugs Disorder by Design

Elizabeth Peatfield

# Drugs Disorder by Design

## Why Britain's War on Drugs Targets the Poor and Protects the Privileged

palgrave
macmillan

Elizabeth Peatfield
Department of Criminal Justice
Liverpool John Moores University
Liverpool, UK

ISBN 978-3-032-07813-1 ISBN 978-3-032-07814-8 (eBook)
https://doi.org/10.1007/978-3-032-07814-8



This Palgrave Macmillan imprint is published by the registered company Springer Nature Switzerland AG
The registered company address is: Gewerbestrasse 11, 6330 Cham, Switzerland

If disposing of this product, please recycle the paper.

*This book is dedicated to my twin sister Amanda.*
*Your recovery from all the challenges you have faced in your life is an inspiration.*
*The way you have changed your life around and taken charge of it is fabulous, and I am in awe of you for doing this.*
*It's been a long, old, complicated road, but you got there kiddo and mum would have been so proud of the woman you have become.*
*Keep growing, keep learning and love yourself, like I love you*
*Your Twinny*
*Lizzbeth*

# Preface

The words *drugs* and *drug user* still evoke a particular image in the public imagination: dirty needles, broken lives, crime-ridden backstreets. It's a powerful image—but it's also deeply misleading. The truth is, nearly all of us are drug users in one way or another. Whether it's the paracetamol we pop for a headache, the coffee we crave to get through the day, or the sugar we scoff in celebration, drug use is part of everyday life. We've just normalised some substances and demonised others—and that double standard is at the heart of this book.

The term *drugs* has been weaponised, reduced to a caricature: someone with a needle in their arm, strung out and broken. But most drug use in the UK is functional, not chaotic. Many people use substances—illegal and legal alike—without serious harm. Some even experience benefit, whether it's with cannabis, MDMA, or psychedelics. But our policies don't make that distinction. They criminalise use rather than understand it.

Every year, I ask my students, "How many of you drink alcohol?" Almost every hand goes up. Then I ask, "How many of you consider yourselves alcoholics?" Silence. The point is simple: using a drug is not the same as abusing it. And yet, our legal and policing frameworks often ignore that nuance.

I come to this topic wearing a few different hats. As a former magistrate, I've seen first-hand how drug laws derail lives—especially those of young, working-class people from minoritised communities. As a criminologist, I've studied how these laws fail to reduce harm and often exacerbate it. And as someone who spent over two decades working Liverpool's night-time economy as a bouncer from the late 80s to the new millennium, I've lived through the evolution of street-level drug trends—from speed and booze in the '80s, to coke and ecstasy in the '90s, to today's surge in ketamine use. I've seen both the communal joy and the very real risks associated with drug use.

One night in particular still haunts me. A young woman, just starting university, died after taking a pill she believed was ecstasy. It had been cut with ketamine—something she was unknowingly allergic to. That tragedy wasn't caused by MDMA. It was caused by prohibition: by the criminalised, unregulated market that produces unknown, unpredictable substances. It was caused by a system that creates harm under the guise of preventing it.

We need to talk honestly about why people use drugs—not just to escape or self-medicate, but because it feels good. Pleasure, connection, curiosity—these too are reasons people take drugs. And yet, our policies deny this reality, feeding a moral panic that has very little to do with evidence or outcomes.

If harm were truly the measure of policy, then alcohol and tobacco—two of the most damaging substances available—would be far more restricted. Instead, they're legal, taxed, and culturally celebrated. Meanwhile, less harmful substances remain outlawed, and their users punished. The hypocrisy is staggering. We're told drug laws are rooted in science. But if you've lived in a city like Liverpool, you'll know that most people you grow up with have used both legal and illegal substances. These acts aren't deviant. They're normal. So why are some branded criminals, while others are left alone—or even applauded?

This book is a call for honesty. It offers critique, but also clarity. You'll find academic analysis, yes—but also stories from courtrooms, club nights, and everyday life. Stories of joy and injustice, of contradictions and courage. I hope they make you think, feel, and maybe even change your mind.

Because if we don't start telling the truth about drugs, we'll keep enforcing a policy that isn't just broken—it's *disorder by design*.

Liverpool, UK Elizabeth Peatfield

# About This Book

This book critically examines the failures and contradictions of UK drug policy, exposing how current laws disproportionately target marginalised communities while overlooking the widespread harms of legal substances like alcohol. Drawing on the author's unique experiences as a magistrate and bouncer, alongside academic research, policy analysis, and lived experience testimonies, it reveals the systemic injustices embedded in drug enforcement. By contrasting the treatment of so-called "problematic" versus "functional" drug users, the book highlights how class, race, and power shape who is punished and who is protected. It also interrogates the influence of moral panic, media narratives, and political ideology on drug legislation, questioning the absence of evidence-based, harm-reduction approaches. Ultimately, the book aims to challenge prevailing assumptions, inform public discourse, and advocate for a more just, ethical, and effective drug policy rooted in health, evidence, and equality.

# Introduction

This book is a blend of academic knowledge, research practice, and lived experience. It draws on decades of observation and involvement with drugs and drug users, both professionally and personally.

Growing up in Liverpool in the early 1960/1970s, I was always surrounded by drugs of one kind or another. To be honest, we all are—it just depends on what we define as a "drug." Many of the people I grew up with, including friends and their parents, used substances in one form or another. Whether it was alcohol, cigarettes, marijuana, or even mushrooms, drug use was part of the social fabric.

No one ever encouraged me to take drugs, but my thinking around their use has always been shaped by the social context I grew up in. That's the crux of it: we all use drugs. Whether you rely on steroids for asthma, take a paracetamol for a headache, enjoy a morning coffee, or use energy drinks to get through the day—unless you're extremely lucky and extremely healthy, you've used a drug at some point.

But the problem isn't drugs. It's the stories we tell about them—who's allowed to use them, and who's punished for doing so. As a former magistrate and a criminologist, I've seen the stark contrast between how society treats "respectable" drug use and how it criminalises and stigmatises others. The same drug, when taken by a white-collar professional, can be overlooked or excused—but in the hands of someone poor, racialised, or already marginalised, it becomes a justification for surveillance, punishment, or exclusion.

So, what is it about certain drugs that causes so much fear and controversy? Why do some substances spark public outrage or moral panic, while others are silently accepted or even promoted? Why do politicians treat drug policy like a game, constantly shifting the narrative without ever tackling the real issues?

I've seen both the benefits of drugs and the dark consequences of addiction. But after all these years (and I am quite old now), I can honestly say: no other area of law and policy feels as random and inconsistent as drug legislation. You'd think drug policy would be guided by scientific research, by principles of harm reduction, or at the very least by health outcomes—but nothing could be further from the truth.

This book sets out to explore those contradictions. It will examine the policies, highlight both good and bad practice, and weave in stories from my many years of working as a bouncer, and from my time engaging with drug users, enforcers, and communities. These personal tales are not here for shock value—they serve as lived illustrations of the policy failures (and occasional successes) that shape the UK's relationship with drugs.

As you read this book, I ask you to honestly reflect on a few key questions: What makes a drug dangerous? Why is it that some substances—like alcohol, arguably one of the most toxic and harmful drugs available—are legal and widely consumed, while others, like ecstasy (which was originally designed to be a safer alternative to alcohol), are banned and heavily criminalised? Yes, I did say designed to be safe—and we'll come back to that.

You also need to consider: What does prohibition really look like to you? What kinds of drug use do you consider acceptable, and what kinds are not—and, more importantly, why? What shapes your view? Is it based on evidence, or on what you were taught to fear?

What harms does prohibition actually cause? And is the enormous investment of time, money, and resources by the criminal justice system to keep many drugs illegal really worth it? These are uncomfortable questions—but essential ones if we want a policy that serves public health and social justice, not just political theatre.

So, let's begin at the beginning.

Where did drug legislation come from? Why was it developed in the first place, and who exactly decided which substances should be criminalised—and which should be accepted, taxed, and sold? The truth is, drug laws were never purely about health, science, or public safety.

From the very start, they were shaped by politics, racism, class prejudice, and colonial power structures. The early waves of legislation weren't introduced to protect people from harm—they were often about protecting the powerful, controlling certain populations, and reinforcing social hierarchies.

To understand how we got to today's messy and contradictory state of affairs, we need to look at the origins of drug control—both in Britain and globally. In doing so, we'll see that the question has rarely been "how dangerous is this drug?" and more often "who is using it — and how can we control them?"

# About the Author

**Dr. Elizabeth Peatfield** is a criminologist and senior lecturer in criminal justice at Liverpool John Moores University, UK, where she specialises in drug policy, criminal justice inequality, and lived experience research. She is Fellow of the Higher Education Academy. Before entering academia, she worked for more than 20 years as a bouncer in Liverpool's vibrant and chaotic nightlife scene and later served as a magistrate, presiding over drug-related cases in England's lower courts.

# Contents

CHAPTER 1

# A Condensed History of British Drug Policy and Legislation (1860–Present)

**Abstract** This chapter offers a critical historical overview of British drug policy and legislation from 1860s to the present, examining how shifting legal frameworks and political ideologies have shaped the national approach to substance use. It traces the evolution from Victorian-era medical regulation through the criminalisation solidified by the Dangerous Drugs Act 1920 and the emergence of the distinctive "British System" of medically supervised drug maintenance in the mid-twentieth century. It then analyses the seismic shift ushered in by the Misuse of Drugs Act 1971, which entrenched a punitive model of prohibition that still governs UK drug policy today.

The chapter explores key developments across subsequent decades, including the rise of recreational drug use in the 1960s, the moral panic of the 1980s, and the complex blend of public health and criminal justice strategies under New Labour. It also critically assesses more recent legislation such as the Psychoactive Substances Act 2016, arguing that symbolic lawmaking has often replaced evidence-led interventions. Special attention is paid to the political manipulation of drug classification, the marginalisation of scientific advisors, and the disproportionate policing of minority and working-class communities.

Moreover, the chapter highlights increasing divergence in drug policy within the UK's devolved administrations. While Scotland, Wales, and Northern Ireland have sought to embed harm reduction within broader



E. Peatfield, *Drugs Disorder by Design*,
https://doi.org/10.1007/978-3-032-07814-8_1

social services, Westminster has remained wedded to prohibitionist strategies. The final section considers international models—especially Portugal's decriminalisation approach—and evaluates growing domestic calls for reform grounded in public health, equity, and empirical evidence.

In sum, the chapter reveals that British drug policy has long struggled to reconcile the competing demands of law enforcement, medical ethics, and social justice. Despite rhetorical nods to harm reduction, criminalisation has remained the dominant response, often at odds with research and lived experience. As drug-related harms persist and political tensions deepen, the need for an honest, compassionate, and evidence-based policy framework is more pressing than ever.

**Keywords** Criminalisation-Harm Reduction · Misuse of Drugs Act 1971 · British System · Devolution · Public Health · Drug Classification · Prohibition · Drug Policy Reform · Evidence-Based Policy

## A Condensed History of British Drug Policy and Legislation (1860–Present)

British drug policy has evolved significantly from the laissez-faire attitudes of the nineteenth century to today's complex and often contradictory framework that oscillates between criminalisation, harm reduction, and public health. The nation's approach to controlled substances has never been linear; rather, it has been shaped by shifting political ideologies, moral panics, imperial interests, medical developments, and international pressures. From the early use of opium in patent medicines and the relative freedom of drug commerce in the Victorian era, through the establishment of strict controls in the early twentieth century, to the punitive but rhetorically health-oriented policies of the twenty-first century, the evolution of UK drug legislation reflects broader social anxieties and governmental priorities.

This chapter traces the development of drug policy in the UK from 1860 to the present day, critically evaluating the major legislative landmarks and the ideological underpinnings that have informed them. It begins by examining the regulatory origins of drug control, such as the Pharmacy Act 1868 and the Dangerous Drugs Act 1920, which laid the groundwork for a legal-medical approach to addiction. It then explores the rise and decline of the so-called "British System," a medical model of addiction management that offered a globally distinctive response to drug dependency. The analysis continues through the politicised turn of the 1971 Misuse of Drugs Act, which remains the cornerstone of modern prohibition, and into the late twentieth and early twenty-first centuries, where public health imperatives have struggled to assert themselves against entrenched criminal justice frameworks.

Critically, this chapter interrogates not only what laws were enacted but also why they were introduced, whose interests they served, and what impact they have had on individuals and communities. By evaluating these developments in historical and policy context, this account aims to shed light on the enduring contradictions within British drug policy—contradictions that remain highly relevant to debates around decriminalisation, harm reduction, and evidence-based reform today.

## Early Regulation: Medicines and Poisons (1860–1920)

The first significant step in British drug policy was the **Pharmacy Act 1868**, which sought to control the sale of poisons and certain drugs such as opium, morphine, and cocaine by restricting their sale to qualified pharmacists (Berridge, 1999). Notably, the act was rooted more in consumer safety than in moral panic or criminality. During the Victorian period, drug use was relatively unproblematic socially, with substances like opium and laudanum used widely and legally across classes (Musto, 1991).

However, concerns about dependency and social impact grew during the late nineteenth and early twentieth centuries, especially in the context of the British Empire and fears about non-white populations' drug habits being a threat to social order (Seddon, 2010). These anxieties culminated in the Dangerous Drugs Act 1920, influenced by Britain's obligations under the 1912 Hague Opium Convention. This Act marked a shift towards prohibitionist logic and introduced criminal penalties for possession and unlicensed supply.

"The 1920 Act formalised the ideological link between drug use and criminality, establishing a framework still recognisable in current policy" (Berridge, 1999; 172).

Medicalisation and the "British System" (1920–1960). Despite the criminalisation introduced by the Dangerous Drugs Act 1920, Britain adopted a relatively liberal and medically oriented approach to addiction management through what came to be known as the British System. Under this framework, doctors were permitted to prescribe controlled drugs such as heroin and morphine to individuals with addiction, provided they were registered and operating under the supervision of the Home Office. This model did not criminalise the addict as such but instead treated addiction as a chronic, relapsing medical condition that could be stabilised through ongoing medical care.

The approach was largely codified following the Rolleston Committee Report of 1926, chaired by Sir Humphry Rolleston. The report was a direct response to ambiguities in the 1920 legislation and growing concern over the professional role of doctors in the care of drug users. The committee concluded that, in certain cases, maintaining an individual on controlled substances might be preferable to withdrawal, particularly where abstinence would lead to severe distress, a breakdown of social functioning, or risk of death (Rolleston, 1926; Stimson, 1987). Rather than promoting abstinence as the only acceptable goal, the Rolleston Report explicitly permitted maintenance prescribing when it served the patient's best interests.

This pragmatic and non-punitive stance placed Britain in sharp contrast to the prohibitionist regimes emerging in the US, where addiction was increasingly viewed as a moral failure and criminal behaviour. In the UK, general practitioners retained the discretion to manage addiction within a clinical framework, and the Home Office issued licences to those authorised to prescribe. This fostered a relatively small and stable population of "notified addicts," the majority of whom were middle-class individuals addicted through medical use rather than recreational experimentation (Berridge, 1999).

Throughout the 1930s to the 1950s, this policy remained largely uncontroversial, with addiction numbers remaining low and largely invisible in public discourse. The British System attracted international attention for its apparent effectiveness and its humane ethos. By allowing controlled access to drugs, the system reduced the need for black market supply and prevented many of the harms associated with criminalisation and social marginalisation.

"The British System represented a unique model of harm minimisation before the term gained traction globally, allowing controlled use under medical guidance and reducing the risks associated with untreated or criminalised addiction" (Spear, 2002, p. 50). However, the system was not without flaws. Oversight was limited, and the decision to prescribe often rested on individual doctor discretion, which in rare cases led to overprescription or exploitation of the system. Additionally, the British System was largely class-bound and gendered—accessible primarily to white, middle-class patients, while those outside these social norms found it more difficult to access consistent medical care (Mold, 2008). Nevertheless, it reflected an early recognition of the complex social and medical nature of addiction—an insight that modern drug policy has, at times ***contestably***, lost sight of.

By reframing drug dependence as a condition requiring therapeutic management rather than moral judgement or criminal punishment, the British System laid a foundation for later harm reduction strategies, such as methadone substitution and needle exchange programmes. While the dominance of prohibitionist ideology in later decades would undermine and complicate this model, its legacy remains significant in contemporary debates on decriminalisation, medically supervised use, and patient-centred approaches to drug policy.

## The Rise of Recreational Use and Moral Panic (1960s–1970s)

The 1960s marked a decisive cultural and political shift in the landscape of drug use and regulation in the UK. This period saw the emergence of a more visible and diverse pattern of drug consumption, particularly among younger people. Drugs such as cannabis, LSD, and amphetamines became central to the countercultural movements of the era, associated with rebellion, civil disobedience, and challenges to traditional authority. The growth of psychedelic culture, inspired by both artistic expression and political disillusionment, was emblematic of broader societal changes. Drug use became entwined with protest against the Vietnam War, critiques of consumerism, and a search for spiritual or personal liberation (Berridge, 2013, p. 85). This changing social context brought drug use out of the medical sphere and into the public eye, triggering growing anxiety among policymakers and the public alike. Sensationalist media coverage amplified concerns about moral decline, youth deviance, and the risks posed by "foreign" drugs and lifestyles. British tabloids frequently moralised about the "dope menace," fuelling the perception that drug use, particularly among working-class and racially marginalised communities, was spiralling out of control (Blackman, 2004, p. 46). The increase in drug-related arrests and prosecutions reinforced the idea that the existing regulatory framework was no longer fit for purpose.

Simultaneously, there was a measurable increase in the number of heroin and amphetamine users in the UK, with a new profile of user emerging: not only patients addicted through iatrogenic exposure, but also young people seeking drugs for recreational and experimental purposes. While the total number of heroin addicts was still relatively small compared to today, the demographic shift caused alarm. A minority of unscrupulous private doctors, notably in London, were accused of overprescribing heroin and cocaine without appropriate oversight. The case of Dr. John Petro in the early 1960s, who was struck off for supplying large quantities of heroin to clients with little regard for therapeutic intent, exemplified the loopholes within the British System (Mold, 2008, p. 115).

In response, the government commissioned the Brain Committee, chaired by Sir Russell Brain, which reported in 1965. The committee recommended stricter controls over prescribing and the establishment of specialised Drug Dependency Units (DDUs) within the NHS. These units were intended to centralise the treatment of addiction and reduce the capacity for general practitioners to prescribe without adequate supervision. This recommendation was implemented through the Dangerous Drugs Act 1967, which marked a transition from a dispersed, discretionary medical model towards a more regulated and institutionalised approach (Spear, 2002, p. 49). The turning point in modern British drug policy, however, came with the enactment of the Misuse of Drugs Act 1971 (MDA). This legislation remains the foundational statute governing the classification, possession, production, and supply of controlled substances in the UK. For the first time, the government adopted a comprehensive classification system, sorting substances into Classes A, B, and C based on their perceived harm to individuals and society. Class A drugs, such as heroin, cocaine, and LSD, attracted the most severe penalties, while Class B and C substances carried progressively lesser sanctions (Seddon, 2010, pp. 98–100).

The MDA fundamentally altered the relationship between the state and the drug-using public. It codified a framework of prohibition and criminalisation, establishing punitive sanctions not just for trafficking but also for simple possession. While the Act did include provisions for medical and scientific exemptions, its overall thrust was to strengthen law enforcement and deterrence through criminal justice measures. Police powers were expanded, and the emphasis shifted from harm reduction and medical maintenance to the containment and punishment of drug use.

"The 1971 Act entrenched a punitive framework, marking a clear departure from the earlier medical model towards criminalisation and moral judgement" (Seddon, 2006, p. 684).

The classification system embedded within the MDA was based on an ostensibly evidence-led rationale, designed to reflect both the physical harms and the social dangers posed by each substance. However, critics have long argued that the classifications have often reflected political expediency more than scientific analysis. For instance, alcohol and tobacco—two substances with well-documented harms—remain legal and widely consumed, while cannabis and MDMA (ecstasy) have faced stringent legal control despite evidence of comparatively lower risks (Nutt et al., 2010, p. 1560).

A key component of the MDA was the establishment of the Advisory Council on the Misuse of Drugs (ACMD), intended to provide expert, independent advice to government ministers on drug classification and emerging trends. The ACMD was created to act as a buffer between political pressure and evidence-based policy. In principle, its remit included advising on which substances should be controlled, the appropriate class for each, and the health and social implications of drug use.

In practice, however, successive governments have frequently ignored or overridden ACMD recommendations when they conflicted with prevailing political narratives. A notable example occurred in the 2000s, when the ACMD recommended the downgrading of ecstasy from Class A to Class B, based on its relatively low mortality rate and limited long-term health effects. The Home Secretary at the time refused to implement the change, citing concerns about "sending the wrong message" (Monaghan, 2008, p. 409). Similarly, the reclassification of cannabis has been a political football. Initially downgraded to Class C in 2004, it was re-upgraded to Class B in 2009 amid public controversy and media panic, despite ACMD opposition.

The sacking of Professor David Nutt in 2009 epitomised the fraught relationship between scientific advice and political control. As chair of the ACMD, Nutt had publicly criticised government decisions that contradicted evidence, famously arguing that alcohol and tobacco caused more societal harm than many controlled drugs. His dismissal revealed the limitations of technocratic governance in the field of drug policy: when evidence clashes with populism or moral panic, the former is often sacrificed (Nutt et al., 2010, p. 1559).

These tensions between medical knowledge and political interests are not new but are rooted in the very design of the 1971 Act. The MDA allowed the state to maintain a semblance of expert-led policy while preserving the power to overrule advice whenever necessary. This duality has enabled the government to appear rational and scientific while retaining ultimate control over a deeply moralised and politicised area of law.

"The establishment of the ACMD created a façade of evidence-based policymaking, but its influence has consistently been limited by political priorities and ideological constraints" (Stevens, 2007, p. 146).

In broader terms, the MDA reflects a shift in the purpose of drug legislation—from managing addiction through health care to controlling behaviour through law enforcement. This move mirrored global trends influenced by the US-led "War on Drugs," which prioritised prohibition, eradication, and punishment over treatment or public health. British drug policy, once notable for its pragmatism and clinical ethos, became increasingly aligned with international conventions that emphasised supply reduction and zero tolerance (Berridge, 2013, p. 176).

The consequences of this shift have been far-reaching. The criminalisation of users, particularly for possession offences, has disproportionately affected marginalised communities, especially Black and working-class youth (Eastwood, Shiner and Bear, 2013, p. 10). Enforcement has often focused on low-level offences rather than targeting organised trafficking networks. Moreover, the emphasis on punitive responses has diverted resources away from prevention, education, and treatment.

Yet, despite the apparent failure of the criminal justice approach to reduce either drug use or drug-related harm, the basic structure of the MDA remains intact over fifty years later. Periodic reviews and reforms have tweaked the framework but have not fundamentally reimagined it. The Act's endurance suggests not only institutional inertia but also a political reluctance to confront the moral and ideological foundations of Britain's drug policy.

## Entrenchment of Prohibition and Racial Disparities (1980s–1990s)

The 1980s and 1990s witnessed intensified drug enforcement under successive Conservative governments, which increasingly linked illicit drug use to moral decline, criminality, and social disorder. The framing of drugs as a societal threat aligned with broader neoliberal policies that emphasised individual responsibility, law and order, and the shrinking of the welfare state. Prime Minister Margaret Thatcher's administration was particularly instrumental in reshaping the discourse around drugs, positioning users not as patients or victims, but as deviants undermining social cohesion (Seddon, 2006, p. 689).

This shift was heavily influenced by the "War on Drugs" rhetoric emerging from the US, where President Reagan's administration framed drug use as a national emergency. British politicians adopted similar language, contributing to a moral panic that demanded visible and punitive responses. The Criminal Justice Act 1988 reflected this climate, introducing tougher penalties including mandatory minimum sentences for repeat drug offences. These measures signalled a clear preference for enforcement-led approaches over prevention or care.

Simultaneously, the arrival of crack cocaine in Britain's inner cities—particularly London, Manchester, and Liverpool—intensified racialised media coverage. Sensationalist reports portrayed Black communities as disproportionately involved in drug-related violence, reinforcing harmful stereotypes and justifying aggressive policing tactics. Stop and search powers were disproportionately used against Black youth, contributing to a significant overrepresentation of ethnic minorities in drug-related arrests and prison sentences (Eastwood, Shiner and Bear, 2013, p. 10).

Despite the punitive rhetoric, the emergence of HIV/AIDS in the mid-1980s forced a partial rethink. Public health concerns about shared needles and bloodborne disease transmission led to the introduction of needle exchange schemes, methadone substitution, and other harm reduction initiatives. These were pragmatic interventions, grounded in epidemiology rather than ideology, and signalled a reluctant but necessary return to health-based strategies in drug policy.

"While rhetoric remained punitive, pragmatic harm reduction strategies were implemented in response to emergent public health crises" (Berridge, 2013, p. 198).

## Modernisation and Contradictions (2000s–2010s)

The Labour government (1997–2010) presided over a significant phase in UK drug policy development, adopting what appeared to be a pragmatic, dual-track approach. While prohibition remained the foundation of statutory control, there was also unprecedented investment in treatment services, harm reduction programmes, and evidence-informed strategies. This approach reflected the influence of New Labour's broader emphasis on "tough on crime, tough on the causes of crime," situating drug use not only as a health issue but also a key factor in criminality, social exclusion, and urban decline (Stevens, 2007, p. 147).

The Updated Drug Strategy 2002 encapsulated this logic by focusing on four key pillars: reducing demand, restricting supply, safeguarding communities, and enhancing treatment. These goals were explicitly linked to reducing drug-related crime, particularly acquisitive offences such as burglary and theft, which were understood to be driven by problematic heroin and crack cocaine use. The introduction of Drug Intervention Programmes (DIPs) sought to channel offenders into treatment as a condition of bail or sentencing. This shift placed the criminal justice system at the heart of public health responses and blurred the line between coercion and care (Duke, 2006, p. 409).

However, while Labour's strategy was rhetorically supportive of evidence-based policy, in practice it was frequently driven by public opinion, media pressure, and political calculus. Nowhere was this more apparent than in the controversy over cannabis reclassification. In 2004, following a review by the Advisory Council on the Misuse of Drugs (ACMD), cannabis was reclassified from Class B to Class C, meaning possession was no longer an arrestable offence. The ACMD had concluded that cannabis, while not harmless, posed relatively low risks compared to other substances and that its continued classification as a Class B drug was disproportionate ACMD XE "ACMD ((Advisory Council on the Misuse of Drugs)" , 2002).

The change was intended to free up police time and refocus efforts on more dangerous drugs. However, it quickly became a lightning rod for political and tabloid backlash, particularly after a handful of high-profile cases linked cannabis use with mental health problems, such as psychosis and schizophrenia. Critics accused the government of sending "the wrong message" to young people, and ministers came under intense pressure to reverse the decision (Stevens, 2007, p. 148).

In 2009, under Prime Minister Gordon Brown, cannabis was reclassified back to Class B—despite the ACMD's continued opposition and growing scientific evidence suggesting that the harms of cannabis, while present, remained lower than those of many legal substances. This reversal highlighted the fragile status of scientific advice within UK drug policymaking.

The clearest illustration of this dynamic came with the sacking of Professor David Nutt, then-chair of the ACMD, in 2009. Nutt had published a paper in *The Lancet* using a multi-criteria decision analysis that ranked alcohol and tobacco as more harmful than LSD, ecstasy, and cannabis (Nutt et al., 2010, p. 1558). He publicly criticised the government for ignoring the scientific consensus and accused ministers of prioritising political optics over evidence. His dismissal by Home Secretary Alan Johnson exposed the deep tension between technocratic expertise and populist governance, reinforcing the idea that drug classification was more about public reassurance than scientific rigour.

"Scientific evidence often plays a secondary role to moral panics and political expediency in shaping UK drug policy" (Monaghan, 2008, p. 409).

Following Labour's defeat in 2010, the Coalition and subsequent Conservative governments introduced further changes, notably the Psychoactive Substances Act 2016 (PSA). This legislation was designed to address the proliferation of novel psychoactive substances (NPS)—often sold in head shops and online under names like "spice," "bath salts," or "legal highs." These substances, while not covered under the Misuse of Drugs Act, often mimicked the effects of banned drugs and were associated with rising hospital admissions, prison disturbances, and deaths (Home Office, 2018, p. 6).

Rather than banning substances individually, the PSA took the novel step of prohibiting any substance capable of producing a psychoactive effect, unless specifically exempt (such as caffeine, nicotine, and alcohol). While this broadened the state's capacity to respond rapidly to emerging threats, it also presented major enforcement challenges. The definition of "psychoactive" was legally and scientifically ambiguous, and several prosecutions collapsed due to the difficulty of proving psychoactivity beyond reasonable doubt (Stevens, 2022, p. 203).

Critics argued that the PSA represented a symbolic rather than substantive intervention, aimed more at reassuring the public and media than at reducing harm. The Home Office's own post-legislative review noted a decline in open sales of NPS, but also admitted that many users had simply shifted to illicit markets, where products were unlabelled and potentially more dangerous (Home Office, 2018, p. 14). Moreover, the PSA appeared to prioritise supply-side enforcement over harm reduction or public education, continuing the long-standing trend of punitive measures masquerading as protective policy.

The Act was also criticised for creating a legal paradox. While banning synthetic cannabinoids like "spice," it left the far more harmful substances alcohol and tobacco untouched, reinforcing public confusion about the relative risks of various substances and undermining the credibility of the state's drug messaging (Nutt, 2012, p. 3).

In sum, the period from 1997 to 2016 reflects a deep ambivalence in UK drug policy: a rhetorical commitment to evidence-based approaches often subverted by moral panic, electoral concerns, and tabloid influence. Harm reduction and treatment initiatives were expanded under Labour, and innovations like the ACMD and multi-agency partnerships gained ground. However, political leaders repeatedly undermined expert advice, especially when it conflicted with populist narratives or risked electoral fallout.

These contradictions were further compounded by legislation like the PSA, which exemplified the tendency to adopt broad, symbolic bans rather than engage with the structural causes of drug-related harm. As such, the period represents a microcosm of the enduring contradictions in British drug policy: progressive in rhetoric, but regressive in practice.

## Devolution, Harm Reduction, and Policy Divergence (2010s–Present)

Devolved administrations have increasingly explored alternative models of drug policy that prioritise harm reduction, public health, and social support, diverging from the more enforcement-led approach favoured by Westminster. Nowhere is this more evident than in Scotland, where a spiralling drug-related death crisis—among the highest in Europe—has forced a re-evaluation of traditional strategies. In response, the Scottish Government has repeatedly called for the decriminalisation of personal possession and the introduction of safe consumption facilities, which would allow individuals to use drugs under medical supervision, thereby reducing overdose deaths and infectious disease transmission (Scottish Government, 2021, p. 6).

Despite widespread support from public health experts, service providers, and police chiefs in Scotland, such innovations have been blocked by the UK government, which retains control over the Misuse of Drugs Act 1971. This has led to a policy impasse, with Scottish ministers arguing that constitutional constraints are undermining their ability to protect lives. A legal case surrounding a proposed Overdose Prevention Centre in Glasgow illustrates the extent of this conflict: although Glasgow City Council and health authorities supported the plan, the Home Office refused to provide legal exemptions, citing the need for consistent national enforcement (Ford, 2022, p. 84).

Elsewhere in the UK, Wales and Northern Ireland have taken quieter but significant steps towards public health integration. In Wales, the substance misuse strategy is explicitly framed around harm reduction, trauma-informed care, and co-production with service users. Welsh authorities have invested in housing-first programmes, mental health support, and culturally sensitive services for women and ethnic minorities. Similarly, Northern Ireland's New Strategic Direction for Alcohol and Drugs (2011–2016) embedded drug policy within broader public health and social care frameworks, emphasising early intervention, education, and local coordination (NISRA, 2017, p. 11).

Meanwhile, England's strategy has remained centrally controlled and predominantly prohibitionist. The UK Government's 10-Year Drug Strategy, *From Harm to Hope* (2021), pledged £780 million in new funding for treatment services, which was broadly welcomed by professionals working in addiction support. However, the strategy retained a strong law enforcement ethos, including expanded drug testing of individuals on arrest, tougher penalties for recreational users, and an explicit focus on disrupting supply chains (HM Government, 2021, p. 14). Notably, the strategy continued to frame drug use—particularly among middle-class professionals—as a matter of moral failure and criminality rather than health or social inequality.

This growing policy divergence has produced a fractured landscape across the UK, with devolved nations increasingly frustrated by the limits of their power to innovate within the current legislative framework. The underlying tension lies in the centralisation of drug law—retained at Westminster—while health and justice are devolved. This disjuncture means that while Scotland can reform services, it cannot decriminalise; Wales can promote harm reduction, but must still operate under a punitive legal system.

"UK drug policy reflects growing divergence between devolved nations prioritising harm reduction and central government adherence to punitive orthodoxy" (Stevens, 2022, p. 205).

This fragmentation raises questions about the future of unified drug legislation in the UK. As devolved administrations continue to innovate around the edges of a rigid legal framework, pressure may mount for further devolution of powers—or even constitutional reform—in the pursuit of evidence-led, humane, and effective drug policy.

## Contemporary Critiques and Calls for Reform

Current debates highlight the ineffectiveness of criminalisation in reducing harm. The UK continues to experience rising drug-related deaths, high levels of reoffending linked to substance misuse, and social inequality exacerbated by enforcement practices (Release, 2020). International comparisons, especially with Portugal, where decriminalisation has reduced deaths and infections, fuel calls for reform (Hughes & Stevens, 2010).

There is also growing awareness of functional drug use and the disproportionate legal focus on vulnerable and marginalised users. Alcohol, a legal substance, causes significantly more harm than many illegal drugs, yet remains under-regulated—a contradiction at the heart of UK drug policy (Nutt et al., 2010).

Proposition: The disparity in treatment between alcohol and illicit drugs illustrates the sociopolitical construction of drug harm, rather than evidence-based classification (Room, 2005).

## Conclusion

From the 1960s onward, British drug policy has undergone significant transformations in law, rhetoric, and strategic emphasis. However, what remains striking across this timeline is the enduring tension between health-based and punitive models, between evidence and political expediency, and between social inclusion and moral discipline. The evolution from the pragmatic "British System" to the expansive criminalisation under the Misuse of Drugs Act 1971 marked a profound shift—not simply in legislative mechanics but in the ideological foundations of the UK's approach to substance use.

The Misuse of Drugs Act 1971 created a classification system that purported to reflect the relative harms of different substances, yet, as the chapter has demonstrated, the act often functioned more as a tool of political signalling than of public health strategy. Its durability over five decades—despite mounting evidence of ineffectiveness—points to a system in which drug control is less about managing harm and more about managing populations, particularly those already subject to social marginalisation. The criminalisation of possession, disproportionately enforced against Black and working-class communities, has not prevented drug use or improved health outcomes. Instead, it has perpetuated cycles of incarceration, stigma, and socio-economic exclusion.

While the 1980s and 1990s intensified this punitive focus under a law-and-order agenda influenced by the US-led War on Drugs, the public health emergency of HIV/AIDS forced a degree of harm reduction pragmatism, albeit begrudgingly. Needle exchanges and methadone programmes were introduced, not because the ideological tide had turned, but because failing to act would have led to even more devastating public health outcomes. This contradiction—rhetorical toughness versus reluctant pragmatism—has remained a defining feature of UK drug policy ever since.

The Labour era (1997–2010) introduced a nuanced dual strategy: while rhetorically embracing evidence and health-led approaches, in practice it often reverted to tabloid-led populism, as seen in the handling of cannabis reclassification and the sacking of Professor David Nutt. The expansion of treatment and integration of drugs policy with criminal justice through the Drug Interventions Programme offered some benefits, but these gains were undermined by the continued moralisation of drug use and by framing policy success around crime reduction rather than user well-being.

The Psychoactive Substances Act 2016 continued this trend of symbolic legislation, outlawing "legal highs" through vague definitions that proved difficult to enforce and arguably pushed users towards more dangerous black-market alternatives. The PSA epitomised a broader pattern: rather than addressing structural determinants of problematic drug use—poverty, trauma, exclusion—policy continues to chase symptoms with legal prohibitions and criminal sanctions.

What has become increasingly clear over the last decade is the policy divergence between devolved nations and Westminster. Scotland, Wales, and Northern Ireland have all sought to embed drug strategy within wider health and social care frameworks, with Scotland particularly vocal in calling for decriminalisation and safe consumption facilities. England, by contrast, has largely remained committed to prohibition, even as drug deaths soar and public trust in policy efficacy wanes. The centralisation of drug law under Westminster while devolving health and justice has created a constitutional bottleneck, stalling the progressive reform efforts in the devolved nations.

The persistence of outdated frameworks also reveals deeper epistemological and ideological problems. The chapter has shown that what counts as a "dangerous drug" is less a product of pharmacology than of historical anxieties, racialised fears, and political utility. That alcohol and tobacco—responsible for far more deaths and social costs—remain legal and lightly regulated while safer substances are criminalised is not a quirk of the system, but a symptom of its politicised foundations.

Calls for reform are now supported not only by harm reduction advocates but by criminologists, public health officials, police chiefs, economists, and even former politicians. The Portuguese decriminalisation model has become a benchmark in reform debates, not because it is perfect, but because it provides empirical evidence that decriminalisation paired with health investment can reduce harm without increasing use. Domestic reviews such as the Dame Carol Black Report (2021) have echoed similar conclusions, calling for whole-system approaches centred on treatment, education, and support rather than punishment.

Yet despite these developments, real reform in UK drug law remains elusive. The political risks of appearing "soft on drugs" continue to outweigh the public health imperative for most policymakers. And so, the UK finds itself caught in a policy double bind: aware that the current system fails but unable or unwilling to embrace change. All of this left me wondering: What are we really punishing? Harm? Risk? Or just illegality for its own sake? From the bench, the pattern was painfully clear: we're using the criminal justice system to manage a public health issue—and we're doing so unevenly, often unfairly, and in ways that compound harm rather than reduce it.

## The Catastrophic Nature of Criminalisation-Personal reflection

On a personal note, I served as a magistrate for many years on the Liverpool bench, and during this time dealt with a lot of drugs and alcohol related crime which have lasting consequences for those accused.

Time and again, I saw people criminalised for simple drug possession, especially young men found with small amounts of cannabis. These weren't hardened criminals—they were students, apprentices, or just young people trying to navigate difficult lives. Yet the outcome was the same: a criminal record that would follow them for years, limiting their chances in employment, education, travel, and even housing.

What struck me even more, though, was that many of the criminal offences we dealt with in court weren't caused by illegal drugs—but by alcohol. In fact, nearly all of the domestic violence cases, criminal damage, and street assaults I sat on involved alcohol to some degree. And many of these were repeat offenders, cycling through the system again and again, not because of cannabis, ecstasy, or cocaine—but because of drink.

The same pattern was true in my other professional life. I also worked as a bouncer for over 20 years, and in that time, the main concern on the doors was intoxication—especially alcohol-fuelled aggression. That's what triggered most of the violence I experienced at work. Although illicit drugs did cause issues from time to time, my overall experience with drug users was often non-violent, even chaotic but generally less aggressive.

Working in big venues like Cream in the 1990s (we averaged 4000 people a night), I saw a lot of drug use—particularly ecstasy and marijuana—but I rarely saw the kind of reckless, violent behaviour that alcohol produced every single weekend. (I'll share a few tales from that era later on—some funny, some grim, and at least one that might make you feel a bit sick.)

And yet, alcohol—arguably one of the most harmful and socially corrosive substances—remains entirely legal, heavily marketed, widely available, and culturally celebrated. Meanwhile, far less harmful substances land people in court or jail, with life-altering consequences.

Another issue I saw emerge on the bench was the rise in drug driving offences, particularly after roadside testing was introduced. (I'll explore this in more detail later.) What concerns me most is that many of these cases involved traces of drugs taken days—sometimes a full week— before the driving offence. These aren't people caught driving under the influence in the traditional sense; they're being prosecuted for the residual presence of drugs in their system, with little or no evidence of impairment.

That time I witnessed first-hand how our criminal justice system handles drug-related offences.

In conclusion, the post-1960 history of British drug policy is a story of missed opportunities, institutional rigidity, and ideological entrenchment. It is also a history that shows glimmers of innovation, moments of pragmatic reform, and increasing recognition of the need for change. The challenge now is to ensure that the next phase of policy is shaped not by fear, stigma, or political calculation, but by evidence, equity, and compassion.

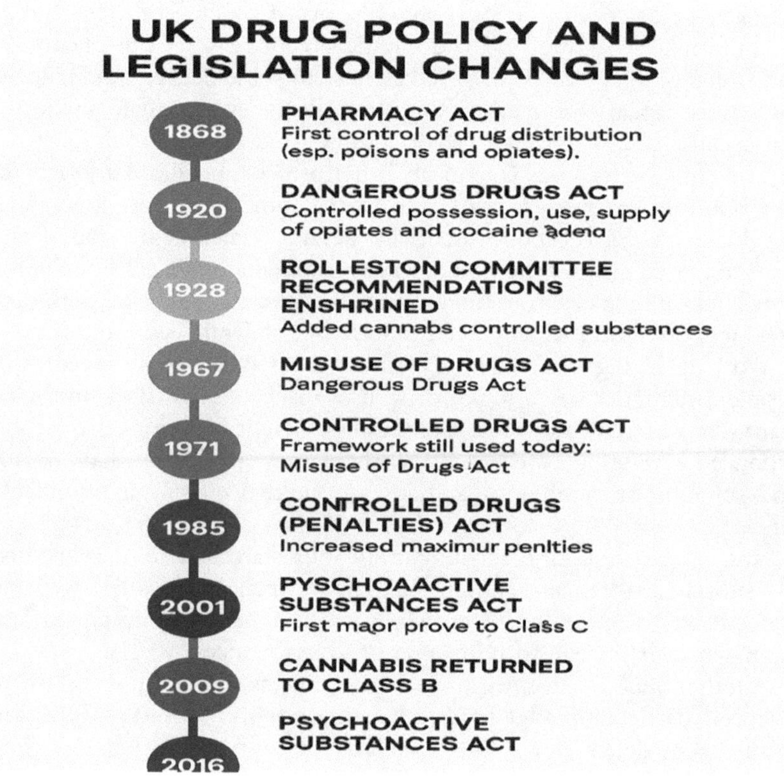

## References


ACMD (Advisory Council on the Misuse of Drugs). (2002). *Cannabis: Classification and public health*. Home Office.

Berridge, V. (1999). *Opium and the people: Opiate use and drug control policy in nineteenth and early twentieth century England* (2nd ed.). Free Association Books.

Berridge, V. (2013). *Demons: Our changing attitudes to alcohol, tobacco, and drugs*. Oxford University Press.

Blackman, S. (2004). *Chilling out: The cultural politics of substance consumption, youth and drug policy*. Open University Press.

Duke, K. (2006). Out of crime and into treatment? The criminalisation of contemporary drug policy since tackling drugs together. *Drugs: Education, Prevention and Policy, 13*(5), 409–415.

Eastwood, N., Shiner, M., & Bear, D. (2013). *The numbers in black and white: Ethnic disparities in the policing and prosecution of drug offences in England and Wales*. Release.

Ford, M. (2022). *Overdose prevention and the limits of devolution: Policy, politics and place*. University of Glasgow Centre for Drug Policy Research.

HM Government. (2021). *From harm to hope: A 10-year drugs plan to cut crime and save lives*. Home Office.

Hughes, C. E., & Stevens, A. (2010). What can we learn from the Portuguese decriminalization of illicit drugs? *British Journal of Criminology, 50*(6), 999–1022.

Mold, A. (2008). *Heroin: The treatment of addiction in twentieth century britain*. Northern Illinois University Press.

Monaghan, M. (2008). Tolerance, guidance and remit: The politicisation of the ACMD. *Drugs: Education, Prevention and Policy, 15*(5), 403–414.

Musto, D. F. (1991). *The American disease: Origins of narcotic control* (3rd ed.). Oxford University Press.

NISRA (Northern Ireland Statistics and Research Agency). (2017). *Statistics from the Northern Ireland drug misuse database: 2016/17*. Department of Health Northern Ireland.

Nutt, D. (2012). *Drugs without the hot air: Minimising the harms of legal and illegal drugs*. UIT Press.

Nutt, D., King, L. A., & Phillips, L. D. (2010). Drug harms in the UK: A multicriteria decision analysis. *The Lancet, 376*(9752), 1558–1565.

Office, H. (2018). *Post-legislative scrutiny of the psychoactive substances act 2016: Review report*. HMSO.

Release. (2020). *A quiet revolution: Drug decriminalisation across the globe*. Release.

Room, R. (2005). Stigma, social inequality and alcohol and drug use. *Drug and Alcohol Review, 24*(2), 143–155.

Rolleston, H. (1926). Report of the Departmental Committee on Morphine and Heroin Addiction.

Scottish Government. (2021). *Drug deaths taskforce: Strategy and evidence review*. Scottish Government.

Seddon, T. (2006). Drugs, crime and social exclusion: Social context and social theory in British drugs–crime research. *British Journal of Criminology, 46*(4), 680–703.

Seddon, T. (2010). *A history of drugs: Drugs and freedom in the liberal age*. Routledge.

Spear, B. (2002). The role of the Rolleston report in UK drug policy. *Addiction, 97*(4), 381–383.

Stevens, A. (2007). Surveillance, regulation and control: Governing drug use in the UK. *International Journal of Drug Policy, 18*(3), 146–148.

Stevens, A. (2022). *Drug policy constellations: A cultural approach to drug policy analysis*. Palgrave Macmillan.

Stimson, G. V. (1987). The future of the "British system" of drug control. *British Journal of Addiction, 82*(1), 43–52.

CHAPTER 2

# Based on Science?

**Abstract** This chapter critically examines the UK's drug classification system under the Misuse of Drugs Act 1971 (MDA), challenging the widely held belief that it is grounded in scientific evidence. While the system claims to categorise substances according to their harm, addiction potential, and societal impact, the reality is far more politically driven. Through an analysis of historical decisions, expert dissent, and international comparisons, the chapter exposes a persistent pattern in which political convenience, moral panic, and media pressure routinely override scientific advice.

One of the most prominent examples of this disconnect is the dismissal of Professor David Nutt in 2009, following his criticism of the government's refusal to reclassify drugs like cannabis and ecstasy in line with harm-based evidence. Nutt's multi-criteria decision analysis demonstrated that legal substances like alcohol and tobacco cause significantly more harm than many Class A drugs. His dismissal, alongside media vilification, underscores the political risks faced by experts who challenge prohibitionist orthodoxy.

The chapter explores how drug classification in the UK often reflects symbolic governance, shaped more by populist sentiment than public health needs. The reclassification of cannabis and the criminalisation of nitrous oxide, both made against the recommendations of the Advisory Council on the Misuse of Drugs (ACMD), illustrate the marginalisation of evidence in favour of political theatre. It also highlights


E. Peatfield, *Drugs Disorder by Design*,
https://doi.org/10.1007/978-3-032-07814-8_2

the consequences of this approach: misaligned enforcement priorities, entrenched stigma, and serious barriers to medical research—particularly for promising compounds like psilocybin and MDMA.

By comparing UK policy to more progressive international models—such as Portugal's decriminalisation strategy and Switzerland's heroin-assisted treatment—the chapter makes the case for evidence-led reform. It argues that UK policy fails not only in harm reduction but also in scientific credibility, public trust, and social justice. The continued criminalisation of low-harm substances disproportionately affects marginalised populations while blocking innovation in mental health care.

Ultimately, this chapter contends that the UK's drug classification system is best understood as a myth of evidence-based policy—a rhetorical device masking ideological control. For reform to be meaningful, policymakers must move beyond moral posturing and engage with scientific evidence, independent expertise, and public health priorities. Until then, the UK's drug laws will remain a cautionary example of how ideology can subvert evidence to the detriment of both science and society.

**Keywords** Drug Classification · Misuse of Drugs Act 1971 · Political Influence · Scientific Evidence · David Nutt · Moral Panic · Media Sensationalism · Harm Reduction · Policy Theatre · Research Barriers

## Introduction: The Myth of the Evidence-Based Classification

The UK government's drug classification system, established under the *Misuse of Drugs Act 1971* (MDA), purports to be grounded in scientific evidence, with the stated aim of categorising substances according to their potential for harm to individuals and wider society. This framework determines the legal status of various drugs, the criminal penalties associated with their possession and supply, and the public health responses deployed to address their use. In principle, the classification of a substance into Class A, B, or C is meant to reflect a rational assessment of its physical and psychological harm, addictive potential, and broader social consequences. However, as this chapter will argue, the reality of how drugs are classified in the UK reveals a profound disconnect between scientific understanding and political practice.

Far from being a neutral, evidence-based system, the UK's approach to drug classification is riddled with inconsistencies, ideological biases, and reactive policymaking. Over the past two decades, a growing body of scientific research and academic critique has exposed the ways in which political expediency, cultural panic, and historical inertia often take precedence over empirical data in shaping policy. Substances that are demonstrably harmful—such as alcohol and tobacco—remain legal and widely consumed, while others with lower harm profiles, including cannabis, ecstasy (MDMA), and psilocybin, continue to be criminalised under the most severe legal categories. This situation raises urgent questions about the legitimacy, efficacy, and social justice implications of the current classification model.

One of the most striking illustrations of the tension between science and policy came in 2009 with the dismissal of Professor David Nutt, then Chair of the Advisory Council on the Misuse of Drugs (ACMD). Nutt had been outspoken in his criticisms of the government's drug policies, particularly its refusal to reclassify substances like cannabis and ecstasy in line with scientific evidence. In a now-infamous lecture at King's College London—later published under the title *Equasy* (Nutt, 2009)—he compared the risks of taking ecstasy to those of horse riding, arguing that the latter caused more harm but faced no legal restrictions. His broader work used multi-criteria decision analysis (MCDA) to demonstrate that alcohol was the most harmful substance overall, while many illegal drugs ranked much lower in terms of personal and societal harm (Nutt et al., 2010).

Rather than engaging with these findings, the government responded with hostility. Then-Home Secretary Alan Johnson accused Nutt of blurring the line between adviser and campaigner and dismissed him from his post. This decision provoked widespread backlash from the scientific community, with multiple members of the ACMD resigning in protest. More disturbingly, it unleashed a tabloid-driven smear campaign against Nutt, in which he was painted as "soft on drugs" and dangerously out of touch with public morality. Newspapers such as *The Daily Mail* and *The Sun* caricatured him as a radical scientist promoting drug use, despite his repeated clarifications that his research was about risk assessment, not endorsement. This episode revealed not only the government's discomfort with dissenting evidence but also the broader mechanisms through which scientific voices are marginalised when they challenge dominant ideological narratives.

The case of Nutt is not an isolated incident but emblematic of a wider problem. UK drug policy has long been shaped by moral panic, political theatre, and media sensationalism. Changes to drug classifications often reflect attempts to placate tabloid campaigns or signal political toughness, rather than careful analysis of harm. The reclassification of cannabis from Class C back to Class B in 2009, despite the ACMD advising otherwise, is a case in point. Similarly, the recent decision to criminalise nitrous oxide, despite repeated ACMD recommendations against such action, demonstrates how populist pressures continue to trump evidence-based policymaking.

This chapter takes as its starting point the claim that the UK's drug classification system is a "myth of evidence-based policy"—a system that invokes scientific language and institutional expertise while routinely ignoring or distorting actual scientific findings. Drawing on academic literature, government reports, and international comparisons, the chapter critically examines the political, cultural, and institutional dynamics that sustain this disconnect. It interrogates the roles of media influence, public fear, and bureaucratic inertia in shaping legislation, and considers how expert advice is often subverted or suppressed when it threatens political orthodoxy.

Ultimately, by unpacking the inconsistencies and contradictions in UK drug classification, this chapter aims to demonstrate that meaningful reform is both necessary and achievable. If drug policy is to truly serve public health, social justice, and scientific progress, it must move beyond symbolism and moral posturing to embrace an honest, evidence-led approach. The stakes are high: continued resistance to reform risks not only scientific credibility but also the health and well-being of countless individuals harmed by punitive and outdated laws.

## The Misuse of Drugs Act 1971: An Overview

The *Misuse of Drugs Act 1971* (MDA) remains the central legal instrument governing drug control in the UK. It divides substances into three classes—A, B, and C—purportedly based on their relative potential for harm. In theory, this classification scheme informs sentencing guidelines, enforcement priorities, and public health interventions, with Class A drugs (e.g. heroin, crack cocaine) deemed the most dangerous and Class C drugs (e.g. certain prescription sedatives) the least. However, while the MDA presents itself as a rational, harm-based framework, a growing body of scientific and sociopolitical critique suggests it functions more as a tool of symbolic governance than a system of evidence-led regulation.

The Act has been consistently criticised for its lack of flexibility and failure to adapt to new scientific findings. As early as 2006, the House of Commons Science and Technology Committee concluded that the classification system lacked transparency, coherence, and scientific validity, noting that ministers had repeatedly overruled the advice of the Advisory Council on the Misuse of Drugs (ACMD) without adequate justification. This issue is exemplified in the government's refusal to downgrade ecstasy (MDMA) from Class A to Class B, despite compelling evidence from the ACMD that it did not warrant the highest level of control (House of Commons Science and Technology Committee, 2006).

Empirical studies, particularly those led by Professor David Nutt, have further exposed the inconsistencies in how substances are classified. Nutt et al. (2010) used a multi-criteria decision analysis (MCDA) to rank 20 legal and illegal drugs based on a range of harms, including physical damage, dependence potential, and social costs. The results were striking: alcohol emerged as the most harmful drug overall, with heroin and crack cocaine following. Conversely, substances such as LSD, ecstasy, and psilocybin were found to pose significantly lower harm—yet all three remain Class A substances under the MDA.

This disconnect raises fundamental questions about the purposes of the Act. If legal status does not correspond to evidence of harm, then the classification system arguably serves other political or ideological functions. Steve Taylor (2016) argues that UK drug law is shaped by what he terms "moral hierarchies of intoxication," in which socially embedded and economically significant substances like alcohol are normalised, while countercultural or racialised drugs are stigmatised and criminalised. This process has little to do with actual pharmacological risk and much more to do with cultural symbolism and political expediency.

These "moral hierarchies" are reinforced by a cycle of tabloid sensationalism and populist policymaking, in which substances are demonised in the press and then reclassified or restricted by government in an attempt to appear "tough on drugs." The reclassification of cannabis from Class C to Class B in 2009—against the advice of the ACMD—is a clear example of this process in action. The legal framework allows ministers to override scientific advice with no formal requirement for transparency, enabling drug classification to function as a form of policy theatre rather than evidence-based public health intervention.

Ultimately, the MDA does not operate as a neutral arbiter of drug harm. Instead, it reflects politically negotiated truths about what types of intoxication are acceptable, who gets punished, and which forms of risk society is willing to tolerate. This has profound implications for public health, criminal justice, and civil liberties—particularly for young people, people who use drugs non-problematically, and marginalised communities who are disproportionately targeted by enforcement.

## The Case of Professor David Nutt

Professor David Nutt, former chair of the Advisory Council on the Misuse of Drugs (ACMD), was dismissed in 2009 by then-Home Secretary Alan Johnson after publicly criticising the UK government's approach to drug classification. Nutt had consistently argued that the classification system under the *Misuse of Drugs Act 1971* was politically driven and failed to reflect the best available scientific evidence. In a lecture delivered at King's College London, later published as "Equasy – An Overlooked Addiction with Implications for the Current Debate on Drug Harms" (Nutt, 2009), he provocatively compared the risks of taking ecstasy (MDMA) to those of equestrian sports, arguing that horse riding posed greater risks of harm. His aim was not to trivialise drug harms but to expose the inconsistent and irrational basis on which the UK's drug laws operate.

Nutt's broader analysis—formalised in subsequent peer-reviewed work (Nutt et al., 2010)—employed multi-criteria decision analysis (MCDA) to rank 20 drugs in terms of their harm to individuals and society. Alcohol emerged as the most harmful substance overall, significantly more so than heroin or crack cocaine. By contrast, ecstasy and LSD—both categorised as Class A drugs under the MDA—ranked among the least harmful. These findings challenged the coherence of the classification system, revealing that legality and enforcement severity bore little relation to actual levels of risk.

The government's reaction was swift and severe. In his dismissal letter, Alan Johnson claimed that Nutt had crossed the line from "adviser to campaigner" and had therefore undermined the credibility of the ACMD (Home Office, 2009). Yet critics argued that Nutt was dismissed not for any breach of protocol, but for stating uncomfortable truths that contradicted government messaging. His sacking exposed the fragility of the "evidence-based policy" narrative, revealing a system in which expert advice could be cast aside whenever it proved politically inconvenient.

The backlash extended well beyond Whitehall. Nutt became the target of an aggressive smear campaign by right-wing tabloids, most notably *The Sun* and *The Daily Mail*. These outlets portrayed him as a reckless radical who was undermining the war on drugs. Headlines mischaracterised his comments, suggesting he was advocating drug use or dismissing the risks faced by young people. In one particularly egregious piece, he was accused of "equating fun with heroin," a wilful misreading of his argument about proportionality and risk perception. The press repeatedly depicted him as "soft on drugs," ignoring his clear statement that he was not endorsing use, but advocating for rational classification grounded in empirical data.

Taylor (2016) observes that such vilification fits a broader pattern in UK drug policy, where expert dissent is met not with engagement, but with personal attacks and media scapegoating. This use of "moral outrage journalism" functions to delegitimise scientific critique, reinforce prohibitionist ideology, and silence debate. The Nutt affair had a chilling effect on other scientists working in the field, many of whom became wary of speaking publicly for fear of similar treatment. Several members of the ACMD resigned in protest, citing government interference and a lack of respect for independent science.

The Nutt episode is not just an anecdote about one man's dismissal; it stands as a cautionary tale about the fragility of science-informed policy in the UK. It illustrates the systemic barriers faced by experts who challenge dominant drug narratives and the weaponisation of the press in discrediting those who threaten the status quo. In doing so, it highlights the urgent need for a more transparent, accountable, and intellectually honest framework for shaping drug legislation—one where truth is not punished, and expertise is not politicised.

## Political Influences on Drug Classification

Political considerations often play a significant role in drug classification decisions, frequently overriding scientific evidence in favour of symbolic gestures. This politicisation is most clearly seen in the reclassification of cannabis from Class C back to Class B in 2009—a move taken against the advice of the Advisory Council on the Misuse of Drugs (ACMD), which had conducted a detailed harm assessment and concluded there was no sufficient justification for reclassification (ACMD XE "ACMD (Advisory Council on the Misuse of Drugs)" , 2008). The decision was widely interpreted as an attempt by then-Home Secretary Jacqui Smith to demonstrate a "tough on drugs" stance amidst media anxiety about so-called "skunk" strains and their alleged links to psychosis, despite the lack of conclusive evidence establishing a direct causal relationship.

As Stevens (2007) argues, UK drug policy has long been reactive to media narratives rather than proactive in applying public health principles. Drug classification changes are often introduced to align with tabloid headlines rather than epidemiological realities. The *Daily Mail*, for example, led aggressive campaigns against cannabis during the mid-2000s, referring to it as a "lethal gateway drug" and attributing complex mental health issues to its use, often without adequate scientific backing. Politicians, in turn, responded to such moral panics, eager to avoid being cast as soft on crime or permissive on drug use (Stevens, 2007; Taylor, 2016).

This media-politics loop turns drug policy into a form of political theatre—what some scholars have termed "policy-making by moral panic" (Critcher, 2003). In such a climate, politicians tend to use drug reclassification or prohibition as an easy win to demonstrate authority or appease conservative voter bases. The symbolic dimension of classification—what Monaghan (2008) calls its "communicative function"—becomes more important than its practical consequences. In this way, classifications become more about expressing condemnation or control than guiding proportionate enforcement or reducing harm.

The Misuse of Drugs Act itself has been criticised as being uniquely vulnerable to politicisation. Unlike many other areas of regulatory law, it allows ministers significant discretion to override expert advice. For example, Section 2(5) of the Act allows the Home Secretary to disregard the ACMD's recommendations, a power exercised multiple times in high-profile decisions, such as the classification of MDMA and cannabis (Seddon, 2011). This has led to calls for the establishment of a more independent, statutory body that could insulate drug policy decisions from political expediency.

Recent debates around the legal status of nitrous oxide (laughing gas) further underscore how political rhetoric can eclipse scientific consensus. Despite the ACMD's repeated conclusion that nitrous oxide posed relatively low harm and that a ban was not warranted, the government pressed ahead with its prohibition in 2023 under the *Anti-Social Behaviour Action Plan*—again, apparently in response to media-fuelled concerns about visible street use and perceived anti-social behaviour, rather than clinical evidence (ACMD XE "ACMD (Advisory Council on the Misuse of Drugs)" , 2023).

The repeated use of drug classification as a political tool not only undermines public confidence in the system but also erodes the integrity of scientific advice. More worryingly, it can lead to real-world harms: from misallocating law enforcement resources to deterring research into potentially therapeutic substances. As Taylor (2016) notes, when classification is used primarily to score political points, the nuanced reality of drug use—particularly among vulnerable or marginalised populations—is lost in favour of simplistic, punitive narratives.

## Impact on Research and Medical Use

The stringent classification of certain substances hampers not only harm reduction efforts but also, scientific research and the exploration of potentially life-changing medical applications. Under the *Misuse of Drugs Act 1971*, substances placed in Class A are deemed to have the highest potential for harm and no recognised therapeutic use. As a result, research into these substances faces intense regulatory scrutiny, cumbersome licensing processes, and significant funding barriers. One of the most notable examples is psilocybin, the active compound in so-called "magic mushrooms," which remains a Class A drug in the UK despite a growing body of scientific evidence supporting its potential therapeutic benefits.

Psilocybin's classification presents a paradox: although it is placed alongside heroin and crack cocaine in terms of legal status, it exhibits a markedly different risk profile. Unlike opioids or stimulants, psilocybin has extremely low toxicity, is non-addictive, and has shown promise in treating a range of psychiatric conditions, particularly treatment-resistant depression and post-traumatic stress disorder (PTSD). As Nutt et al. (2013) pointed out in a *Nature Reviews Neuroscience* article, the scheduling of psychedelics such as psilocybin under Schedule 1—defined as drugs with no medical value—creates "exceptionally difficult" conditions for researchers seeking to conduct even basic safety studies, let alone clinical trials.

More recently, Nutt has led a series of groundbreaking studies through Imperial College London's Centre for Psychedelic Research, where he and his colleagues have demonstrated that psilocybin can produce significant and sustained improvements in patients with treatment-resistant depression (Carhart-Harris et al., 2021). In clinical trials comparing psilocybin-assisted therapy to conventional antidepressants such as SSRIs, psilocybin has shown at least comparable, and often superior, results with fewer side effects (Carhart-Harris & Nutt, 2017). This line of research has also begun to explore the use of psilocybin in alleviating PTSD symptoms, where early-phase studies indicate that the compound can help individuals process traumatic memories and reduce associated anxiety and emotional numbness (Reiff et al., 2020).

However, the regulatory framework in the UK has not kept pace with these developments. Researchers must obtain a Schedule 1 licence from the Home Office to legally possess and study psilocybin, a process that is costly and time-consuming. Institutions must also install special security measures for storage, adding further barriers to entry for academic teams. These restrictions have led to what Nutt has famously described as "the worst censorship of research since the Catholic Church banned the telescope" (Nutt, 2012). The result is a chilling effect that deters promising research and delays the development of innovative treatments for some of the most debilitating mental health conditions.

This state of affairs contrasts sharply with developments in other jurisdictions. In the US, for example, the Food and Drug Administration (FDA) granted psilocybin "Breakthrough Therapy" status for depression in 2018, fast-tracking its evaluation for clinical use. Similar regulatory shifts are occurring in Canada and parts of Europe, suggesting that the UK's intransigence may lead to a competitive disadvantage in the emerging field of psychedelic medicine.

Furthermore, Taylor (2016) argues that the resistance to reclassifying or descheduling psilocybin and similar substances is not merely bureaucratic inertia but reflects a deeper ideological commitment to punitive drug policies. The framing of psychedelics as dangerous or subversive substances, rooted in the moral panics of the 1960s and 70 s, continues to shape public and political attitudes, despite scientific evidence to the contrary. This disconnect between evidence and policy not only undermines the UK's scientific credibility but also deprives patients of access to potentially transformative therapies.

## International Comparisons and Alternative Approaches

Other countries have adopted more evidence-based approaches to drug policy, challenging the punitive models that still dominate in the UK. Portugal, for instance, decriminalised the possession of all drugs for personal use in 2001, shifting its focus from punishment to public health. Rather than face criminal charges, individuals found in possession of small quantities are referred to dissuasion panels composed of legal, medical, and social work professionals who can recommend treatment or other interventions. The results have been significant: within a decade of implementation, drug-related deaths plummeted, rates of HIV transmission via injecting drug use dropped dramatically, and overall levels of drug use remained stable or declined, particularly among young people (Greenwald, 2009; Hughes & Stevens, 2010).

Portugal's model also reduced stigma around drug use, allowing users to seek help without fear of legal repercussions. The approach not only demonstrated compassion but was grounded in cost-effectiveness, reducing pressures on the criminal justice system and allowing resources to be redirected towards health services. Its success has influenced policy discussions in multiple jurisdictions.

In Switzerland, a heroin-assisted treatment programme for long-term dependent users has been in operation since the 1990s and has demonstrated reductions in crime, improved health outcomes, and successful reintegration of users into employment and stable housing (Uchtenhagen, 2010). Participants receive medically regulated doses of heroin in supervised clinical settings, eliminating many of the harms associated with street use and illegal procurement. In Canada, a harm reduction approach has evolved to include supervised consumption sites, decriminalisation pilots, and the prescription of pharmaceutical alternatives to street opioids—measures introduced to combat a devastating opioid overdose crisis.

These international models stand in stark contrast to the UK's continued reliance on prohibition and criminal penalties, even as domestic drug-related deaths hit record highs and public health indicators worsen. The evidence is clear: humane, health-led policies work. The question is whether the UK has the political courage to follow suit.

## Conclusion and Recommendations

The UK's current drug classification system, governed by the *Misuse of Drugs Act 1971*, presents itself as a rational, evidence-based framework for controlling substances that pose harm to individuals and society. However, a critical analysis of its history, application, and outcomes reveals a structure steeped in political expediency, cultural prejudice, and media-driven moral panic rather than in scientific integrity. From the unjustified reclassification of cannabis to the suppression of research on psilocybin, and the public vilification of experts like Professor David Nutt, the evidence consistently points to a system that prioritises political narratives over harm reduction, medical innovation, or public health.

The case of psilocybin—currently classified as a Class A substance despite growing scientific consensus on its therapeutic potential—exemplifies the way in which outdated legal categories actively inhibit potentially life-saving medical research. Meanwhile, harmful yet legal substances like alcohol and tobacco continue to receive political protection despite their far greater societal toll. This inconsistency not only erodes public trust but also undermines the credibility of the UK's entire drug control framework.

International comparisons further underscore the inadequacies of UK policy. Countries such as Portugal, Switzerland, and Canada have moved towards models that prioritise evidence, compassion, and harm reduction over punishment and stigma. These models have yielded measurable improvements in public health, social stability, and individual outcomes. By contrast, the UK continues to see record drug-related deaths and stagnation in addiction treatment outcomes, despite decades of punitive policy.

To realign drug classification with scientific evidence and public health priorities, the following recommendations are proposed:

1. Establish an Independent Statutory Advisory Body.

The current Advisory Council on the Misuse of Drugs (ACMD) operates in a consultative capacity, but ministers retain the power to ignore its recommendations without justification. To ensure evidence is meaningfully integrated into policy, the UK should establish an independent, statutory body with protected autonomy to review classifications, conduct impact assessments, and oversee reforms. This model could mirror NICE (the National Institute for Health and Care Excellence) in its relationship to medical guidance.

2. Implement Transparent, Evidence-Based Review Mechanisms.

All drug classifications should be subject to regular, independent reviews grounded in current scientific understanding of pharmacological harm, dependency potential, and social impact. A formal review cycle—every five years, for example—would ensure the system evolves with research rather than lagging behind it. Such a mechanism must also account for functional patterns of use, recognising the difference between recreational, dependent, and therapeutic consumption.

3. Deschedule or Reschedule Drugs with Proven Medical Value.

Substances such as psilocybin, MDMA, and cannabis—with growing evidence of their therapeutic potential—should be urgently re-evaluated and reclassified to facilitate medical research and clinical trials. This includes removing them from Schedule 1 and ensuring that research institutions are not burdened by excessive licensing costs and security requirements that hinder innovation and treatment development.

4. Decriminalise Personal Possession.

Drawing from the Portuguese model, the UK should decriminalise the possession of small quantities of drugs for personal use. This reform would reframe drug use as a health issue rather than a criminal one, reduce the burden on the justice system, and enable early interventions for problematic use. Decriminalisation should be paired with investment in mental health services, addiction support, and social care. We will address this more in later chapters on criminalisation.

5. Introduce Public Education Campaigns Based on Scientific Literacy.

Public understanding of drug harms is often shaped by sensationalist media coverage rather than balanced, evidence-based information. A national campaign grounded in scientific literacy—using infographics, school-based education, and community outreach—would help to shift public attitudes, reduce stigma, and support a more honest conversation about substance use.

6. Protect and Amplify Scientific Voices.

The treatment of Professor David Nutt exemplifies how scientific dissent is often met with censorship rather than critical engagement. Policymaking must explicitly protect the role of independent researchers and ensure that political discomfort does not silence or distort legitimate academic findings. Engaging scientific advisors in public discourse, rather than sidelining them, will foster more robust, transparent policymaking.

## Final Reflections

Ultimately, a modern, humane, and effective drug policy must be grounded in reality, not rhetoric. The evidence is clear: the UK's current classification system is not only outdated but actively counterproductive. It criminalises individuals unnecessarily—often targeting already marginalised populations—and misallocates resources that could be better spent on health, education, housing, and treatment services. The system also obstructs scientific and medical progress, stalling promising innovations in mental health care and pain management, while placing unnecessary and expensive barriers on academic research. Most fundamentally, it fails to reduce harm: drug-related deaths in the UK have continued to rise to record levels, and problematic use has not been curtailed by prohibition. Instead, the punitive model fuels stigma, drives users underground, and deters people from seeking help when they need it most.

Reform is not only possible but urgent. A growing body of international evidence demonstrates that alternative models—based on decriminalisation, harm reduction, and sustained public health investment—are not only viable but far more effective at achieving the very outcomes UK policymakers claim to prioritise. Portugal's decriminalisation framework, Switzerland's heroin-assisted treatment, and Canada's public health-led overdose response all point to models that reduce harm, improve lives, and restore dignity to those most affected. Ignoring this evidence does not just reflect intellectual laziness or political conservatism—it constitutes an ethical failure, particularly in light of the harms caused by criminalisation and the persistent racial and social inequalities it exacerbates.

The pathway forward lies in listening to science, learning from international experience, and prioritising health over punishment. This means replacing ideological posturing with honest public dialogue, empowering independent scientific advisors, and building a drug policy that reflects the complex, messy realities of drug use in the twenty-first century. It means recognising that drug use exists along a spectrum—functional, recreational, problematic—and that our laws must reflect that nuance, not erase it.

Such a transformation will not be easy, and it will inevitably face resistance from entrenched political, economic, and media interests. But the alternative is to maintain a broken system—one that damages lives, wastes public funds, and leaves the UK increasingly isolated from the progressive and pragmatic policy developments taking place across the globe.

Without such reform, the UK risks not only falling behind in global health innovation but continuing to inflict avoidable harm on the very people its policies purport to protect. The time for change is not tomorrow—it is now.

## References

Advisory Council on the Misuse of Drugs (ACMD). (2008). *Cannabis: Classification and public health*. Home Office.

Advisory Council on the Misuse of Drugs (ACMD). (2023). *Nitrous oxide: A review of the evidence*. Home Office.

Carhart-Harris, R. L., & Nutt, D. J. (2017). Serotonin and brain function: a tale of two receptors. *Journal of Psychopharmacology*, 31(9), 1091–1120.

Carhart-Harris, R.L. et al. (2021). Trial of psilocybin versus escitalopram for depression. *New England Journal of Medicine, 384*(15), 1402–1411.

Critcher, C. (2003). *Moral panics and the media*. Open University Press.

Greenwald, G. (2009). *Drug decriminalization in Portugal: Lessons for creating fair and successful drug policies*. Cato Institute.

Home Office. (2009). *Guidance on the Misuse of Drugs Act 1971*. London: Home Office.

House of Commons Science and Technology Committee. (2006). *Drug classification: Making a hash of it? Fifth report of session 2005–06*. The Stationery.

Hughes, C. E., & Stevens, A. (2010). What can we learn from the Portuguese decriminalization of illicit drugs? *British Journal of Criminology, 50*(6), 999–1022.

Monaghan, M. (2008). Appreciating cannabis: The paradox of evidence in evidence-based policy making. *Policy and Politics, 36*(2), 295–311.

Nutt, D. (2009). Equasy – An overlooked addiction with implications for the current debate on drug harms, *Journal of Psychopharmacology, 23*(1), 3–5.

Nutt, D.J. (2012). *Drugs-without the hot air: Minimising the harms of legal and illegal drugs*. Cambridge: UIT Cambridge.

Nutt, D., King, L. A., Nichols, D. E., & Nichols, C. D. (2013). Effects of schedule I drug laws on neuroscience research and treatment innovation. *Nature Reviews Neuroscience, 14*(8), 577–585.

Nutt, D., King, L. A., & Phillips, L. D. (2010). Drug harms in the UK: A multicriteria decision analysis. *The Lancet, 376*(9752), 1558–1565.

Reiff, C.M. et al. (2020). Psychedelics and psychedelic-assisted psychotherapy, *JAMA Psychiatry, 77*(7), 695–704.

Seddon, T. (2011). Explaining drug policy: Towards an historical sociology of policy change. *International Journal of Drug Policy, 22*(6), 415–419.
Stevens, A. (2007). Survival of the ideas that fit: An evolutionary analogy for the use of evidence in policy. *Social Policy and Society, 6*(1), 25–35.
Taylor, S. (2016). *Drug Law and policy in the UK: The politics of misinformation.* Routledge.
Uchtenhagen, A. (2010). Heroin-assisted treatment in Switzerland: A case study in policy change. *Addictive Behaviours, 35*(10), 913–918.

CHAPTER 3

# The War on Some Drugs, Who Really Pays the Price?

**Abstract** This chapter provides a critical analysis of the disproportionate impacts of UK drug policy on marginalised communities, particularly Black, Asian, and minority ethnic (BAME) groups and individuals living in socio-economically deprived areas. Despite the rhetorical framing of drug laws as neutral mechanisms of public health and safety, evidence shows that their implementation entrenches structural inequalities. Through an interdisciplinary synthesis of academic research, government reviews, and policy critiques, the chapter examines how race, class, and geography intersect to shape differential experiences of policing, prosecution, and punishment.

Focusing on stop and search practices, sentencing disparities, and access to treatment, the chapter demonstrates how drug enforcement disproportionately targets visible, street-level use in racialised and impoverished communities. Conversely, middle-class functional users—who consume similar substances in private, socially sanctioned settings—are rarely subject to criminal sanctions. This selective enforcement not only perpetuates injustice but also undermines public health objectives by criminalising the very communities most in need of support.

The chapter also explores how corporate and institutional actors, particularly within the pharmaceutical industry, escape the scrutiny applied to individual users, despite their role in large-scale drug-related harms. Drawing on case studies including the opioid crisis, it argues that the political economy of drug policy protects power and punishes poverty.



E. Peatfield, *Drugs Disorder by Design*,
https://doi.org/10.1007/978-3-032-07814-8_3

Moreover, it highlights the role of media narratives in shaping public perception—framing affluent drug users as experimental or harmless, while depicting poorer, racialised users as dangerous or deviant.

Importantly, the chapter situates these issues within broader calls for reform. It considers alternative models of harm reduction and decriminalisation, drawing on examples from Scotland, Portugal, and global best practice. The chapter concludes by arguing that meaningful reform must go beyond piecemeal decriminalisation and address the structural determinants of drug misuse—such as housing, health care, education, and employment—through a health-centred and socially just policy framework.

Ultimately, this chapter exposes the UK's drug enforcement regime as a system of selective criminalisation, not a rational tool for managing harm. It calls for a paradigm shift in both policy and institutional culture: one that acknowledges the deep inequities in current practice and seeks to redress them through evidence, equity, and compassion.

**Keywords** UK Drug Policy · Racial Disparities · Criminalisation · Harm Reduction · Functional Users · Stop and Search · Class Inequality · Night-Time Economy · Decriminalisation · Corporate Impunity

## Introduction

The formulation and enforcement of drug policy in the UK have historically been shaped by a combination of legal, political, and moral imperatives, often underpinned by punitive ideologies. Yet increasingly, scrutiny has turned towards the uneven impacts of these policies—notably their disproportionate effects on marginalised communities. Despite political rhetoric framing drug policy as a neutral instrument of public health and safety, a growing body of evidence suggests otherwise. Black, Asian and minority ethnic (BAME) individuals, people experiencing poverty, and those in socio-economically disadvantaged areas are consistently overrepresented at every stage of the drug enforcement process—from police surveillance to sentencing and incarceration (Lammy, 2017; Release, 2022).

This chapter critically explores the uneven terrain of UK drug policy, focusing particularly on the intersection of race, class, and justice. It argues that while the stated aim of drug legislation is to protect individuals and communities from the harms of substance misuse, the implementation of these laws has entrenched cycles of inequality and exclusion. Drawing on empirical data, government reports, and academic analysis, the chapter illuminates how policies that are ostensibly about reducing harm often perpetuate systemic bias. In contrast, more privileged populations—functional drug users from middle- and upper-class backgrounds—often consume the same or similar substances without fear of police or judicial intervention (Stevens, 2020).

At the heart of this analysis is the concept of disproportionality. Stop and search practices, for example, remain a key site of racialised policing. Under Section 60 of the Criminal Justice and Public Order Act 1994, officers are granted discretionary powers to stop individuals without specific suspicion. In practice, these powers are disproportionately applied to Black and minority ethnic individuals, with Black people in England and Wales nine times more likely to be stopped and searched than white people (Home Office, 2021). Crucially, these searches do not result in higher discovery rates of illicit substances, exposing the racial bias that underpins such interventions (Release, 2022; Walker, 2023). The effects are not merely procedural—they extend into the daily lives of those policed, cultivating distrust in authorities, damaging community relations, and contributing to a criminal record that may follow an individual indefinitely.

These policing patterns cannot be divorced from broader socio-economic dynamics. Marginalised communities are more likely to be targeted because of the visibility of their drug use and the geographical concentration of enforcement in deprived areas. According to the Runnymede Trust (2021), young Black men living in inner-city neighbourhoods are significantly more likely to be arrested for low-level drug possession, despite no evidence suggesting higher usage rates than their white peers. This suggests that drug policy enforcement is influenced less by actual patterns of drug use and more by spatial, racial, and class-based profiling.

Moreover, the disparities do not end at arrest. Courtroom data reveals consistent sentencing inequities. The Lammy Review (2017) found that Black men were 240% more likely to receive custodial sentences for drug offences than white men for comparable crimes. Sentencing outcomes are influenced by "risk narratives" that depict minority defendants as more dangerous or less rehabilitative, leading to harsher penalties (Eastwood et al., 2016). These narratives are often shaped by the implicit biases of predominantly white institutions, including the judiciary and legal services.

In stark contrast, drug use among affluent, predominantly white populations is frequently overlooked or treated with leniency. Functional users—those who use drugs recreationally without apparent disruption to their lives—are rarely subject to police intervention, even when engaging in illegal behaviours such as cocaine use or non-prescribed stimulant use. Cannabis, in particular, is increasingly seen by sections of the population as a benign substance, with many no longer considering it a "real" drug (Release, 2022). This perception is reinforced by empirical evidence: Nutt et al. (2010) ranked alcohol as significantly more harmful to individuals and society than cannabis, LSD, or ecstasy. Nevertheless, it is poorer, racialised communities who are more likely to suffer criminal consequences for cannabis possession.

The selective enforcement of drug laws points towards a deeper structural issue: the criminalisation of poverty and racialised identity. As Monaghan and Yeomans (2016) argue, the same substances consumed in different contexts—socially versus publicly, discreetly versus visibly—produce very different outcomes depending on the user's social positioning. This double standard is not only unfair; it undermines public health goals by driving marginalised users away from support services and reinforcing the stigma that prevents effective harm reduction.

This chapter will proceed by exploring the policing practices that most starkly illustrate racial and class-based disparities, the courtroom dynamics that perpetuate sentencing inequalities, and the growing cultural acceptance of drug use among elites. It will also consider the systemic failure of UK policy to address the social determinants of drug misuse, such as unemployment, poor housing, and lack of access to health care. Through this analysis, the chapter makes a case for urgent reform—not just of drug laws themselves, but of the wider institutional cultures that apply them. By shifting from punitive approaches to health-centred, evidence-based models, and by ensuring accountability in policing and prosecution, drug policy could begin to serve all communities more equitably.

Ultimately, the chapter sets out to show that UK drug policy does not fail because it is ineffective in reducing drug use—it fails because it systematically punishes the most vulnerable while ignoring the privilege that insulates others. This is not a war on drugs; it is a war on the poor, dressed in the language of justice.

## Drug Policies Disproportionate Impact on Marginalised Communities

Policing strategies in the UK have been persistently criticised for disproportionately targeting Black, Asian and minority ethnic (BAME) communities, particularly in relation to drug offences. One of the most controversial practices is the use of stop and search powers under Section 60 of the Criminal Justice and Public Order Act 1994, which allows police officers to stop individuals without reasonable suspicion in designated areas. Although framed as a necessary tool for reducing violent crime, this power is regularly used in drug enforcement and is widely regarded as racially biased (Walker, 2023). According to the Home Office (2021), Black people were nine times more likely to be stopped and searched than white people in England and Wales in 2020–21. Yet, crucially, the rate of drug discovery during these searches is lower for Black individuals than for white individuals, undermining the claim that disparities are based on intelligence-led policing (Release, 2022).

This racial disproportionality is not a new trend. The Equality and Human Rights Commission (2019) has highlighted systemic concerns around the over-policing of ethnic minorities, pointing to a lack of accountability and oversight in how discretionary police powers are exercised. The persistent use of stop and search, despite minimal evidence of its effectiveness in reducing drug misuse or serious crime, has been interpreted as an example of institutional racism—a term first formally applied to policing by the Macpherson Report (1999) following the inquiry into the murder of Stephen Lawrence. This practice not only leads to unnecessary criminalisation but also erodes trust between law enforcement and BAME communities, making collaborative public health interventions more difficult to implement (Stevens, 2020).

Further compounding these issues, stop and search is often concentrated in socio-economically deprived areas—locations that are disproportionately populated by ethnic minority groups. This creates a double disadvantage where both race and class intersect to increase the likelihood of criminal justice intervention. According to the Runnymede Trust (2021), young Black men living in urban poverty are especially vulnerable to being swept into the criminal justice system for low-level drug possession, despite evidence suggesting they are not more likely to use drugs than their white peers.

These disparities continue into the courtroom. The Lammy Review (2017), an independent investigation into the treatment of BAME individuals in the criminal justice system, found that Black men were 240% more likely to be given a prison sentence for a drug offence than white men, even when controlling for the type of offence and prior convictions. Similarly, sentencing data from the Ministry of Justice (2020) indicates that Black and mixed-ethnicity defendants are more likely to receive immediate custody for drug-related offences than white defendants, and their average sentence lengths are also longer.

The reasons for these judicial disparities are multifaceted. One key factor is the existence of "risk narratives" within the criminal justice system, where BAME defendants are often perceived as inherently more dangerous or non-compliant, leading to more punitive outcomes (Eastwood et al., 2016). Additionally, systemic biases such as the underrepresentation of ethnic minorities in the judiciary and legal professions contribute to the perpetuation of these inequalities. Cultural misunderstandings, language barriers, and reduced access to high-quality legal representation further marginalise defendants from minority backgrounds.

Intersecting with racial injustice is the role of socio-economic deprivation in shaping drug-related encounters with the criminal justice system. Areas of high unemployment, limited access to education, and inadequate housing—factors more prevalent in minority communities—are associated with increased vulnerability to problematic drug use (Garside, 2020). However, punitive drug policies often fail to address these structural conditions. Instead, enforcement disproportionately targets visible street-level offences, such as cannabis possession, while ignoring less visible but equally harmful patterns of drug use among affluent populations (Monaghan & Yeomans, 2016).

This emphasis on criminalisation over social intervention creates a feedback loop. A young person caught with a small amount of cannabis may acquire a criminal record, making it more difficult to access employment, education, or housing—all factors known to protect against drug misuse and reoffending. As noted by the Public Accounts Committee (2022), the failure to adopt a holistic, evidence-based approach to drug misuse has resulted in poor outcomes, with higher rates of recidivism and sustained social exclusion for those most vulnerable.

Moreover, there is evidence to suggest that BAME individuals are less likely to be referred to or engage with drug treatment services.

Barriers include stigma, distrust of public institutions, and a lack of culturally appropriate services (Black, 2021). In failing to account for these factors, current drug policy not only punishes but also neglects minority groups, exacerbating health inequalities and undermining the potential for rehabilitation.

In summary, the UK's enforcement-led drug policy has disproportionately criminalised BAME individuals, both through over-policing and judicial bias. Socio-economic deprivation compounds this inequality, creating a system in which those already disadvantaged by race and poverty are more likely to be prosecuted, imprisoned, and excluded from public health support. These outcomes demand urgent reform towards a more equitable, health-based approach to drug misuse.

## Functional Users, Normalised Drug Culture, and Corporate Impunity

One of the most significant yet under-acknowledged features of UK drug policy is the selective scrutiny applied to different classes of drug users. While marginalised communities are aggressively policed for visible, street-level drug use, a growing segment of functional drug users—predominantly from middle- and upper-class backgrounds—experience little to no legal repercussions for the same or similar behaviours. Functional users are individuals who incorporate drugs into their recreational or professional lives without significant disruption to their daily routines. This includes, for example, middle-class professionals using cocaine at social gatherings, students using stimulants to aid academic performance, or cannabis being consumed for relaxation, creative enhancement, or stress relief.

The rising normalisation of certain drugs, particularly cannabis, has shifted public perceptions to the extent that many no longer regard such substances as "real" drugs at all. A recent survey by Release (2022) found that a substantial number of university students and young professionals viewed cannabis as less harmful than alcohol or tobacco, a view echoed in broader public opinion surveys. This perception is supported by empirical evidence; Nutt et al. (2010), using a multi-criteria decision analysis model published in *The Lancet*, ranked alcohol as the most harmful drug overall, significantly more so than cannabis, ecstasy or LSD. These findings have fuelled ongoing debates over the appropriateness of the UK's drug classification system and whether it reflects actual harm or outdated social values.

Despite shifting attitudes, enforcement continues to be applied unevenly. According to the Home Office (2021), cannabis remains the most commonly used illicit drug in the UK across all ethnic and socio-economic groups. However, police data reveal that Black individuals are far more likely to be stopped, searched and prosecuted for cannabis possession than their white counterparts (Release, 2022). Crucially, this disparity exists despite similar or lower rates of cannabis use among Black populations. The disproportionality suggests that enforcement is less about the behaviour itself and more about the visibility and social positioning of the user.

Drug use in private residences, corporate offices, and exclusive festivals is far less likely to attract law enforcement attention than the same behaviours in public housing estates or urban neighbourhoods with high police presence (Stevens, 2020). As Bourgois (1995) argues, this represents a form of "symbolic violence" in which societal structures criminalise the survival strategies of the poor while excusing the leisure activities of the privileged. This selective enforcement fosters a two-tiered system of justice: one that tolerates drug use among the affluent as harmless experimentation or lifestyle choice, and another that treats drug use among the working class and racially minoritised as evidence of criminality and moral failure.

Moreover, the increasing popularity of microdosing psychedelics, the use of prescription stimulants for productivity, and the commercialisation of cannabidiol (CBD) products are examples of how drug use among the wealthy has been medicalised or aestheticised. In contrast, the same substances when found in the possession of working-class individuals are often pathologised. As Monaghan and Yeomans (2016) note, drug-taking among elites is frequently narrated in the media as controlled, informed, and safe, while drug-taking among the poor is constructed as reckless, dangerous and deviant.

Compounding this inequity is the limited scrutiny applied to corporate actors who profit from and contribute to drug-related harms on a massive scale. Pharmaceutical companies, particularly those involved in opioid manufacturing, have played a central role in one of the most devastating public health crises of recent decades. Purdue Pharma's aggressive marketing of OxyContin in the US, which downplayed addiction risks, has been widely documented and legally challenged (Black, 2021). While the UK has not experienced an opioid crisis of the same magnitude, the prescription of synthetic opioids such as fentanyl, tramadol, and oxycodone has risen sharply over the past two decades, with opioid-related deaths increasing in parallel (Public Accounts Committee, 2022).

Despite this, pharmaceutical companies rarely face criminal charges for their role in fuelling addiction. The contrast between the legal impunity of corporate actors and the severe penalties meted out to individuals caught in possession of heroin or crack cocaine is striking. The disparity reflects a structural bias in UK drug policy: harm caused by powerful institutions is treated as a regulatory issue, while harm linked to impoverished individuals is treated as criminal (Eastwood et al., 2016).

The influence of pharmaceutical lobbying in delaying regulatory reforms and framing drug debates also contributes to the protection of corporate interests. As Garside (2020) notes, successive UK governments have been reluctant to challenge pharmaceutical companies despite mounting evidence of overprescription, often due to the economic and political influence these companies wield. Even when firms are fined or publicly criticised, these penalties pale in comparison to the social and legal sanctions faced by individual drug users.

This class-based double standard extends to how legality itself is conferred. The development of the UK's medical cannabis market, for instance, illustrates how access to certain drugs is increasingly mediated by wealth and social capital. Although medical cannabis was legalised in 2018, the vast majority of prescriptions remain privately issued and unaffordable for most working-class patients. At the same time, thousands continue to be arrested for growing or possessing cannabis without a prescription, even when used for therapeutic purposes (Black, 2021). This inconsistency reveals a troubling contradiction: cannabis is both a legal medicine and an illegal drug, depending not on the substance itself but on who is using it, why, and whether they can afford a doctor.

The role of the media in sustaining these contradictions must also be recognised. Recreational drug use among celebrities, influencers, and tech entrepreneurs is often portrayed as quirky or enlightened, while reports of drug use in deprived areas are routinely framed as symptomatic of social breakdown or gang violence. This moral hierarchy is deeply racialised and classed. As the Runnymede Trust (2021) argues, public attitudes are shaped not just by facts but by cultural narratives that valorise the "right kind" of drug user and vilify the "wrong" one.

In conclusion, the UK's drug enforcement regime is deeply shaped by class and corporate privilege. Functional users from middle- and upper-class backgrounds enjoy a level of social and legal tolerance that is systematically denied to working-class and racially minoritised individuals. At the same time, corporations that profit from addictive substances face minimal accountability for the public health consequences of their products. As drug use becomes more socially acceptable in certain contexts—particularly cannabis—these disparities become increasingly indefensible. Addressing this hypocrisy requires more than tinkering with classifications; it demands a fundamental reorientation of drug policy around principles of equity, public health, and social justice.

## Critiques and Calls for Reform

A growing body of academic literature critiques the UK's punitive drug policies, advocating for a shift towards harm reduction and public health approaches. Studies suggest that decriminalisation and the provision of support services can more effectively address drug misuse and its associated harms than criminalisation. These perspectives emphasise the need for evidence-based policies that prioritise health outcomes over punitive measures.

Government-commissioned reviews, such as the Lammy Review and reports by the Public Accounts Committee, have acknowledged the shortcomings of current drug policies and their disproportionate impact on marginalised communities. Recommendations from these reviews include the implementation of culturally competent treatment services, the reduction of racial disparities in the criminal justice system, and the adoption of harm reduction strategies. However, the translation of these recommendations into policy has been slow and inconsistent.

## Scotland's Drug Death Crisis and the Role of "Civilised" Society

Scotland currently has the highest rate of drug-related deaths in Europe, a public health crisis that has prompted significant scrutiny of the country's existing drug laws and health interventions. According to the National Records of Scotland (2023), 1051 drug misuse deaths were registered in 2022—a slight decrease from 2021 but still nearly three times higher than the UK average. This devastating trend has forced a revaluation of drug policy in Scotland, with increasing emphasis placed on harm reduction, decriminalisation, and the need for a health-led approach to drug use.

The Scottish Government has consistently framed the drug crisis as a public health emergency, calling for policy tools that prioritise care over punishment. Among the most prominent proposals has been the introduction of supervised drug consumption facilities (DCRs)—medically monitored spaces where people can consume pre-obtained drugs safely. The rationale for these centres is grounded in substantial international evidence. In Canada, Germany, and Switzerland, DCRs have been shown to reduce overdose fatalities, prevent the spread of bloodborne viruses such as HIV and hepatitis C, and facilitate entry into addiction treatment and social support services (Potier et al., 2014).

Despite strong support from public health experts and the Scottish Government, the legal authority to open such facilities remains reserved to Westminster. Under the Misuse of Drugs Act 1971, operating a DCR could be considered facilitating the use of controlled substances—a criminal offence under UK law. This legal impasse has led to increasing tensions between the Scottish and UK governments. In 2023, Scotland's Lord Advocate, Dorothy Bain KC, made a landmark decision to allow a DCR pilot in Glasgow by signalling that it would not be in the public interest to prosecute those operating or using the facility (Crawford, 2023). This marks a significant step forward in devolved harm reduction strategies, though the pilot remains in early stages.

Parallel to the push for DCRs, Scotland has also led calls for the decriminalisation of personal drug possession. A 2021 report by the Scottish Affairs Committee recommended a radical overhaul of UK drug policy, arguing that criminalising drug users exacerbates stigma, reduces the likelihood of individuals seeking help, and places undue strain on the criminal justice system (UK Parliament, 2021). In response, the Scottish Government has explored the use of Recorded Police Warnings (RPWs) as a de facto form of decriminalisation for simple possession offences. Introduced nationally in 2021, RPWs allow officers to issue warnings rather than arrests, shifting the state response from criminal justice to health and social care (Scottish Government, 2021).

Evidence from Portugal, which decriminalised personal drug use in 2001, supports the logic behind this approach. Following the reform, Portugal saw reductions in drug-related deaths, HIV infections, and incarceration rates, alongside increased uptake of voluntary treatment (Hughes & Stevens, 2010). While Scotland has not adopted a full

Portuguese model, the direction of travel indicates a willingness to experiment with alternative strategies grounded in public health evidence.

Importantly, this shift in Scottish policy has been driven not only by government action but by the sustained advocacy of civil society organisations. Groups such as Release, Transform Drug Policy Foundation, and Scottish Drugs Forum have been instrumental in highlighting the failures of punitive drug policy and advancing evidence-based reforms.

Release, for example, has long advocated for decriminalisation, the expungement of drug-related criminal records, and the establishment of safe consumption spaces in the UK. In its reports The Colour of Injustice (Eastwood et al., 2016) and A Quiet Revolution (2016), Release presents empirical data showing racial and socio-economic disparities in drug enforcement, while providing case studies from countries that have successfully implemented health-based alternatives. These publications serve as tools for both public education and policy lobbying.

Similarly, the Transform Drug Policy Foundation has played a critical role in shaping the discourse around legal regulation and harm reduction. Its report How to Regulate Stimulants (2021) outlines a pragmatic framework for reducing the harms associated with unregulated drug markets by controlling the production and distribution of substances such as MDMA and cocaine. Although politically controversial, Transform's evidence-based approach has helped shift conversations from moral panic to pragmatic reform.

In Scotland specifically, Scottish Drugs Forum (SDF) and Crest Advisory have collaborated with healthcare providers, people with lived experience, and local authorities to support harm reduction initiatives on the ground. SDF has launched training programmes to develop peer naloxone distribution networks, recognising that community responders are often the first on the scene during an overdose (Scottish Drugs Forum, 2022). Research suggests that widespread naloxone availability can reduce opioid-related deaths by as much as 30% (McDonald & Strang, 2016).

Civil society organisations also play a key role in challenging stigma, a major barrier to treatment and recovery. A 2020 study by the Glasgow Centre for Population Health found that individuals labelled as "junkies" or "addicts" often internalise negative stereotypes, which undermines their self-worth and willingness to seek help (Carnegie et al., 2020). Campaigns such as "See Beyond" and "You Are Not Alone" have sought to humanise people who use drugs and reframe addiction as a health issue, not a criminal failing.

Moreover, third-sector actors are often pioneers in service innovation. Projects such as Safe Space in Glasgow, a mobile health unit providing sterile injecting equipment and referrals to support services, are examples of how civil society fills gaps left by overstretched public systems. While not officially designated DCRs, these initiatives demonstrate the feasibility and acceptability of harm reduction in Scottish communities.

Nevertheless, the capacity of civil society to effect change is not without constraints. Funding remains a persistent challenge, particularly for organisations that advocate policies seen as politically contentious. Moreover, while civil society actors have proven adept at influencing public opinion and policy debate, implementation often stalls at the level of intergovernmental coordination. The tension between devolved health powers and reserved drug laws under the UK's constitutional framework continues to limit Scotland's ability to enact full-scale reform.

Despite these obstacles, the trajectory of drug policy in Scotland stands in contrast to the UK Government's continued reliance on criminalisation. The UK Government's 10-Year Drug Strategy, launched in 2021, reaffirmed an enforcement-led approach, including intensified policing and stricter sentencing for supply offences (HM Government, 2021). Critics argue this strategy misses the opportunity to engage with the evidence amassed in countries and jurisdictions—like Scotland—that are taking a more progressive stance.

In summary, Scotland's experience highlights both the urgency and potential of reforming drug policy through a public health lens. The high rate of drug-related deaths has galvanised political and civil society efforts to adopt harm reduction measures, including supervised consumption sites and de facto decriminalisation. Civil society organisations have been central to these developments, offering research, advocacy, and frontline services that directly impact lives. While legal barriers and funding issues persist, Scotland's evolving drug policy provides a compelling case study in the possibilities of humane, evidence-based reform.

## Authors Reflection—The Fallout of Drugs in the NTE-

One of the most persistent challenges faced by drug users—and those of us who have worked around them—is the arbitrary distinction between "good" drugs and "bad" drugs, and by extension, "good" users and "bad" users. These categories are shaped not by pharmacology, but by politics, media narratives, and cultural acceptability. In my years working as a bouncer—through the late 1980s, the 1990s, and into the new millennium—I saw these labels in action, and I watched the drug landscape in the night-time economy (NTE) change dramatically.

In the '80 s, drug use on the doors I worked was mostly a mix of booze and speed, with only occasional use of cocaine—a substance that was still considered expensive and elite. By the '90 s, the dominant combination had shifted to booze and cocaine, particularly among city centre crowds. Alongside this, the dance and rave generation emerged, bringing with it a wave of ecstasy use. What was notable then was a subset of clubbers who would avoid alcohol altogether—their nights fuelled solely by MDMA, music, and movement. It wasn't necessarily safer, but it was a different culture, often more communal and less aggressive.

But by the late '90 s and early 2000s, things changed again. Ketamine began to appear in increasing quantities, and unlike other substances, its street price began to fall. Today, ketamine use in the NTE is endemic—partly because it remains relatively cheap compared to almost everything else. And with the criminalisation of new substances over time, we saw a predictable pattern: adaptation. What was once simply MDMA became something else entirely. Pills were increasingly cut with other substances—ketamine, caffeine, baby powder, or even LSD—and pressed into tablets stamped with cartoon logos like doves or monkeys to appear playful, approachable, and safe. But of course, they weren't always safe.

I remember one night all too clearly. I was working the doors at a major club—one that genuinely tried to take drug safety seriously. A young woman, just starting university, came to the venue with a friend. She took one tablet while queuing to get in. That tablet killed her. It had been cut with ketamine, which she was unknowingly allergic to. She didn't even know it was in the pill.

We did everything we could, but it was too late. She was rushed to hospital but dies there later that night. Eighteen years old.

The heartbreak of that night stayed with me—with all of us who were working. For her family, the pain must be unimaginable and enduring. But what made it worse for me was knowing it wasn't the MDMA she thought she'd taken that killed her. It was the adulterant—a direct consequence of criminalisation pushing the market underground and unregulated.

We, the staff, were left shaken for years. We'd seen people take "the knock" before—a term we used for when someone became seriously ill from a dodgy batch—but this was different. This was a death that didn't need to happen. A life lost, not to a drug per se, but to a broken system that refuses to treat drug use as a public health issue.

## Conclusion

The UK's current drug policy framework, built on the foundations of the Misuse of Drugs Act 1971, continues to fail in both efficacy and equity. Designed at a time when drug use was framed as a moral panic rather than a public health concern, the Act entrenched punitive measures that have disproportionately impacted marginalised communities—especially Black, Asian, and minority ethnic (BAME) groups, and those living in socio-economically deprived areas. While the ostensible aim of drug legislation is to protect public health and reduce harm, in practice, it has facilitated the over-policing of certain groups and the criminalisation of poverty and racial identity.

One of the most striking elements of this disproportionate impact is the persistent use of stop and search powers. These have been demonstrably exercised in racially biased ways, with Black individuals being nine times more likely to be stopped and searched than white individuals, despite similar or lower rates of drug use (Home Office, 2021; Release, 2022). This pattern exemplifies how structural racism is embedded within law enforcement strategies and contributes to a broader culture of surveillance and mistrust between the police and minority communities. Furthermore, such encounters often result in minimal drug finds, highlighting the inefficacy of the approach as a tool of drug control (Walker, 2023).

Beyond policing, these disparities extend into the courtroom and correctional systems. The Lammy Review (2017) made clear that Black men were significantly more likely to be given custodial sentences for comparable drug offences than their white counterparts. These sentencing disparities stem not only from racial bias but also from risk narratives and cultural misunderstandings that influence judicial decision-making. When coupled with barriers such as inadequate legal representation and the underrepresentation of BAME individuals in legal professions, the justice system becomes an engine of cumulative disadvantage.

At the same time, the chapter has highlighted how UK drug policy largely ignores the reality of drug use among functional users—those who are affluent, often white, and able to consume drugs in ways that are socially or privately insulated from law enforcement. Cocaine use at professional gatherings, stimulant use among university students, or cannabis consumption by middle-class adults rarely attracts police intervention or judicial sanction. Instead, such drug use is either medicalised, aestheticised, or overlooked. This double standard reflects a class-based hypocrisy within the enforcement of drug laws and fuels a moral hierarchy of drug use—one that vilifies the poor and excuses the privileged (Monaghan & Yeomans, 2016; Stevens, 2020).

Corporate actors, particularly those in the pharmaceutical industry, are similarly shielded from scrutiny. The opioid crisis, driven in large part by aggressive pharmaceutical marketing, has led to thousands of preventable deaths. Yet, companies that profit from the production and distribution of addictive substances often escape criminal accountability. Their harms are framed as regulatory oversights rather than crimes, while individuals caught with small amounts of illicit drugs face life-altering consequences (Black, 2021; Public Accounts Committee, 2022). This imbalance exposes the political economy of drug control—where power and capital can deflect blame, but marginalisation attracts punitive attention.

Critiques from academia, civil society, and independent governmental reviews have converged on a call for reform. The body of evidence produced by organisations like Release, the Transform Drug Policy Foundation, and government reviews such as the Lammy Review and the Scottish Affairs Committee reports underscores the failure of punitive models and the need for a public health-oriented approach. Harm reduction strategies, such as supervised drug consumption facilities, decriminalisation of personal use, naloxone distribution, and culturally competent treatment services, offer an alternative rooted in evidence rather than ideology (Potier et al., 2014; Scottish Drugs Forum, 2022).

Moreover, international models provide robust support for this transition. Portugal's decriminalisation framework has demonstrated tangible benefits, including reductions in drug-related deaths, HIV infections, and incarceration rates (Hughes & Stevens, 2010). Scotland's more recent movement towards harm reduction, including the planned introduction of supervised drug consumption rooms and increased use of recorded police warnings for possession, represents a divergence from the Westminster status quo and illustrates what can be achieved with political will and civil society engagement (Crawford, 2023).

However, these reforms must go beyond shifting enforcement priorities. They must address the root causes of problematic drug use, including poverty, housing insecurity, trauma, and lack of access to mental health services. A genuinely equitable drug policy must be embedded in a broader agenda of social justice, with investments in education, employment, and health care acting as preventative interventions against the circumstances that often lead to drug misuse. Without this, even the most progressive harm reduction strategies risk becoming band-aid solutions.

Equally vital is the need for accountability and transparency in the institutions tasked with enforcing drug policy. Police forces must be held to account for racially biased practices, courts must adopt sentencing policies that correct for historic injustices, and corporate actors must face real consequences for public health harms caused by their products. These are not merely procedural reforms but moral imperatives in the pursuit of justice.

In conclusion, the UK's drug policy is not simply outdated—it is discriminatory and dangerous in its current form. It perpetuates cycles of inequality by criminalising already vulnerable communities while permitting privileged groups and corporate interests to operate with impunity. The solution is not more punishment but more compassion, not more surveillance but more support. Implementing evidence-based reforms that address the structural and systemic causes of drug misuse—and ensuring they are applied equitably across all communities—is essential for building a more just, humane, and effective drug policy.

## References

Black, C. (2021). *Review of drugs: Phase two report*. Home Office. Retrieved May 4, 2025, from https://www.gov.uk/government/publications/review-of-drugs-phase-two-report

Bourgois, P. (1995). *In search of respect: Selling crack in El barrio*. Cambridge University Press.

Carnegie, R., Thomson, H., & Walsh, D. (2020). *Drugs, deprivation and health in glasgow: A review of the evidence*. Glasgow Centre for Population Health.

Crawford, C., 2023, September 22. 'Lord advocate clears way for drug consumption rooms in Scotland'. *The Herald*. Retrieved May 4, 2025, from https://www.heraldscotland.com

Eastwood, N., Fox, E., & Rosmarin, A. (2016). *The colour of injustice: 'Race', drugs and law enforcement in England and Wales*. Release.

Garside, R. (2020). *The misuse of drugs act 1971: Forty years of failure*. Centre for Crime and Justice Studies. Retrieved May 4, 2025, from, https://www.crimeandjustice.org.uk/publications/misuse-drugs-act-1971-forty-years-failure

HM Government. (2021). *From harm to hope: A 10-year drugs plan to cut crime and save lives*. Home Office. Retrieved May 4, 2025, from https://www.gov.uk/government/publications/from-harm-to-hope-a-10-year-drugs-plan

Home Office. (2021). *Drug misuse: Findings from the 2019/20 crime survey for England and Wales*. Home Office.

Hughes, C. E., & Stevens, A. (2010). What can we learn from the Portuguese decriminalization of illicit drugs? *British Journal of Criminology, 50*(6), 999–1022.

Lammy, D. (2017). *The lammy review: An independent review into the treatment of, and outcomes for, black, asian and minority ethnic individuals in the criminal justice system*. Ministry of Justice. Retrieved May 4, 2025, from https://www.gov.uk/government/publications/lammy-review-final-report

McDonald, R., & Strang, J. (2016). Are take-home naloxone programmes effective? systematic review. *Addiction, 111*(7), 1177–1187.

Monaghan, M., & Yeomans, H. (2016). Mixing drink and drugs: Policy implications of polydrug use. *Drugs: Education, Prevention and Policy, 23*(2), 113–122.

National Records of Scotland. (2023). *Drug-related deaths in Scotland in 2022*. NRS. Retrieved May 4, 2025, from https://www.nrscotland.gov.uk/statistics-and-data/statistics/statistics-by-theme/vital-events/deaths/drug-related-deaths-in-scotland

Nutt, D., King, L. A., & Phillips, L. D. (2010). Drug harms in the UK: A multicriteria decision analysis. *The Lancet, 376*(9752), 1558–1565. https://doi.org/10.1016/S0140-6736(10)61462-6

Potier, C., Laprévote, V., Dubois-Arber, F., Cottencin, O., & Rolland, B. (2014). Supervised injection services: What has been demonstrated? A systematic literature review. *Drug and Alcohol Dependence, 145*, 48–68.

Public Accounts Committee. (2022). *Drug treatment and recovery: Twelfth report of session 2022–23. HC 72*. House of Commons. Retrieved May, 4, 2025, from https://publications.parliament.uk/pa/cm5803/cmselect/cmpubacc/72/report.html

Release. (2022). *Cannabis policing and young people in the UK*. Release.

Runnymede Trust. (2021). *Overpoliced and underprotected: The road to racial justice*. Runnymede Trust.

Scottish Drugs Forum. (2022). *Naloxone peer network: Annual report*. SDF. Retrieved May 4, 2025, from https://www.sdf.org.uk

Scottish Government. (2021). *Recorded police warnings for possession offences: Policy framework*. Scottish Government.

Stevens, A. (2020). Rethinking UK drug policy. *British Journal of Criminology, 60*(4), 913–927.

UK Parliament, 2021. Problem drug use in Scotland: Scottish affairs committee report. HC 1048. House of Commons. Retrieved May 4, 2025, from https://committees.parliament.uk/publications/6881/documents/72433/default/

Walker, C. (2023). Stop and search statistics and racial disparities: A review. *Policing and Society, 33*(2), 145–164.

CHAPTER 4

# Functional vs. Problematic Drug Users in the UK: A Policy Blind Spot

**Abstract** This chapter critically examines the ideological, structural, and policy-driven distinctions between *functional* and *problematic* drug users in the UK. It argues that UK drug policy is founded upon a punitive and moralistic framework that disproportionately targets socially marginalised individuals—those experiencing poverty, addiction, and visible public drug use—while largely ignoring the significant proportion of users who integrate drug consumption into otherwise stable, productive lives. The chapter deconstructs this dichotomy, exploring how the visibility and perceived deviance of problematic users have shaped a criminal justice-led approach, while functional users—typically middle- or upper-class, white, and discreet—are rendered invisible to policy and immune from enforcement.

Using an interdisciplinary framework that draws from criminology, public health, media studies, and political sociology, the chapter highlights how punitive drug enforcement practices reinforce broader social inequalities. The analysis incorporates Situational Action Theory (Wikström et al., 2012) to explain how environmental contexts and visibility mediate criminalisation, showing that where and how drug use occurs is often more consequential than what is used. Empirical data, including studies on stop-and-search practices, arrest patterns, and sentencing disparities, reveal that Black and working-class individuals are disproportionately subject to punitive sanctions, despite similar or lower rates of drug use compared to more privileged groups.


E. Peatfield, *Drugs Disorder by Design*,
https://doi.org/10.1007/978-3-032-07814-8_4

The chapter critically assesses the UK government's drug strategies—particularly the 2017 and 2021 frameworks—and finds them to be reactive, overly focused on addiction and acquisitive crime, and resistant to adopting proven harm reduction approaches. The emphasis on abstinence-based "recovery" models serves to reinforce stigma and marginalises both functional users and those whose recovery goals do not conform to abstinence. While purporting to adopt a public health orientation, the government's approach remains rooted in outdated moral binaries that categorise drugs as inherently harmful and users as either victims or villains.

A key contribution of the chapter is its focus on the ideological erasure of functional drug users. Drawing on the work of Duff (2012) and Nutt et al. (2010), it explores how the existence of controlled, non-problematic drug use challenges the foundational justifications for prohibition. Functional users often demonstrate a higher degree of responsibility and health-consciousness in their drug use than many legal substance users. Yet they are omitted from official discourse because their presence complicates simplistic narratives of drug use as disorder. This omission enables the continued marginalisation of problematic users while allowing the privileged to escape scrutiny, thus reinforcing the status quo.

The chapter also critiques the moral economy underpinning the legal classification of substances in the UK. Substances like alcohol and tobacco—responsible for significant health and social harms—remain legal and culturally embedded, while less harmful drugs such as cannabis, MDMA, or psilocybin remain criminalised due to historical prejudice and political expediency. This inconsistency reflects a policy landscape more concerned with moral order and political optics than with evidence-based harm reduction.

Finally, the chapter proposes a shift from punitive drug policy to a comprehensive public health model that accounts for the full spectrum of drug use. This includes the decriminalisation of possession for personal use, expanded access to harm reduction services (such as drug checking and supervised consumption rooms), and a re-evaluation of the legal status of substances based on scientific risk assessments. It calls for the inclusion of all user voices in drug policy development, recognising the legitimacy of controlled, functional use alongside support for those experiencing problematic patterns.

Until such reforms are implemented, the UK's drug policy will remain a mechanism of social control—a war not on drugs, but on the poor. The chapter concludes that addressing this injustice is not only a matter of effectiveness but of equity, dignity, and human rights.

**Keywords** Functional Drug Use · Problematic Drug Use · Drug Policy · Criminalisation · Harm Reduction · Social Inequality · Situational Action Theory · Moral Panic · Public Health Approach

## Introduction

Drug use in the UK is frequently conceptualised through a binary framework that conflates legality with morality and pathology. This simplistic dichotomy frames substance use as either licit and socially acceptable (such as alcohol or prescribed pharmaceuticals), or illicit and indicative of deviance or addiction. Such a framework fails to capture the nuanced reality of drug-taking behaviours across British society and distorts public understanding and policy formulation. Most notably, it obscures the substantial presence of *functional* drug users—those who consume substances without significant disruption to their daily routines or social functioning—and reinforces disproportionate scrutiny and criminalisation of *problematic* users, who are more likely to experience addiction, social exclusion, or interaction with the criminal justice system (Monaghan, 2012; Stevens, 2011).

While both categories represent different points on a spectrum of drug use, only one is typically visible in public discourse and policy. Functional users, are often portrayed as middle-class professionals or students using drugs such as cannabis, cocaine, or prescription stimulants in moderate and controlled ways, are frequently omitted from public concern and state intervention (Lancaster et al., 2017). These individuals often enjoy socioeconomic privilege, live in stable environments, and have the resources to avoid detection or criminalisation. In contrast, problematic users are often portrayed as those whose substance use is marked by dependency, homelessness, mental ill health, or criminal behaviour—are portrayed as burdens on public services, moral failures, or threats to public order (Neale et al., 2011). It is this latter group that drug policy disproportionately targets, reinforcing a moralistic and punitive approach that does little to address underlying social determinants of problematic use.

The evolution of UK drug policy illustrates the dominance of this binary. From the Misuse of Drugs Act 1971 to the most recent *From Harm to Hope* strategy (Home Office, 2021), the government's approach has oscillated between prohibitionist and abstinence-based models, rarely acknowledging the spectrum of drug use or the presence of non-disruptive, recreational users. The emphasis has typically been on the visible harms associated with problematic drug use—crime, anti-social behaviour, and overdose deaths—rather than the social context in which all forms of drug use occur. This focus not only distorts the reality of drug use but also contributes to the stigmatisation and marginalisation of already vulnerable populations.

Furthermore, the UK's criminal justice response to drug use reinforces this bias. Studies have consistently shown that policing practices, such as stop and search, disproportionately affect working-class communities and ethnic minorities, particularly Black people, despite similar or lower levels of drug use among these groups compared to their white counterparts (Eastwood et al., 2013; Release, 2016). As a result, problematic users, already more likely to be visible due to socio-economic disadvantage, are further subjected to punitive sanctions that can entrench cycles of marginalisation. Conversely, functional users, whose use is often shielded by class privilege and discretion, are far less likely to be subjected to surveillance or sanction.

The concept of "policy silence" is critical here. As Stevens (2011) notes, drug policies frequently maintain silence on patterns of use that do not conform to the dominant narrative of chaos and dependency. This silence serves a legitimising function, reinforcing the state's justification for punitive measures by presenting drug use as uniformly harmful. It also reflects what Seddon (2006) calls the "politics of visibility," where only those forms of drug use that cause public nuisance or are difficult to ignore receive attention. In this schema, problematic users become hyper-visible and pathologised, while functional users remain invisible, their experiences and risks unacknowledged in both data collection and intervention strategies.

This invisibility also has epistemological consequences. Academic and policy research overwhelmingly focuses on problematic users, given their accessibility through treatment centres, prisons, and public services. By contrast, functional users, who often do not seek help or experience acute harms, remain under-researched and poorly understood. This has resulted in a knowledge gap that reinforces the policy gap—without robust evidence on the prevalence, practices, and outcomes of functional use, policy continues to operate on assumptions rather than comprehensive understanding (Duff, 2012).

The failure to account for functional use is not just a gap in empirical understanding—it is a political choice. As Nutt et al. (2010) famously demonstrated in their multi-criteria decision analysis of drug harms, legal classification of substances in the UK does not correlate with their actual risk to individuals or society. Alcohol, for instance, was ranked as more harmful than heroin or crack cocaine when considering social costs. Yet alcohol remains legal and widely consumed, in large part due to its cultural embeddedness and economic value. The same logic protects many functional users of illegal substances, who, despite engaging in criminalised behaviours, do so in ways that are socially acceptable or economically inconsequential to the state.

The socio-economic stratification of drug policy is therefore a form of structural inequality. Those who are most likely to suffer from problematic drug use—people experiencing poverty, trauma, or mental illness—are also the most likely to be criminalised and excluded. Those who use drugs functionally—often wealthier, white, and socially mobile—are effectively exempt from this scrutiny. As Wacquant (2009)) argues, this reflects a broader pattern in neoliberal governance where the state uses punitive mechanisms to regulate the poor while insulating the privileged.

From a criminological perspective, this aligns with Garland's (2001) notion of the "culture of control," in which public policy increasingly focuses on managing perceived risk and disorder rather than addressing root causes. In this paradigm, problematic drug users become both the object and justification of surveillance, discipline, and exclusion. Meanwhile, functional users do not fit the archetype of risk and are thus omitted from both discourse and intervention. The result is a two-tiered system in which the same behaviour—drug use—is treated radically differently depending on the user's social position.

The policy implications of this are profound. By focusing on the visible harms of problematic users while ignoring the breadth of functional use, the UK misses critical opportunities for harm reduction, early intervention, and evidence-based education. It also perpetuates stigma and inequality, reinforcing the notion that drug use is inherently deviant rather than socially constructed and contextually variable.

This essay therefore argues that current UK drug policy functions more as a mechanism of social control than as a public health initiative.

It sustains a punitive focus on a marginalised minority while permitting, through inaction or denial, the widespread and often safer use of substances among the socially privileged. Addressing this imbalance requires not only a re-evaluation of enforcement and treatment priorities, but also a rethinking of the cultural narratives and moral assumptions that underpin drug policy itself.

## Defining Functional and Problematic Use

A functional drug user is typically defined as someone who incorporates drug use into their daily life in a controlled and non-disruptive manner. This type of user continues to meet key social and occupational responsibilities, often excelling in work, maintaining stable relationships, and avoiding contact with the criminal justice system (Lancaster et al., 2017). Functional users may take drugs recreationally or strategically—for example, to increase productivity, social confidence, or relaxation—and do so in ways that do not visibly interfere with their broader lifestyle or social obligations (Duff, 2012; Werse & Bernard, 2016). Because they do not draw attention through disruptive behaviours or dependence-related crises, they are frequently overlooked in both policy and research.

In contrast, problematic drug users are marked by patterns of harmful consumption and social instability. These individuals often experience addiction, repeated encounters with the criminal justice system, unemployment, homelessness, and comorbid physical or mental health conditions (Neale et al., 2011; ACMD XE "ACMD (Advisory Council on the Misuse of Drugs)" , 2019). Their substance use may be a coping mechanism for structural disadvantage, trauma, or exclusion, rather than a deliberate enhancement of social or professional functioning. The divergence in experience between these two categories of users is not merely behavioural—it reflects deep socio-economic divisions that shape both drug use and institutional responses to it.

This dichotomy—functional versus problematic—is not merely a sociological observation but holds significant consequences for how drug users are perceived by society and managed by the state. Functional users tend to be drawn from middle- and upper-class demographics. They include professionals who use cocaine recreationally, students using modafinil or Ritalin for academic performance, or parents who microdose psychedelics for mental well-being (Monaghan, 2012; Power, 2013). Such users often have stable housing, private healthcare access, and supportive social networks. These privileges enable them to manage potential risks associated with drug use discreetly and reduce the likelihood of detection or harm.

By contrast, problematic users are disproportionately drawn from economically marginalised groups. They are more likely to live in deprived neighbourhoods, experience unstable housing, and rely on overstretched public services. Their drug use is often intertwined with histories of abuse, adverse childhood experiences, and systemic neglect (Public Health England, 2020; Stevens, 2011). Moreover, they are more likely to use cheaper, high-risk substances such as heroin, crack cocaine, or synthetic cannabinoids—substances that not only carry greater physical risks but also attract more aggressive policing and legal sanction (Eastwood et al., 2013; Release, 2016).

This socio-economic stratification plays a central role in determining visibility and risk of criminalisation. Functional users are often protected by discretion, private spaces, and the presumption of innocence tied to their class and race. A white middle-class professional caught with a small quantity of cocaine is likely to be treated with leniency or even avoided altogether by police intervention. In contrast, a working-class Black man stopped and searched in a public space is far more likely to be arrested and prosecuted for a similar offence, despite comparable levels of drug use across ethnic groups (Shiner et al., 2018).

The different responses to these groups are shaped by long-standing societal narratives that link drug use with moral failure, criminality, and disorder—narratives that disproportionately apply to the poor and racialised populations (Seddon, 2006; Wacquant, 2009). This is reflected in British policy approaches, which have historically relied on punitive measures targeting the most visible and vulnerable drug users. The Misuse of Drugs Act 1971, the cornerstone of UK drug legislation, criminalises possession of controlled substances without reference to the user's context, motivations, or capacity to function (Stevens, 2011). While the law is theoretically blind to status, in practice it is enforced with profound social bias.

The consequences of this uneven enforcement are multifaceted. Criminalisation can entrench social exclusion, making it harder for problematic users to access housing, employment, or treatment. A criminal record can serve as a long-term barrier to reintegration, exacerbating the very conditions that contribute to harmful drug use in the first place (ACMD XE "ACMD (Advisory Council on the Misuse of Drugs)" , 2019). Functional users, by contrast, can continue their use without legal repercussions or stigma, maintaining their social capital and avoiding the structural violence that state intervention often brings.

This disparity also influences the direction of drug policy. Because problematic users are more visible and politically constructed as threats, policy responses tend to focus on this group, with interventions centred around crime reduction, abstinence, and moral rehabilitation. Functional users, who may constitute the majority of drug users, are rendered invisible in this policy landscape (Lancaster et al., 2017; Stevens, 2020). This silence allows governments to uphold prohibitionist frameworks under the guise of protecting public health, while ignoring the full spectrum of drug use behaviours and their varying harms.

Indeed, this dichotomy enables a moral economy of drug use. Functional users are implicitly granted a license to consume, provided their behaviour does not disrupt dominant norms. Problematic users, conversely, are treated as both morally and socially defective, deserving of coercive treatment or punishment. This division upholds middle-class values and the legitimacy of state power, allowing drug policy to act as a mechanism of social control rather than harm reduction (Garland, 2001; Wacquant, 2009).

Moreover, the absence of functional users from public discourse leads to policy distortions. Harm reduction strategies—such as drug checking, safe consumption spaces, and wider education campaigns—could benefit both categories of users. However, the association of drug policy with problematic use leads to limited political appetite for such interventions. Policymakers remain hesitant to introduce reforms that might appear to condone recreational drug use, even when evidence supports their efficacy in reducing harm (Transform Drug Policy Foundation, 2021).

In short, the functional/problematic dichotomy is not simply a matter of user behaviour but a reflection of class, race, and structural inequality. It is a lens through which drug use is interpreted, regulated, and sanctioned. Functional users are afforded discretion, invisibility, and privilege. Problematic users are subjected to surveillance, stigma, and punishment. Recognising this disparity is essential to developing a drug policy grounded in equity, evidence, and compassion.

## Representations in Media and Policy

Media portrayals have long constructed the drug user as deviant, criminal, and morally deficient. These representations have deep historical roots in British society, stretching back to the mid-twentieth century when drugs were increasingly associated with urban disorder, racialised communities, and youth rebellion (Seddon, 2006; Taylor, 2008). Contemporary media continues this legacy, focusing disproportionately on problematic use—depicting addiction, chaos, criminality, and dependency—while rendering functional users either invisible or selectively romanticised as bohemian "creative geniuses" or successful professionals whose drug use is framed as eccentric rather than threatening (Blackman, 2004).

This dualism has significant implications for how society understands drug use and how the state responds to it. Functional users, whose use occurs in private, professional, or middle-class contexts, are largely exempt from public scrutiny and thus policy concern. In contrast, problematic users—disproportionately drawn from marginalised, racialised, and working-class populations—are highly visible and repeatedly framed as societal threats. This contrast reinforces existing social hierarchies and informs punitive drug policy through a process of moral panic and deviancy amplification.

The concept of **moral panic**, first developed by Stanley Cohen (1972), helps explain the media and political focus on problematic drug users. A moral panic occurs when a group or behaviour is framed as a threat to societal values and interests, leading to exaggerated media coverage, increased public anxiety, and a demand for swift political action. Drug users, especially those involved in visible or chaotic consumption, have long served as "folk devils" in this process. The heroin users of the 1980s, crack users of the 1990s, and more recently spice users among the homeless have all been scapegoated as symbols of societal decline (Coomber et al., 2013). This framing invites simplistic and punitive responses, such as zero-tolerance policies, rather than nuanced public health interventions.

Closely linked to moral panic is **deviancy amplification**, a theory introduced by Jock Young (1971), which describes how societal reactions to deviant behaviour can intensify the very behaviours they seek to control. When the media sensationalises drug use among certain communities, it not only stigmatises those users but also justifies increasingly coercive policing and criminal justice responses. These measures, in turn, marginalise users further, deepening cycles of poverty, exclusion, and dependency. Young's original work on drug use in Notting Hill demonstrated how police pressure and media scrutiny led to the entrenchment of drug subcultures rather than their dissolution—a dynamic still evident today in the way urban drug scenes are policed and publicised.

Modern drug policy in the UK remains heavily influenced by these dynamics. The 2017 *Drug Strategy* continues to emphasise abstinence, recovery, and enforcement, with little attention given to harm reduction or the lived realities of non-problematic users (Home Office, 2017). Functional users, who consume significant quantities of illegal substances in private and professional settings, are conspicuously absent from the strategy's objectives and risk assessments (Release, 2016). This selective visibility supports what Stevens (2011) terms **"policy myopia"**—a form of institutional blindness that directs attention and resources towards the most visible and socially marginal forms of drug use, while ignoring the broader spectrum.

Media coverage plays a pivotal role in shaping this myopia. A content analysis by Hughes et al. (2011) revealed that British tabloids and broadsheets consistently frame drug stories around crime, danger, and degradation, with a particular focus on low-income areas and racialised populations. By portraying drug use through a narrow lens of deviance and disorder, the media not only distorts public perception but also reinforces a punitive policy environment. When functional users appear in media narratives, they are often detached from the drug discourse altogether, described as "burned-out artists" or "party animals," implicitly excused from the harsh moral judgments levied against problematic users.

These narratives have tangible policy consequences. Public pressure generated by moral panics often leads to knee-jerk legislation that exacerbates inequalities. For instance, the classification of ecstasy (MDMA) as a Class A drug under the Misuse of Drugs Act 1971 was not based on comparative evidence of harm but rather on political expediency in the face of media-fuelled fear during the 1990s "rave" moral panic (Nutt et al., 2007). Similarly, the criminalisation of synthetic cannabinoids like "spice" followed media hysteria over "zombie-like" behaviour in urban centres, rather than any measured assessment of harm or context (Ralphs & Gray, 2018). These decisions often ignore academic consensus and instead cater to tabloid sensationalism.

Functional drug users—those who manage their use with relative control and discretion—are not only overlooked but are also systemically protected by their class status. As Monaghan (2012) notes, middle-class recreational users often benefit from a presumption of rationality and agency; their drug use is framed as a personal choice or lifestyle preference rather than a symptom of deviance. This framing protects them from the stigmas and sanctions applied to users from less privileged backgrounds. For example, a banker caught with cocaine at a party may be dismissed as foolish or unlucky, whereas a working-class youth found with the same drug in a public space is far more likely to be prosecuted and publicly vilified.

This disparity is not only moral but institutional. Policing practices such as stop and search are disproportionately applied in deprived areas and among Black communities, despite consistent data showing similar or lower rates of drug use compared to white populations (Shiner et al., 2018). In this way, the state reproduces and legitimises social inequality, enforcing drug laws in ways that disproportionately harm the already disadvantaged. The result is a two-tiered system of drug justice: one that punishes visibility and poverty, while excusing discretion and privilege.

From a Foucauldian perspective, this bifurcation serves a regulatory function within neoliberal governance. Drug policy does not merely respond to harm; it constructs and maintains social order by defining who is considered "deserving" or "undeserving" of state intervention. Functional users are allowed autonomy and discretion because they align with the values of productivity and self-discipline central to neoliberal subjectivity (O'Malley & Valverde, 2004). Problematic users, by contrast, are positioned as morally and economically deficient—requiring coercion, rehabilitation, or exclusion.

This regulatory logic is reinforced by the language of "recovery" in recent policy discourse. As Lancaster et al. (2017) argue, recovery is often framed not as a personal journey but as a moral imperative—one that requires abstinence, contrition, and conformity. Such framing aligns with conservative notions of responsibility and self-control, and marginalises harm reduction approaches that accept non-abstinence-based outcomes. Consequently, problematic users are pressured into treatment models that may not reflect their needs or realities, while functional users are permitted to operate outside the system altogether.

To move beyond this distorted policy landscape, it is essential to challenge the narratives and assumptions that underpin it. This means confronting media sensationalism, interrogating the moral foundations of drug policy, and recognising the full spectrum of drug use behaviour. It also means investing in media literacy, academic engagement, and participatory policymaking that includes the voices of users themselves—both functional and problematic.

## The Classed and Racialised Nature of Drug Enforcement

Drug policy in the UK does not apply equally across social groups. While legislation such as the *Misuse of Drugs Act 1971* is nominally universal, its enforcement reflects stark disparities along socio-economic lines. Numerous studies confirm that stop-and-search practices, arrests, and prosecutions for drug possession disproportionately affect working-class individuals and residents of deprived areas, despite these groups not using drugs at significantly higher rates than more affluent populations (Eastwood et al., 2013; Shiner et al., 2018). These enforcement patterns expose an enduring structural bias in UK drug policy: one that is not rooted in evidence of harm, but in the visibility and perceived disorder associated with certain social environments.

Functional users—who are typically white, middle- or upper-class, and discreet in their use—are far less likely to be subject to criminal justice scrutiny. Their consumption often occurs in private settings, such as homes, university accommodation, or professional events, and includes substances such as cannabis, powder cocaine, or modafinil. These users benefit from social insulation and access to informal networks that reduce the likelihood of detection and prosecution (Monaghan, 2012). Conversely, problematic users—more often based in public spaces and deprived urban areas—are far more visible and are policed accordingly. This divide between "discreet and contained" versus "visible and public" drug use has been central to shaping how the criminal justice system deploys its resources (Stevens, 2011).

This enforcement imbalance reflects what Loïc Wacquant (2009) refers to as **neoliberal penality**, whereby the state disciplines and punishes the poor while protecting the autonomy of the affluent. In this context, problematic users serve as symbolic scapegoats for wider social anxieties—about disorder, decline, and moral failure. The state, through criminalisation, performs a ritualistic reassertion of social control. Functional users, being economically productive and socially integrated, are not framed as threats and thus escape both policy and enforcement focus.

The issue is not simply who uses drugs, but where, how, and under what social and environmental conditions.

To further understand how certain groups become overrepresented in drug enforcement statistics, we can turn to **Situational Action Theory (SAT)**, developed by Wikström et al. (2012). SAT argues that criminal behaviour results from the interaction between individual propensity and exposure to criminogenic settings. In this framework, people are not inherently deviant or criminal; rather, crime emerges from the convergence of moral decision-making processes and environmental contexts. Applied to drug policy, SAT helps explain why problematic users—often located in deprived, surveilled, and high-stress environments—are more likely to be criminalised than their functional counterparts, even when engaging in similar behaviours.

Under SAT, the concept of "moral context" is crucial. Functional users often operate in environments where drug use is normalised or tolerated—for example, within university subcultures or creative industries—making the behaviour less likely to be perceived as deviant by users or observers (Wikström et al., 2012). Conversely, problematic users are embedded in moral contexts where drug use is framed as symptomatic of moral failure or criminal intent. The same act—possessing or using a substance—thus carries different meanings and consequences depending on its setting and the social actors involved.

The theory also emphasises the role of **perceived action alternatives**. Functional users may perceive a range of legitimate options for coping with stress or engaging in leisure, with drug use as one non-disruptive choice among many. Problematic users, facing limited social and economic opportunities, may view drug use as one of the few viable means of escape, relief, or social connection (Neale et al., 2011). These differing perceptions shape not only behaviour but also how that behaviour is judged and sanctioned by the state.

Policing practices further reinforce this divide. Research by Shiner et al. (2018) shows that stop-and-search is disproportionately applied in poorer and more ethnically diverse neighbourhoods. Although SAT does not focus on race or class per se, it provides a mechanism for understanding how location and social setting mediate the likelihood of law enforcement encounters. Areas deemed "criminogenic" are more heavily patrolled, and residents within them are more likely to be stopped, searched, and arrested—even if their behaviours are no different from those in less policed communities. In effect, the environment amplifies the criminalisation risk.

This environmental focus is consistent with findings from Webb and Burrows (2009), who found that drug enforcement was often concentrated in urban council estates and city centres, places already burdened by surveillance and social stigma. These environments become "moral geographies" where certain behaviours are pathologised and punished. Meanwhile, middle-class suburbs, private residences, and elite institutions—where functional drug use frequently occurs—are largely exempt from the same level of scrutiny.

Situational Action Theory also aligns with routine activity theory, in which crime is more likely to occur (or be detected) when motivated offenders and suitable targets converge in the absence of capable guardianship (Cohen & Felson, 1979). In marginalised communities, visible drug use in public spaces often coincides with high levels of policing and surveillance, making arrest and criminalisation more likely. In contrast, functional users are rarely subject to "capable guardianship" in their own homes or private gatherings, thus reducing the chance of detection and sanction.

This dynamic contributes to the selective criminalisation of poverty and public visibility, rather than of drug use per se. As Garland (2001) has argued, modern criminal justice systems are increasingly oriented towards managing risk and regulating behaviour through preemptive measures. Policing, under this model, becomes a form of social sorting, identifying and targeting those who are easiest to monitor and discipline—typically the poor, the homeless, and the socially marginalised.

The consequences of this uneven application of drug policy are long-term and deeply damaging. A criminal record for drug possession can limit access to employment, education, housing, and travel, entrenching the very disadvantage that problematic users already experience (ACMD XE "ACMD (Advisory Council on the Misuse of Drugs)" , 2019). Functional users, by contrast, are far more likely to recover from drug-related incidents without long-term consequences. This reinforces what has been described as a two-tiered system of justice—one that criminalises the visible poor while tolerating the discreet behaviour of the wealthy (Stevens, 2020).

Moreover, these patterns distort public perceptions and policy priorities. By focusing on visible drug use among the poor, the state perpetuates the myth that drugs are primarily a working-class problem, obscuring the widespread use of illicit substances across all social strata. This misperception informs policy that targets symptomatic behaviours rather than structural causes, such as housing insecurity, mental health services, and social inequality.

In conclusion, the uneven enforcement of UK drug policy reflects not only class and environmental bias but also the situational dynamics outlined in contemporary criminological theory. Situational Action Theory provides a valuable lens for understanding how different environments and individual contexts interact to produce unequal outcomes in drug law enforcement. By focusing on where and how drug use occurs—not just who uses—SAT reveals a system that punishes visibility and disadvantage, while excusing privilege and discretion. Reform must therefore address not only the legal framework but the social and spatial dynamics that shape its enforcement.

## The Policy Focus on Problematic Use

UK drug policy is largely reactive, designed to respond to individuals who are already deeply embedded in cycles of addiction, homelessness, and criminality. Rather than adopting a proactive stance rooted in prevention, education, and early intervention, government strategies have historically focused on crisis containment. Funding for treatment and support services tends to be disproportionately directed at individuals in acute distress, often following criminal justice involvement, overdose, or other high-risk events (ACMD, 2019). This model mirrors a broader pattern in social policy, whereby intervention only occurs after significant harm has already materialised, reflecting a "late-stage" response system that is neither efficient nor equitable.

This approach has clear limitations. Crisis-based responses are costly, less effective in the long term, and tend to overlook broader social and structural determinants of drug use. Individuals experiencing severe addiction often require complex, multi-agency interventions that involve not only substance misuse services but also housing support, mental health care, and trauma-informed treatment. However, such services remain underfunded and fragmented, leading to gaps in provision and inconsistent outcomes (Public Health England, 2020). Meanwhile, less visible or functional users who may benefit from preventative or low-threshold services are excluded from the system entirely.

The UK government's 2021 drug strategy, *From Harm to Hope*, claims to represent a "public health" turn in drug policy. However, a closer examination reveals a continued fixation on problematic drug users, particularly those engaged in acquisitive crime (Home Office, 2021). The strategy's core aims—"breaking drug supply chains," "delivering a world-class treatment and recovery system," and "achieving a generational shift in demand"—suggest that public health is still secondary to crime control. The bulk of the new funding announced in the strategy was earmarked for criminal justice-linked interventions, such as court-ordered treatment and prison-based programmes, reinforcing the notion that drug use is first and foremost a matter for law enforcement.

The language of "recovery" used throughout the strategy further undermines its public health credentials. Recovery is frequently framed in moralistic terms, connoting abstinence, redemption, and conformity to socially sanctioned lifestyles. While recovery can be meaningful for many people, when presented as the only desirable outcome, it marginalises those who use drugs in non-problematic ways or who pursue harm reduction rather than abstinence (Lancaster et al., 2017). It also implicitly blames individuals for their substance use, overlooking the structural and social contexts—such as poverty, trauma, and exclusion—that often underpin drug-related harm.

This narrow conception of recovery contributes to a lack of investment in essential harm reduction infrastructure. Services such as supervised consumption rooms, drug-checking facilities, heroin-assisted treatment (HAT), and widespread naloxone provision are well-evidenced in terms of reducing mortality, disease transmission, and public drug use (EMCDDA, 2018). Yet in the UK, these interventions remain politically controversial and underfunded. Despite the mounting evidence base, including support from international health bodies and pilot schemes in countries such as Canada and Switzerland, UK policymakers have largely resisted their implementation (Transform Drug Policy Foundation, 2021).

The omission of functional users from policy considerations exacerbates this situation. Functional users—who may engage in occasional recreational use or use substances to manage mental health or enhance productivity—are not recognised in service planning. They are unlikely to seek formal treatment but could benefit from harm reduction initiatives such as anonymous drug checking, peer-led education, or confidential health advice (Measham, 2020). Ignoring this group not only limits the reach of public health efforts but also perpetuates the binary distinction between "addicts" and "normal" people, further embedding stigma into the policy landscape.

The failure to scale harm reduction approaches also has wider public health implications. For example, the limited distribution of naloxone—a life-saving opioid antagonist—means that overdose deaths remain high, despite this being a preventable outcome (Office for National Statistics (ONS), 2023). Supervised consumption rooms, which have been shown to reduce syringe litter, public drug use, and emergency service demand, are still not legal in the UK, even in areas experiencing acute overdose crises such as Glasgow (Harris & Rhodes, 2012). The resistance to such measures is not grounded in evidence but in political and moral opposition, often rooted in the fear of appearing "soft on drugs."

Ultimately, UK drug policy continues to prioritise moralistic and punitive approaches over pragmatic, health-led strategies. Functional users, despite constituting a significant portion of drug consumption, are effectively rendered invisible. Problematic users are constructed as objects of rescue or discipline, depending on their level of compliance with the abstinence-based model. The result is a policy landscape that is unbalanced, ineffective, and unjust—one that fails to reflect the complexity of drug use and the diversity of user experiences.

## Functional Use and the Policy Vacuum

Functional drug use poses a significant conceptual and political challenge to UK drug policy. It directly undermines the simplistic and moralistic narrative that drug use is inherently dangerous, inevitably leads to dependency, and thus warrants criminalisation. By demonstrating that many individuals use illicit substances without visible harm to themselves or others—and often while maintaining employment, relationships, and civic responsibilities—functional users call into question the foundational assumptions of prohibitionist drug policy. Their existence contradicts the dominant framing of the drug user as chaotic, criminal, or morally deviant. As Duff (2012) argues, the absence of functional users from policy discourse is not accidental but ideological; it helps sustain a prohibition model by denying the possibility that controlled, non-problematic use is both possible and relatively common.

This erasure serves several political functions. It simplifies policymaking by reducing a complex behavioural spectrum into a binary—between abstainers (good) and addicts (bad)—and legitimises enforcement by pathologising all forms of illegal drug use. Functional use complicates this dichotomy by presenting drug users who do not conform to the stereotype and who, in some cases, experience positive effects from their use, such as enhanced social engagement, stress relief, or cognitive performance (Werse & Bernard, 2016). Acknowledging such use would necessitate a shift from punitive to pragmatic responses—something that remains politically unpalatable in a landscape dominated by "tough on crime" rhetoric.

A further problem lies in the mismatch between a drug's legal classification and its actual harm. The most commonly consumed legal substances in the UK—alcohol and tobacco—are among the most harmful in terms of both individual and societal impact. In their widely cited multi-criteria decision analysis, Nutt et al. (2010) ranked alcohol as more harmful than heroin or crack cocaine when considering both direct and indirect harms. Tobacco also scored higher than several controlled substances, yet both are legally available, heavily marketed, and socially normalised. This inconsistency reveals the moral and historical roots of drug legislation, where decisions are less influenced by scientific evidence and more by cultural attitudes, racialised fears, and political expediency (Buchanan, 2010; Seddon, 2010).

Functional users of illicit substances often manage their drug-taking more responsibly than users of legal substances. Many take conscious steps to moderate intake, source quality substances, and avoid mixing drugs in dangerous combinations (Measham, 2020). For example, participants in drug-checking services—where individuals voluntarily submit substances for chemical analysis—demonstrate high levels of care and health-conscious behaviour. This contradicts the dominant policy narrative that illegal drug users are inherently reckless or in need of moral correction. Instead, it suggests that when given the right information and autonomy, people can and do make safer choices—whether the drug is legal or not.

Yet UK policy remains rooted in outdated moral binaries, in which certain substances are arbitrarily deemed acceptable and others demonised. These distinctions are often historically contingent. Cannabis, for instance, was associated with Black jazz musicians and immigrant populations during the early twentieth century and was criminalised largely for symbolic and racialised reasons rather than health concerns (Taylor, 2008). Cocaine, once legal and even promoted in medical contexts, became reclassified as public panic associated it with working-class crime and social disorder. In contrast, alcohol retained its legal status despite being a major contributor to domestic violence, liver disease, and public disorder. This moral economy of drugs continues to influence contemporary policy, ensuring that legality reflects social norms more than pharmacological risk.

By ignoring functional use, UK drug policy misses an opportunity to develop a more nuanced, evidence-led approach that acknowledges the realities of drug consumption across the population. Rather than demonising all users or ignoring safe use practices, a rational policy would regulate substances based on harm, support informed choice, and invest in harm reduction across the spectrum of use. Recognising the existence of functional users is a crucial step towards such a transformation.

## Policy Recommendations

A genuinely evidence-based policy would acknowledge the spectrum of drug use and respond proportionately. This means:

Decriminalisation of possession for personal use, following models such as Portugal's, to reduce the harms of criminalisation (Hughes & Stevens, 2010).

Investing in harm reduction across the spectrum of use, including drug checking, peer education, and safe spaces for use.

Shifting media narratives to reflect the diversity of drug use and reduce stigma.

Targeting structural determinants of problematic use, such as poverty, housing insecurity, and mental health service gaps.

Regulating currently illegal drugs, enabling safer use and diminishing the unregulated market.

Such changes would require a significant cultural shift, challenging deeply ingrained moral and class-based prejudices. However, the failure to do so perpetuates injustice and squanders public health opportunities.

## Authors Reflection Growing Up Around Drugs

Growing up in Liverpool in the 1970s, I was always aware of drugs—although I didn't always recognise them as such. That's the problem for many people when they try to make sense of what's allowed and what isn't. My parent smoked cigarettes and occasionally enjoyed a glass of brandy, lime, and lemonade. My nanna, who we lived with, had a nightly can of Mackeson stout with a wee dram of whisky in it—and, on more than one occasion, she even popped a splash of whisky into my milk bottle when I wouldn't settle. You'd never be allowed to do that now, of course—but historically, babies were also given opium to help them sleep.

Around me, plenty of people also smoked weed. Back then, the strains had more balanced cannabinoids and less of the high-potency CBD-dominant varieties we see now. I'd argue that prohibition has played a part in pushing the market towards high-strength strains like skunk—stripped of the helpful compounds and packed with potentially harmful ones.

This kind of casual, everyday use was common then—and still is, in many ways, today. I still live in Liverpool, and when I walk out of my front door, I can smell skunk straight away. Among my friends and wider social circle, many still smoke marijuana or enjoy a drink. Some even dabble in cocaine at the weekend—but as we've all got older, most of us have left those nights behind. It's more my students now who are part of the night-time economy (NTE), and many of them still experiment with various substances—as young people often do.

But here's the important bit: very few of the people I've known over the years have become addicted. The overwhelming majority were, and still are, functional users.

Of course, that's not to say addiction isn't real or devastating. My sister was very seriously addicted to heroin in the 1980s. Thankfully, she recovered—but she still lives with the physical consequences of her addiction. That said, if everyone who had ever used a drug ended up addicted, the problem we face today would be far greater than it actually is.

It comes back to the same question I often ask my students: if you enjoy a glass of red wine, does that make you an alcoholic? Most people would say no—and rightly so. It's the same with other drugs.

Drug use may well be shaped by class—what you can afford versus what you can't—but in truth, this is a classless, raceless, genderless issue. Anyone and everyone has taken drugs in one form or another. It just depends on what you personally enjoy, what's available in your social setting, or whether you're drinking a coffee (which is legal) rather than taking something illicit.

## Conclusion

The UK's drug policy is built upon a fundamentally partial and punitive understanding of drug use—an approach that disproportionately targets problematic users while ignoring or even excusing functional ones. This dichotomy is not a neutral oversight but a reflection of deeply ingrained structural inequalities within British society. The current model of enforcement and intervention prioritises visibility and perceived disorder, resulting in the criminalisation of the poor, the racialised, and the socially excluded, while allowing affluent users to engage in illegal activity with relative impunity (Eastwood et al., 2013; Shiner et al., 2018).

At the heart of this policy imbalance is a long-standing refusal to acknowledge the diversity of drug users and the contexts in which they operate. Functional users—those who consume drugs without significant disruption to their personal or professional lives—represent a substantial proportion of overall use, yet they remain largely invisible in policy discussions (Lancaster et al., 2017). These users are often shielded by socio-economic privilege, social discretion, and private environments. They tend to be white, middle- or upper-class, and embedded within educational or professional institutions where drug use is viewed as a manageable risk rather than a moral or legal crisis (Monaghan, 2012). Because their use does not disrupt the public order or provoke media panic, they are exempt from the surveillance and punishment that defines the experience of many problematic users.

Conversely, problematic users—those experiencing dependency, homelessness, mental illness, or poverty—are the focal point of state intervention. This is not because they represent the majority of drug users or even the most dangerous cases, but because their use is visible, often chaotic, and closely linked with social disorder (Stevens, 2011). As a result, these individuals are disproportionately subject to policing, prosecution, and incarceration, reinforcing what Loïc Wacquant (2009) describes as "neoliberal penality": a system in which the state abandons welfare in favour of punitive control over those deemed unproductive or deviant.

This bifurcation between functional and problematic users mirrors and reproduces class-based and racial inequalities. Studies have shown that Black individuals are nine times more likely to be stopped and searched for drugs than white individuals, despite comparable rates of use (Shiner et al., 2018). Working-class communities are more likely to be subject to aggressive drug enforcement strategies, such as hotspot policing and zero-tolerance campaigns, whereas wealthier areas are policed more leniently, or not at all, for similar offences. The result is a system in which drug law enforcement becomes a tool for regulating poverty and reinforcing existing hierarchies rather than addressing public health needs (Seddon, 2006).

Moreover, this punitive model is not supported by evidence of effectiveness. Decades of criminalisation have failed to reduce either drug consumption or associated harms. Instead, they have contributed to record-high drug-related deaths, increased incarceration rates, and diminished access to health services for those most in need (ACMD XE "ACMD (Advisory Council on the Misuse of Drugs)" , 2019; ONS, 2023). The stigma attached to drug use discourages individuals from seeking help, while the criminalisation of possession—often for small, personal-use quantities—creates lifelong barriers to employment, education, and housing. These outcomes are particularly severe for those already marginalised, thereby deepening cycles of exclusion.

In contrast, functional users largely escape these consequences. Their behaviour is often rationalised or medicalised rather than criminalised. For example, a student using Ritalin to study or a banker taking cocaine recreationally may never encounter the criminal justice system, even though both are technically committing offences under the Misuse of Drugs Act 1971. This uneven enforcement results not from differences in behaviour or harm, but from differences in status and visibility. It also reinforces the illusion that illegal drug use is a pathology of the poor, when in fact it is distributed across all segments of society.

Addressing this imbalance requires a fundamental reorientation of drug policy—from a punitive model aimed at controlling behaviour through criminal sanctions to a public health framework that recognises the full spectrum of drug use. A health-based approach would treat drug use as a social and medical issue, rather than a moral failing or criminal act. It would prioritise harm reduction, access to services, and evidence-based education, while also recognising that not all drug use is inherently problematic (Transform Drug Policy Foundation, 2021).

Such a shift would also demand the decriminalisation of personal use and possession, a policy already adopted in multiple countries with significant success. Portugal, for example, decriminalised all drugs in 2001, leading to reductions in overdose deaths, HIV transmission, and incarceration rates without a corresponding increase in use (Hughes &

Stevens, 2010). Decriminalisation removes the stigma and legal barriers that prevent users—both functional and problematic—from accessing help or engaging with services. It also allows law enforcement to focus on serious offences, such as trafficking and exploitation, rather than punishing individuals for personal decisions.

A more equitable policy would also involve investing in harm reduction services that benefit all users. This includes supervised consumption sites, drug-checking facilities, heroin-assisted treatment, and widespread naloxone distribution. These interventions are backed by robust evidence and have been implemented successfully in countries such as Canada, Switzerland, and the Netherlands (EMCDDA, 2018). Yet in the UK, such services remain politically contentious and underfunded, largely because they challenge the moralistic underpinnings of current policy.

Crucially, reform must also involve reframing the public discourse around drug use. The media, policymakers, and public institutions must move beyond moral panic and stigma, embracing a narrative that acknowledges the complexity of drug use and the humanity of users. This includes recognising the legitimacy of controlled, non-problematic use, as well as the structural conditions that contribute to problematic patterns. Only by broadening the discourse can we dismantle the punitive framework that has dominated UK policy for decades.

Until this happens, the so-called war on drugs will continue to function as a war on the poor. It will criminalise poverty, racialise deviance, and perpetuate a system in which justice is not blind, but acutely attuned to class and status. Functional users will continue to benefit from invisibility and privilege, while problematic users will bear the full weight of a system that punishes vulnerability. Reform is not only a matter of efficacy—it is a matter of justice.

## References


Advisory Council on the Misuse of Drugs (ACMD). (2019). *Drug-related harms in homeless populations and how they can be reduced*. Home Office.

Blackman, S. (2004). *Chilling out: The cultural politics of substance consumption, youth and drug policy*. Open University Press.

Buchanan, J. (2010). *Understanding drug misuse: Models of care and control*. Palgrave Macmillan.

Cohen, L. E., & Felson, M. (1979). Social change and crime rate trends: A routine activity approach. *American Sociological Review, 44*(4), 588–608.

Cohen, S. (1972). *Folk devils and moral panics: The creation of the mods and rockers*. MacGibbon and Kee.

Coomber, R., Moyle, L., & South, N. (2013). The normalisation of drug supply: The social supply of drugs as the "other side" of the history of normalisation. *Drugs: Education, Prevention and Policy, 20*(3), 210–219.

Duff, C. (2012). The social life of drugs. *International Journal of Drug Policy, 23*(3), 167–172.

Eastwood, N., Shiner, M., & Bear, D. (2013). *The numbers in black and white: Ethnic disparities in the policing and prosecution of drug offences in England and Wales*. Release.

European Monitoring Centre for Drugs and Drug Addiction (EMCDDA). (2018). *Health and social responses to drug problems: A European guide*. Publications Office of the European Union.

Garland, D. (2001). *The culture of control: Crime and social order in contemporary society*. Oxford University Press.

Harris, M., & Rhodes, T. (2012). Venous access and care: Harnessing pragmatics in harm reduction for people who inject drugs. *Addiction, 107*(6), 1090–1096.

Hughes, C., Lancaster, K., & Spicer, B. (2011). How do media represent drug use and drug users? *Drugs and Alcohol Today, 11*(4), 197–206.

Hughes, C. E., & Stevens, A. (2010). What can we learn from the Portuguese decriminalization of illicit drugs? *British Journal of Criminology, 50*(6), 999–1022.

Lancaster, K., Duke, K., & Ritter, A. (2017). Producing the "problem of drugs": A cross-national comparison of "recovery" discourse in UK and Australian drug policy. *International Journal of Drug Policy, 44*, 36–43.

Measham, F. (2020). City checking: Piloting the UK's first community-based drug safety testing (drug checking) service in 2 city centres. *British Journal of Clinical Pharmacology, 86*(3), 420–428.

Monaghan, M. (2012). *The politics of drugs: Perceptions, power and policies*. Palgrave Macmillan.

Neale, J., Nettleton, S., & Pickering, L. (2011). Recovery from problem drug use: What can we learn from the sociologist Erving Goffman? *Drugs: Education, Prevention and Policy, 18*(1), 3–9.

Nutt, D., King, L.A., Saulsbury, W. and Blakemore, C. (2007). Development of a rational scale to assess the harm of drugs of potential misuse. *The Lancet, 369*(9566), 1047–1053.

Nutt, D., King, L. A., & Phillips, L. D. (2010). Drug harms in the UK: A multicriteria decision analysis. *The Lancet, 376*(9752), 1558–1565.

O'Malley, P., & Valverde, M. (2004). Pleasure, freedom and drugs: The uses of "pleasure" in liberal governance of drug and alcohol consumption. *Sociology, 38*(1), 25–42.

Office for National Statistics (ONS). (2023). *Deaths related to drug poisoning in England and Wales: 2022 registrations*. Newport.

Office, H. (2017). *2017 drug strategy*. HM Government.

Office, H. (2021). *From harm to hope: A 10-year drugs plan to cut crime and save lives*. HM Government.

Power, M. (2013). Drugs and the neoliberal subject: Governmentality, consumption and citizen agency. *Critical Social Policy, 33*(2), 198–217.

Public Health England. (2020). *Adult substance misuse treatment statistics 2019 to 2020*. PHE.

Ralphs, R., & Gray, P. (2018). Spice use among young homeless populations in the UK: A qualitative study. *Drugs: Education, Prevention and Policy, 25*(5), 420–427.

Release. (2016). *A quiet revolution: Drug decriminalisation across the globe*. Release.

Seddon, T. (2006). Drugs, crime and social exclusion: Social context and social theory in British drugs–crime research. *British Journal of Criminology, 46*(4), 680–703.

Seddon, T. (2010). *A history of drugs: Drugs and freedom in the liberal age*. Routledge.

Shiner, M., Carre, Z., Delsol, R., & Eastwood, N. (2018). *The colour of injustice: 'Race', drugs and law enforcement in England and Wales*. Release and Stopwatch.

Stevens, A. (2011). *Drugs, crime and public health: The political economy of drug policy*. Routledge.

Stevens, A. (2020). The "public health turn" in drug policy debate in the UK: Is it supported by the evidence and has it changed the debate? *British Journal of Criminology, 60*(5), 1187–1206.

Taylor, S. (2008). Outside the outsiders: Media representations of drug use. *Probation Journal, 55*(4), 369–387.

Transform Drug Policy Foundation. (2021). *21st century drugs: A new approach for a new era*. Transform.

Wacquant, L. (2009). *Punishing the poor: The neoliberal government of socialiInsecurity*. Duke University Press.

Webb, L., & Burrows, J. (2009). *Policing drug markets*. Home Office.

Werse, B., & Bernard, C. (2016). Recreational drug users in Europe: Patterns, perceptions, and policy responses. In R. Colson & H. Bergeron (Eds.), *European drug policies: The ways of reform* (pp. 69–87). Routledge.

Wikström, P.-O., Oberwittler, D., Treiber, K., & Hardie, B. (2012). *Breaking rules: The social and situational dynamics of young people's urban crime*. Oxford University Press.

Young, J. (1971). *The drugtakers: The social meaning of drug use*. Paladin.

CHAPTER 5

# Who Benefits from the Criminalisation of Drug Users?

**Abstract** This chapter critically examines the multifaceted beneficiaries of the UKs continued criminalisation of drug users, highlighting how punitive drug policy serves the interests of powerful institutions while disproportionately harming the marginalised. Despite mounting evidence supporting harm reduction and decriminalisation approaches, the UK persists in enforcing a criminal justice-led model that centres on prohibition, surveillance, and punishment. This approach has been widely discredited on grounds of efficacy, public health, and justice, yet it endures due to the political, institutional, economic, and symbolic gains it provides to key stakeholders.

The chapter begins by analysing the role of political actors in sustaining the "tough on drugs" narrative, which functions as a form of moral posturing and political theatre. By framing drug users as a societal threat, politicians are able to appeal to conservative values and middle-class fears, deflecting attention from deeper structural inequalities. Drawing on the work of theorists such as Seddon and contemporary commentators like David Nutt and Stuart Taylor, the chapter explores how drug users have been scapegoated to maintain hegemonic social order.

Law enforcement is also identified as a major beneficiary of drug criminalisation. Police forces gain institutional legitimacy and funding through high arrest rates for drug possession—crimes that are relatively easy to detect and prosecute. The use of stop-and-search powers disproportionately targets racialised and working-class communities, reinforcing



E. Peatfield, *Drugs Disorder by Design*,
https://doi.org/10.1007/978-3-032-07814-8_5

systemic inequalities and generating a steady stream of low-level offenders into the criminal justice system. Moreover, the existence of drug-related crime provides a rationale for aggressive policing and broader surveillance in marginalised areas.

The chapter also considers the economic interests underpinning the UK's punitive drug policy. The partial privatisation of the penal system and the outsourcing of probation, drug treatment, and testing services have created a carceral economy in which the management of drug users becomes a source of profit. Corporations such as Serco and G4S benefit from contracts to run prisons and deliver criminal justice services, while private treatment providers gain from court-mandated rehabilitation and monitoring schemes. These arrangements produce a system that prioritises compliance and control over care, with limited incentives to adopt more humane or effective models.

The media is shown to play a pivotal role in perpetuating these dynamics by fuelling moral panics, stigmatising drug users, and obscuring the prevalence of drug use among privileged populations. Sensationalist reporting reinforces public fears and provides political cover for continued criminalisation, while failing to highlight the social, economic, and racial disparities embedded in drug law enforcement.

In conclusion, the chapter argues that the criminalisation of drug users functions less as a policy tool for reducing harm and more as a mechanism for sustaining inequality and institutional power. A transition towards a public health-based model would require confronting these entrenched interests and acknowledging the political economy of punishment. Only by doing so can the UK begin to adopt a rational, compassionate, and evidence-based approach to drug policy—one that prioritises social justice over control.

**Keywords** Drug policy · Criminalisation · Harm reduction · Social inequality · Carceral economy · Law enforcement · Media representation · Moral panic · Public health · Political symbolism

## Introduction

The UK's drug policy has long favoured a criminal justice approach, focused on prohibition, deterrence, and punishment. Rooted in the 1971 Misuse of Drugs Act and later reinforced through the 1980s "war on drugs"rhetoric, the prevailing framework treats drug use as a criminal matter rather than a public health issue. Individuals caught in possession of controlled substances are often subject to police surveillance, criminal charges, and imprisonment, even when their use poses little harm to others. This punitive approach has remained largely intact despite mounting domestic and international evidence supporting harm reduction, decriminalisation, and health-led strategies (Transform Drug Policy Foundation, 2022).

In recent years, countries such as Portugal and Canada have implemented progressive reforms that focus on treatment, prevention, and social support rather than incarceration. These models have shown promising results, including reduced rates of drug-related deaths, HIV transmission, and reoffending (Hughes & Stevens, 2010; Stevens, 2011). However, the UK government has resisted similar changes, continuing to criminalise possession and focusing enforcement efforts disproportionately on low-level users rather than high-level traffickers or organised crime syndicates.

This persistence in criminalising drug users cannot be explained solely by ignorance of evidence or policy inertia. Instead, it reflects the existence of powerful interests—political, institutional, and economic—that benefit directly or indirectly from maintaining a punitive status quo. Criminalisation allows the state to demonstrate authority and control, reinforcing narratives of moral order and social discipline. It offers political actors a platform to appeal to "law and order" constituencies while avoiding deeper engagement with the socio-economic causes of drug use such as poverty, trauma, and exclusion.

Moreover, the criminal justice system itself, including police forces, courts, and private prison contractors, has developed bureaucratic and financial dependencies on the enforcement of drug laws. Police departments often rely on drug arrests to meet performance targets and justify funding, while private firms profit from incarceration and mandated treatment services. These stakeholders have little incentive to support decriminalisation, which could jeopardise resources, employment, and institutional authority (Monaghan, 2012; Seddon, 2006).

The media, too, plays a role in perpetuating the status quo, framing drug users—especially those who are homeless, poor, or racialised—as dangerous or morally defective. These narratives obscure the reality that many drug users are functional members of society who are never policed or prosecuted, particularly if they are white, middle-class, or using drugs in private settings (Measham & Shiner, 2009). In doing so, the media reinforces a dichotomy between the "deserving" and "undeserving" user, which in turn justifies selective enforcement and sustains public support for criminalisation.

In practice, this system produces profoundly unequal outcomes. Marginalised communities, particularly Black, Asian, and minority ethnic groups, are disproportionately stopped, searched, and prosecuted for drug offences, despite similar or lower rates of drug use compared to white populations (Shiner et al., 2018). The result is a cycle of criminalisation that undermines employment, housing, and social mobility—further entrenching disadvantage and exclusion.

This essay critically examines the range of actors who benefit from the criminalisation of drug users in the UK. Drawing on criminological theory, policy analysis, and empirical research, it identifies the mechanisms through which these actors derive symbolic authority, institutional legitimacy, and financial profit. In doing so, it challenges the assumption that drug criminalisation serves public safety or community well-being. Instead, it argues that the continued punishment of drug users serves the interests of the powerful at the expense of the marginalised, and that meaningful reform requires a fundamental reorientation of the UK's approach to drugs.

## Political Capital and the Maintenance of Moral Authority

Politicians often derive substantial symbolic power from being "tough on drugs." Drug policy has historically provided fertile ground for moral entrepreneurship, allowing political actors to frame themselves as guardians of public decency and societal order. The association of drug use with criminality permits them to perform moral stewardship, appealing to conservative values and middle-class fears about disorder, urban decline, and social deviance. As Seddon (2006, p. 38) observes, the conceptualisation of drug use as a moral failing—rather than a manifestation of health or social need—has long been utilised to legitimise punitive governance and expand state control.

In this framework, drug users are portrayed not as citizens in need of care, but as deviant threats to the moral and physical fabric of society. This portrayal resonates strongly with tabloid media narratives and reinforces the public perception that harsh penalties are necessary to uphold public order. The punitive ethos remains deeply embedded in political discourse, despite widespread evidence demonstrating that such strategies are ineffective, discriminatory, and ultimately harmful (Nutt, 2012; Stevens, 2011). As Taylor (2016) points out, political narratives continue to scapegoat drug users while ignoring the underlying causes of drug-related harm such as poverty, trauma, and mental ill health.

The "war on drugs" rhetoric provides an accessible and emotive political stance, especially during times of economic or social instability. Its simplicity makes it politically expedient: the notion that the state must "crack down" on drug use offers a clear moral binary between good and evil, order and chaos. By demonising drug users, policymakers can shift attention away from systemic issues like unemployment, housing shortages, and welfare cuts—issues for which they might bear political responsibility. This sleight of hand enables governments to posture as responsive and protective, without enacting costly or unpopular structural reforms (Taylor, 2023).

The political utility of drug criminalisation has been particularly salient in British politics since the 1971 Misuse of Drugs Act, which entrenched prohibition as the primary response to drug use. Successive governments—Conservative, Labour, and coalition alike—have used drug policy as a way to symbolise their commitment to "law and order." Even in the face of growing scientific and public support for reform, major parties have continued to resist liberalisation, wary of alienating voters or appearing soft on crime (Stevens, 2011, p. 6). The political risks of decriminalisation are seen as outweighing the potential social benefits, especially in a media environment primed to vilify any deviation from the punitive norm.

David Nutt, former chair of the Advisory Council on the Misuse of Drugs (ACMD), famously clashed with the Labour government in 2009 over the scientific inaccuracies underpinning UK drug classification. Nutt argued that the government had repeatedly ignored empirical evidence in favour of political expedience, maintaining drug schedules that did not correspond to relative harms (Nutt et al., 2010). In his landmark article, *Equasy – An overlooked addiction with implications for the current debate on drug harms*, Nutt (2009) compared the harms of horse riding to those of ecstasy to highlight the irrationality of existing classifications. His sacking following these remarks underscored the extent to which drug policy in the UK is driven by ideology and political optics, rather than evidence-based reasoning.

Nutt has since argued that fear, stigma, and media pressure continue to distort public understanding of drugs, reinforcing the political value of prohibition. In his view, politicians cling to punitive models not because they are effective, but because they are electorally safe (Nutt, 2012). Reform, by contrast, requires political courage—something in short supply when tabloid newspapers can mobilise moral panic at a moment's notice. This dynamic was evident in the government's swift rejection of ACMD recommendations to downgrade cannabis and ecstasy, despite scientific consensus that both substances were less harmful than alcohol or tobacco.

The use of drug policy for political symbolism is deeply entwined with mechanisms of social control. Criminalisation facilitates the ongoing surveillance and regulation of marginalised groups. Through stop-and-search powers, discretionary policing, and zero-tolerance strategies, the state exercises control over populations already subject to economic and racial disadvantage. Shiner et al. (2018) highlight how Black people in England and Wales are nine times more likely to be stopped and searched for drugs, despite no higher prevalence of use compared to white people. In this way, the drug laws act as a pretext for maintaining spatial and racial hierarchies.

Stuart Taylor (2016) develops this argument by showing how drug policy has historically been racialised and class-based. He traces the roots of modern prohibition to colonial anxieties about moral degeneration and the control of the "dangerous classes." In the contemporary UK context, Taylor argues that drug criminalisation continues to perform a disciplining function, targeting the working class, racialised youth, and the urban poor through a framework of moral suspicion and carceral paternalism. This framework ensures that certain groups remain under constant scrutiny, while others—particularly white, middle-class recreational users—are left unpoliced and unpunished (Taylor, 2016).

The preservation of hegemonic order through criminalisation becomes especially apparent when examining the selective enforcement of drug laws. For example, university students using cocaine at house parties or professionals using prescription stimulants to enhance productivity are rarely subjected to criminal sanctions. These users benefit from private spaces, legal representation, and class privilege. Meanwhile, the visible, public, and chaotic drug use often associated with homelessness or poverty is treated as a policing priority. This selective enforcement perpetuates social stratification under the guise of criminal justice (Measham & Shiner, 2009).

Moreover, politicians are complicit in maintaining a two-tiered system that punishes problematic users while effectively tolerating functional use among the elite. This hypocrisy is rarely addressed in public discourse, as doing so would require a fundamental reckoning with how privilege operates within drug policy. Instead, drug users continue to be cast as either dangerous criminals or pitiable addicts, never as complex individuals shaped by structural forces.

Even when attempts are made to shift the narrative—such as pilot diversion schemes in Durham or Thames Valley—central government often withholds support or stymies progress through funding restrictions and regulatory hurdles. Politicians may pay lip service to the principles of harm reduction but frequently revert to punitive posturing under pressure from tabloids or political rivals. This was evident in the Conservative government's 2021 ten-year drug strategy, which allocated significant funding to treatment but continued to frame drug use as a criminal issue requiring aggressive enforcement (Home Office, 2021).

In sum, political actors benefit significantly from the continued criminalisation of drug users. The punitive model allows them to signal authority, maintain control over marginalised populations, and avoid grappling with structural inequality. It is a system that trades in symbolic victories while producing real-world harm—perpetuating cycles of criminalisation, stigma, and exclusion. As long as drug policy remains a tool of political theatre rather than social justice, meaningful reform will be resisted, and the most vulnerable in society will continue to pay the highest price.

## Law Enforcement and Institutional Incentives

One of the primary institutional beneficiaries of drug criminalisation is law enforcement. The war on drugs provides a broad and enduring mandate for police intervention, enabling the use of aggressive, discretionary tactics such as stop and search—often deployed under the authority of the Police and Criminal Evidence Act 1984 and the Misuse of Drugs Act 1971. These powers permit officers to stop individuals based on "reasonable suspicion," a concept that is both highly subjective and disproportionately applied to racialised and working-class individuals. As (Eastwood et al., 2013, p. 12) observe, drug offences are particularly attractive to police forces because they are among the easiest to detect: they typically do not require a victim or complainant, and evidence can often be obtained through a quick search or visible paraphernalia.

This dynamic creates a perverse incentive structure whereby police can meet arrest and performance quotas by focusing on low-level drug users rather than more complex, resource-intensive crimes. As Stuart Taylor (2016) notes, drug enforcement acts as "low-hanging fruit" for officers under pressure to demonstrate productivity. These visible metrics—arrest rates, seizure counts, and stop-and-search figures—can then be used to justify operational funding, secure political backing, and reinforce the legitimacy of the police in public discourse, even though these activities do little to reduce drug-related harm or disrupt supply chains.

The institutional logic of drug policing is further sustained by the availability of targeted government funding linked to enforcement. Programmes such as the Home Office's drug strategy budgets have historically included specific allocations for police-led crackdowns, "county lines" disruption, and high-visibility operations. In some cases, forces have received additional funding on the basis of their drug enforcement track record, reinforcing a cycle in which criminalisation becomes not just a legal tool but a financial asset. This monetary incentive structure is rarely scrutinised, yet it underpins a model of policing that prioritises visible enforcement over long-term community health outcomes.

Moreover, drug policing provides an ideal gateway for broader surveillance and intelligence-gathering. The criminalisation of drug possession allows officers to stop and search individuals with relative ease, providing opportunities not just for arrest but also for data collection, intimidation, and spatial control—particularly in deprived or racialised communities (Shiner, 2015). This function of drug law enforcement goes beyond crime prevention; it acts as a mechanism of social regulation. Surveillance becomes normalised in targeted communities, and certain demographics—especially young Black men—come to be regarded as inherently suspicious or pre-criminal. As a result, drug enforcement serves as both a cause and consequence of broader policing disparities.

Indeed, recent research has highlighted the racialised application of stop-and-search powers in the UK. Shiner et al. (2018) show that Black people are nine times more likely to be stopped and searched for drugs than white people, despite similar levels of drug use across ethnic groups. These disparities cannot be explained by crime patterns alone; rather, they reflect institutionalised biases that frame drug use among Black and working-class individuals as inherently more dangerous or criminal. The consequences of this policing are severe: criminal records for minor possession offences can limit employment, education, housing, and travel opportunities, thus compounding cycles of marginalisation.

In addition to ideological and institutional motivations, drug-related policing offers material benefits for individual officers and departments. Specialist drug units are often well-resourced, and drug operations can involve overtime payments, specialist training, and increased status within the force. Tactical units such as Serious and Organised Crime Teams frequently rely on drug raids to demonstrate operational effectiveness. These raids are not only performative but can also generate income through asset seizure. Under the Proceeds of Crime Act 2002, police forces can retain a portion of confiscated assets—including cash, vehicles, and property—creating a direct financial incentive to pursue drug offences. As Seddon et al. (2008) note, this turns drug policing into a revenue-generating enterprise, raising serious ethical concerns about the impartiality and motivations of law enforcement.

The existence of these economic incentives presents a structural barrier to reform. Were the UK to move towards decriminalisation or a health-led approach—as advocated by organisations such as Release and the Transform Drug Policy Foundation—entire subfields of policing would be rendered redundant or require radical transformation. Officers specialising in narcotics enforcement might face job insecurity; training protocols would need overhaul; and institutional cultures that valorise control, confrontation, and hierarchy would be challenged. In this sense, criminalisation is not merely a legal or political choice, but an embedded institutional practice with deep professional and economic roots.

Further complicating reform efforts is the symbolic role of drug enforcement within police-community relations. In many communities, high-visibility policing is equated with order, safety, and authority. Even if these perceptions are not borne out by empirical reductions in crime, they serve to reinforce public support for drug crackdowns, especially among groups less likely to be targeted themselves. Political leaders often exploit this perception to defend drug enforcement budgets and resist calls for change. As Taylor (2016) argues, this creates a feedback loop in which the symbolic appeal of enforcement eclipses its practical failings.

Meanwhile, the opportunity cost of drug criminalisation is profound. Resources devoted to low-level enforcement could be redirected towards prevention, education, or treatment services—interventions that are shown to be more effective in reducing harm and improving community well-being (Nutt, 2012). Yet, the current structure of law enforcement funding and performance measurement disincentivises such a shift. Police are rewarded not for reducing harm, but for demonstrating activity—often in the form of arrests and seizures. This activity is inherently easier to pursue among street-level users than high-level suppliers, further skewing enforcement priorities.

In conclusion, the institutional benefits of drug criminalisation for law enforcement are multifaceted. From performance metrics and financial gain to surveillance authority and symbolic capital, policing in the UK is deeply enmeshed with punitive drug policy. This entanglement creates strong disincentives for reform, as any move towards decriminalisation threatens the institutional logic and material interests that sustain current practices. Unless these incentives are critically interrogated and restructured, law enforcement will remain a powerful force in the preservation of a punitive, unequal, and ultimately ineffective drug policy regime.

## Private Sector and the Carceral Economy

The criminalisation of drug users also benefits a growing private sector intricately linked to the penal system. Over the past three decades, the UK has increasingly embraced the marketisation of justice. Through the partial privatisation of prisons, the outsourcing of probation, drug treatment, and security services, a carceral economy has emerged in which incarceration and supervision are not merely tools of social control but also sources of profit (Scott & Codd, 2010). Within this economy, the continued criminalisation of drug possession and low-level supply offences ensures a consistent supply of detainees—especially individuals who are poor, socially excluded, and unable to navigate their way out of the criminal justice system.

The commodification of incarceration reflects a broader neoliberal trend in British governance, particularly accelerated during periods of austerity. In the wake of the 2008 financial crisis, successive UK governments promoted the outsourcing of public services as a cost-saving and efficiency-enhancing strategy. However, critics argue that such measures have instead created perverse incentives, where the profit motives of corporations conflict with principles of justice, rehabilitation, and human dignity (Cavadino & Dignan, 2006). Nowhere is this tension more apparent than in the treatment of drug users, who are frequently cycled through private-sector-managed prisons, mandatory treatment programmes, and court-ordered testing schemes—all of which generate revenue for contractors.

Firms such as Serco, G4S, and Sodexo operate several of the UK's privately managed prisons and hold extensive contracts for ancillary services such as prisoner transport, electronic tagging, and probation supervision. The presence of drug users within these facilities helps sustain occupancy levels and justifies continued investment in prison infrastructure. From a business perspective, drug users—particularly those convicted of simple possession or breach of probation orders—represent a low-risk, cost-efficient population. They are typically non-violent, pose minimal management challenges, and have high rates of recidivism, making them ideal clients within a system that profits from volume and turnover (Jewkes & Moran, 2014).

This business model mirrors that of the US private prison system, albeit on a smaller scale. Nevertheless, the principles are similar: the more people arrested and detained for low-level offences, the greater the demand for beds, security staff, logistics, and monitoring services. Under such a model, reducing drug criminalisation would represent a threat to profitability. It would shrink the pool of eligible detainees and reduce the justification for future prison expansion. As such, private sector stakeholders have a vested interest in maintaining or even expanding the criminalisation of drug users.

Importantly, the private sector's involvement in drug-related criminal justice processes extends well beyond prison walls. Drug testing and treatment services—often contracted out to private firms—are increasingly embedded within probation and court orders. For individuals subject to community sentences or Drug Rehabilitation Requirements (DRRs), attendance at treatment or submission to regular testing is a condition of compliance. Failure to meet these conditions can result in breach proceedings and subsequent imprisonment. This creates a captive market in which service providers are guaranteed a steady stream of participants under legal compulsion (Monaghan, 2012).

The profitability of drug testing and treatment contracts is enhanced by the standardisation of services and the use of remote technologies. Firms offering urine or saliva tests can administer them at scale, often using automated systems and centralised laboratories. Treatment providers, including some private clinics and charities operating under contract, frequently deliver group-based interventions at low cost, with limited tailoring to individual needs. While some services undoubtedly offer care and support, the overall model remains geared towards compliance rather than recovery, risk management rather than harm reduction.

In this context, the goals of public health are subordinated to the imperatives of control and efficiency. The needs of drug users—many of whom have complex histories of trauma, mental illness, and social exclusion—are often poorly served by these interventions. Rather than addressing underlying causes of use, programmes may focus narrowly on abstinence and behavioural compliance. Stuart Taylor (2016) critiques this model as a form of "therapeutic coercion," in which the appearance of care masks the reality of compulsion. Users are not helped so much as managed, and the distinction between treatment and punishment becomes increasingly blurred.

There is also growing concern that these dynamics reproduce and deepen social inequalities. The burden of mandatory testing and treatment disproportionately falls on the poorest and most marginalised users—those unable to afford legal representation, private counselling, or detox services. By contrast, wealthier and more socially connected users are often able to avoid criminal penalties altogether. This two-tier system, sustained by a mixture of discretion and privilege, ensures that the private sector's revenue model is largely funded through the surveillance and control of the underclass (Eastwood et al., 2013).

Beyond the criminal justice system, other industries have also profited from the expansion of drug-related enforcement. Insurance companies, security firms, and housing providers all play a role in monitoring and penalising individuals with drug convictions. A criminal record for a drug offence can lead to higher insurance premiums, loss of housing eligibility, and exclusion from employment opportunities—all of which contribute to the ongoing marginalisation of drug users. In turn, this marginalisation makes them more vulnerable to reoffending and further entrenchment in the criminal justice system, sustaining demand for private services.

Even academic and policy research institutions have, at times, benefited from the criminalisation paradigm. Evaluations, pilot projects, and consultancy services related to criminal justice and drug treatment attract government and philanthropic funding. While much of this work is grounded in efforts to reduce harm or promote reform, it is important to acknowledge that the very existence of these research markets depends on the continuation of a punitive framework. As Monaghan (2012) warns, the criminalisation of drug users has become so deeply institutionalised that even efforts to "improve" or "reform" the system may inadvertently reinforce it.

Furthermore, private sector influence on drug policy is not confined to service delivery; it increasingly extends into lobbying and policy advocacy. Some corporations have sought to position themselves as "partners" in public safety, offering to deliver "innovative solutions" to complex social problems. This language, borrowed from corporate social responsibility discourse, masks the reality that these firms often prioritise shareholder value over social impact. In doing so, they contribute to the framing of drug use as a problem to be managed, not a symptom to be understood.

Finally, the entrenchment of private interests in drug policy presents significant obstacles to reform. Any serious effort to decriminalise or depenalise drug use would require not only legal and political change but also economic restructuring. Contracts would need to be terminated or renegotiated, services re-integrated into the public sector, and funding models redesigned around health and well-being rather than control and punishment. Such changes would face intense resistance from stakeholders with financial interests in the status quo.

In conclusion, the private sector is a major, albeit often overlooked, beneficiary of the UK's punitive drug policy. From prison management and probation supervision to testing and treatment provision, the criminalisation of drug users sustains a lucrative industry premised on human containment. While some private actors may offer competent or even compassionate services, the overall structure incentivises volume over value, compliance over care, and punishment over prevention. As long as profit can be extracted from the policing, processing, and punishing of drug users, the private sector will remain a powerful force resisting meaningful reform. Any attempt to transform UK drug policy must therefore reckon not only with outdated laws and harmful rhetoric but with the economic interests that have become embedded in its very enforcement.

## Media Sensationalism and Public Anxiety

The media plays a pivotal role in shaping public attitudes towards drug use, often conflating users with criminality and social decay. Tabloid newspapers, in particular, have long profited from moral panic narratives, portraying drug users as deviant, dangerous, and irresponsible. Such portrayals reinforce public fears and legitimise continued criminalisation (McRobbie & Thornton, 1995).

This media framing benefits news outlets through increased sales and digital engagement. Sensational headlines, graphic imagery, and "before and after" drug user portraits generate high traffic and emotional responses. In doing so, the media contribute to a feedback loop where public support for punitive policies is maintained or intensified, offering political cover for continued enforcement.

Moreover, by focusing on problematic or visible drug use—such as heroin addiction, crack use, or homelessness—media representations obscure the prevalence of functional drug use among middle- and upper-class populations (Parker et al., 1998). This skewed portrayal ensures that criminalisation is primarily directed at the socially marginal, preserving the privileges of functional users who consume privately and without detection.

Media-Induced Moral Panics and Their Impact.

The concept of moral panic, as articulated by sociologists such as Stanley Cohen and later expanded by McRobbie and Thornton (1995), describes how media amplification of certain issues can lead to heightened public concern and policy responses disproportionate to the actual threat. In the context of drug use, media outlets often highlight isolated incidents or extreme cases, framing them as indicative of a broader societal crisis.

For instance, the death of Leah Betts in 1995 after taking ecstasy received extensive media coverage, with images of her in a coma widely circulated. This coverage contributed to a moral panic around ecstasy use, despite statistical evidence indicating that such fatalities were rare (Blackman, 2004). The media's focus on Betts, a young, white, middle-class woman, also underscores how certain narratives are amplified over others, often neglecting the experiences of more marginalised drug users.

Such moral panics can lead to reactive policy measures. The UK's Misuse of Drugs Act 1971 has been amended multiple times in response to media-fuelled concerns, often without robust evidence to support the changes. This reactive policymaking underscores the media's influence in shaping drug legislation.

Stigmatisation Through Language and Imagery.

Media representations frequently employ stigmatising language and imagery when discussing drug users. Terms like "junkie," "addict," or "drug fiend" are commonplace in tabloid reporting, reinforcing negative stereotypes and dehumanising individuals who use drugs. This language contributes to public stigma, which can deter individuals from seeking treatment and support (Lloyd, 2013).

Imagery used in media reports often depicts drug users in states of distress or degradation, further entrenching negative perceptions. Such portrayals neglect the diverse experiences of drug users, many of whom lead functional lives and contribute positively to society. By focusing solely on negative stereotypes, the media fails to provide a balanced view, perpetuating misconceptions about drug use and its impacts.

Obscuring Functional Drug Use Among Privileged Groups.

While media coverage often centres on visible, problematic drug use, it largely ignores or downplays drug consumption among middle- and upper-class individuals. Research indicates that drug use is prevalent across all socio-economic groups, with substances like cocaine and cannabis commonly used in professional and social settings (Parker et al., 1998).

This selective reporting creates a dichotomy where drug use among the privileged is normalised or even glamorised, while use among the marginalised is criminalised and stigmatised. Such disparities in media representation contribute to unequal enforcement of drug laws, with policing and punitive measures disproportionately targeting disadvantaged communities.

The Role of Media in Shaping Public Opinion and Policy.

Media narratives significantly influence public opinion, which in turn affects policymaking. Surveys have shown that public perceptions of drug users are often shaped by media portrayals, leading to support for punitive approaches over harm reduction strategies (UKDPC, 2010).

This public sentiment provides political cover for continued criminalisation, as policymakers align with perceived public opinion to maintain electoral support. Consequently, evidence-based approaches to drug policy, such as decriminalisation or harm reduction, struggle to gain traction in the face of media-driven public resistance.

The Need for Balanced and Evidence-Based Reporting.

To counteract the negative impacts of current media representations, there is a pressing need for balanced and evidence-based reporting on drug use. Journalists and media outlets should strive to present nuanced narratives that reflect the complexity of drug use and its social determinants.

Incorporating voices of individuals with lived experience, public health experts, and researchers can provide more comprehensive coverage. Highlighting successful harm reduction initiatives and decriminalisation efforts in other countries can also inform public discourse and challenge prevailing punitive paradigms.

In summation, the Media representations play a critical role in shaping public perceptions and policies related to drug use in the UK. The prevalent focus on sensationalist narratives and negative stereotypes contributes to the stigmatisation and criminalisation of drug users, particularly among marginalised groups. By obscuring the realities of functional drug use among privileged populations, the media perpetuates unequal enforcement and hinders the adoption of evidence-based policies. Addressing these issues requires a concerted effort to promote balanced reporting and public education, fostering a more informed and compassionate approach to drug policy.

## Author's Reflection: Lived Experience and Shifting Perspectives

Working as a bouncer, I saw first-hand how drug-taking behaviour changed depending on the club, the crowd, and whatever substance happened to be "in fashion" at the time. It was clear that drugs weren't just about addiction or danger—they were deeply social, cultural, and situational. In some clubs, cocaine use was as routine as ordering a pint. In others, MDMA defined the mood of the night. And yet, behind the door, it was rarely the drugs that caused the trouble—it was usually the alcohol.

In court, as a magistrate, I saw a different side of the same system: lives ruined for low-level possession, often uncovered through random stop and searches or minor traffic stops. I watched as people were criminalised not for causing harm, but for being caught—usually young, often racialised, nearly always disadvantaged. I saw drivers banned and prosecuted under drug-driving laws that, frankly, have little basis in science when it comes to measuring actual impairment. The law assumes that trace presence equals intoxication, and in doing so, it makes criminals out of people with no intent to offend.

All of this has shaped how I think about drugs, drug users, and drug abusers. But what we rarely talk about—and what's missing from most policy conversations—is the damage caused by legal substances: sugar, fats, energy drinks. These are addictive, harmful, and heavily marketed. They burden the NHS, alter our behaviour, and impact mental and physical health—but they are largely ignored by the drug policy establishment.

The way we classify substances today doesn't prevent harm—it obscures it. Our current system doesn't reflect scientific understanding, it doesn't protect public health, and it certainly doesn't serve justice. It costs too much money for poor results and ruins far too many lives in the process.

It's time to ask: if this is the best we can do—why are we still doing it?

## Conclusion: Sustaining Inequality Through Criminalisation

The criminalisation of drug users in the UK is neither neutral nor accidental. It is a deeply embedded feature of the country's sociopolitical landscape—one that serves a diverse range of vested interests. From politicians eager to appear "tough on crime," to police forces incentivised to focus on drug possession for performance statistics, to private corporations profiting from incarceration and testing, and media outlets generating engagement through sensationalism, the current punitive regime is supported by a web of interconnected stakeholders. These beneficiaries do not necessarily uphold drug criminalisation because it is effective at reducing harm. Rather, they sustain it because it provides symbolic authority, institutional legitimacy, financial reward, and a means of exerting control over marginalised populations.

Despite decades of research and international examples illustrating the ineffectiveness—and in many cases, the destructiveness—of punitive drug laws, the UK has remained resistant to change. This reluctance cannot be solely attributed to ignorance or inertia. Instead, it must be recognised as a product of structural and ideological investments in a carceral approach to drug use. Decriminalisation, or a shift towards a health-based model, would not merely require legislative reform; it would necessitate a fundamental reorganisation of political narratives, policing priorities, economic contracts, and media framing. In short, it would disrupt the comfortable arrangements of power, profit, and authority that the criminalisation of drug users has come to represent.

Throughout this chapter, we have seen that drug policy in the UK functions less as a coherent public health strategy and more as a mechanism for managing social order in an illusion of control. It selectively punishes those who are most visible—homeless people, racialised communities, the unemployed—while largely ignoring or tolerating drug use among the socially privileged. This selective enforcement is not merely coincidental; it reflects a long-standing moral economy in which poverty, race, and deviance are intertwined in public discourse, often through the lens of media-fuelled panic.

Law enforcement plays a central role in perpetuating this inequality. By targeting drug possession—especially of substances like cannabis, crack, and heroin—in highly policed neighbourhoods, police forces reinforce cycles of criminalisation and exclusion. The data is unambiguous: Black people are nine times more likely to be stopped and searched for drugs in England and Wales, despite using drugs at similar rates to white people (Shiner et al., 2018). These practices do not make communities safer; they fracture trust, alienate youth, and contribute to the broader erosion of civil liberties.

Institutional Dependencies and Economic Incentives go beyond the symbolic power of drug criminalisation and lie a series of institutional dependencies that have become integral to the functioning of the UK's criminal justice and public sector economies. Police departments use drug arrests to boost performance metrics; courts process thousands of drug-related cases annually, keeping administrative systems active and justifying funding; private firms such as Serco and G4S run prisons and probation services, their revenue partially dependent on drug-related convictions; and drug testing companies profit from compulsory monitoring regimes.

These industries have developed a financial stake in the continued punishment of drug users. As highlighted earlier in the chapter, even treatment and rehabilitation services—ostensibly health-focused—are often designed around compliance with court orders, rather than genuine therapeutic support. The expansion of public-private partnerships within the justice system, particularly under austerity-era reforms, has only deepened the commodification of incarceration and control. The result is a carceral economy that thrives on the presence of drug users, particularly those from socially marginalised groups.

Drug criminalisation also serves political interests by providing a stage for moral entrepreneurship. Politicians routinely invoke the spectre of drugs to signal authority, deflect criticism, or stir public emotion. "Tough on drugs" rhetoric offers a ready-made platform that resonates with large swathes of the electorate, particularly when amplified by a willing media. In this context, rational debate and evidence-based policy are often subordinated to emotional appeals and political expedience.

As David Nutt's work (2012) has made clear, drug scheduling in the UK frequently bears little resemblance to scientific assessments of harm. Alcohol and tobacco, among the most damaging substances in terms of public health, remain legal and widely marketed, while less harmful drugs like psilocybin or MDMA are treated as highly dangerous and subject to severe penalties. This disconnect between evidence and policy underscores the role of ideology in shaping drug law—a role that is often obscured by the illusion of rational governance.

The media plays an indispensable role in maintaining this illusion. As explored in the previous section, tabloid coverage of drug use tends to focus on extreme cases, visible users, or tragic deaths, often devoid of broader context. These narratives reinforce stereotypes and stoke fear, creating fertile ground for punitive responses. In turn, the public—fed a steady diet of alarmist headlines and distorted imagery—comes to support criminalisation as a necessary response to perceived moral decline.

The human cost of this punitive regime is staggering and the cost of maintaining this tenuous status quo will continue to rise. Thousands of individuals are criminalised each year for low-level drug offences, many of them receiving fines, community orders, or prison sentences that significantly disrupt their lives. These sanctions have long-term consequences: they limit access to housing, employment, education, and social services; they exacerbate mental health problems; and they perpetuate cycles of poverty and exclusion.

Public health outcomes also suffer. Fear of arrest deters many users from seeking medical help in the event of overdose. Harm reduction initiatives such as needle exchanges, supervised consumption rooms, and drug-checking services are underfunded or politically controversial, despite clear evidence of their efficacy (Transform Drug Policy Foundation, 2022). Meanwhile, the UK continues to experience high levels of drug-related deaths, particularly in areas of acute deprivation such as Scotland and the North of England.

At the societal level, the criminalisation of drug users diverts resources away from more constructive interventions. Police time, court capacity, and public money are spent on enforcing possession laws that have minimal impact on supply or demand. These resources could be reallocated to education, social care, mental health services, and genuine addiction treatment—investments that would offer far greater returns in terms of community safety and well-being.

If drug policy is to align with public health and harm reduction principles, it must confront the uncomfortable truth that criminalisation disproportionately serves the interests of the powerful while exacerbating the marginalisation of vulnerable groups. Addressing this reality demands political courage—the willingness to challenge entrenched narratives, resist institutional inertia, and prioritise long-term societal well-being over short-term electoral gains. Crucially, it also requires acknowledging a fundamental, yet often ignored, fact: many people use drugs for pleasure. This reality must inform our approach, as drug use is not simply a problem to be eradicated but a persistent aspect of human behaviour. In light of this, the case for a more pragmatic, compassionate, and evidence-based framework becomes ever more urgent.

International models provide useful inspiration. Portugal, for example, decriminalised personal drug possession in 2001, shifting the response from criminal justice to public health. Since then, it has seen reductions in overdose deaths, HIV transmission, and drug-related incarceration (Hughes & Stevens, 2010). Canada and parts of the US are also experimenting with legal regulation, particularly of cannabis, with early results suggesting improved public health outcomes and reductions in criminal justice costs.

These models are not without challenges, but they demonstrate that alternatives to criminalisation are not only possible—they are often more effective, humane, and just. Adopting such approaches in the UK would require substantial investment in health and social infrastructure, a reimagining of the role of police, and a cultural shift in how drug use is understood. Crucially, it would also demand a decoupling of drug policy from the political theatre, institutional incentives, and media-driven moral panics that have long defined it.

In conclusion, the criminalisation of drug users in the UK is a policy that masks its failures behind the appearance of control. It offers symbolic comfort while producing real harm. It enriches and empowers certain institutions and individuals, while systematically disadvantaging the poorest and most marginalised. To dismantle this system will not be easy. It will involve confronting not just outdated laws, but the entire architecture of power and profit that sustains them.

However, the cost of inaction is too great. As the death toll from preventable overdoses rises, as prisons overflow with non-violent offenders, and as communities continue to suffer under punitive surveillance, the imperative for reform grows stronger. A drug policy grounded in justice, compassion, and evidence is not only possible—it is urgently necessary.

## References


Blackman, S. (2004). *Chilling out: The cultural politics of substance consumption, youth and drug policy*. McGraw-Hill Education.

Cavadino, M., & Dignan, J. (2006). *Penal systems: A comparative approach*. SAGE Publications.

Eastwood, N., Shiner, M., & Bear, D. (2013). *The numbers in black and white: Ethnic disparities in the policing and prosecution of drug offences in England and Wales*. Release. Retrieved May 5, 2025, from https://www.release.org.uk/publications/numbers-black-and-white

Home Office. (2021). *From harm to hope: A 10-year drugs plan to cut crime and save lives*. HM Government. Retrieved May 7, 2025 from https://www.gov.uk/government/publications/from-harm-to-hope-10-year-drugs-plan

Hughes, C. E., & Stevens, A. (2010). What can we learn from the Portuguese decriminalization of illicit drugs? *British Journal of Criminology, 50*(6), 999–1022. https://doi.org/10.1093/bjc/azq038

Jewkes, Y., & Moran, D. (2014). Should prisons be "normalised"? *The Howard Journal of Criminal Justice, 53*(3), 247–262. https://doi.org/10.1111/hojo.12064

Lloyd, C. (2013). *The stigmatisation of problem drug users: A narrative literature review*. UK Drug Policy Commission. Retrieved January 2, 2025, from https://www.ukdpc.org.uk/wp-content/uploads/Policy%20report%20-%20Stigma%20-%20full%20report.pdf

McRobbie, A., & Thornton, S. L. (1995). Rethinking "Moral Panic" for multi-mediated social worlds. *British Journal of Sociology, 46*(4), 559–574. https://doi.org/10.2307/591571

Measham, F., & Shiner, M. (2009). The legacy of "normalisation": The role of class, gender and ethnicity in shaping drug use pathways. *British Journal of Criminology, 49*(5), 764–777. https://doi.org/10.1093/bjc/azp038

Monaghan, M. (2012). *The politics of drugs: Perceptions, power and policy*. Palgrave Macmillan.

Nutt, D. (2009). Equasy–An overlooked addiction with implications for the current debate on drug harms. *Journal of Psychopharmacology, 23*(1), 3–5. https://doi.org/10.1177/0269881108099658

Nutt, D. (2012). *Drugs without the hot air: Minimising the harms of legal and illegal drugs*. UIT Cambridge.

Nutt, D., King, L. A., Saulsbury, W., & Blakemore, C. (2010). Development of a rational scale to assess the harm of drugs of potential misuse. *The Lancet, 376*(9752), 1558–1565. https://doi.org/10.1016/S0140-6736(10)61462-6

Parker, H., Aldridge, J., & Measham, F. (1998). *Illegal leisure: The normalisation of adolescent recreational drug use*. Routledge.

Scott, D., & Codd, H. (2010). *Controversial issues in prisons*. Open University Press.

Seddon, T. (2006). Drugs, crime and social exclusion: Social context and social theory in British drugs–crime research. *British Journal of Criminology, 46*(4), 680–703. https://doi.org/10.1093/bjc/azi079

Seddon, T., Ralphs, R., & Williams, L. (2008). *Risk, security and the 'criminalisation' of young people's drug use*. Criminal Justice Matters, Centre for Crime and Justice Studies.

Shiner, M. (2015). Drug policy reform and the reclassification of cannabis in England and Wales: A cautionary tale. *International Journal of Drug Policy, 26*(7), 696–704. https://doi.org/10.1016/j.drugpo.2014.12.010

Shiner, M., Carre, Z., Delsol, R., & Eastwood, N. (2018). *The colour of injustice: 'Race', drugs and law enforcement in England and Wales*. Release. Retrieved April 12, 2025, from https://www.release.org.uk/publications/Colour-of-Injustice

Stevens, A. (2011). *Drugs, crime and public health: The political economy of drug policy*. Routledge.

Taylor, S. (2016). From the social supply of drugs to the cultural value of drugs: An exploration of the roles of drug dealers in the UK recreational drug market, drugs: education. *Prevention and Policy, 23*(3), 219–227. https://doi.org/10.3109/09687637.2015.1128889

Taylor, S. (2023). *Drugs, deviancy and the construction of social problems: Critical issues in social harm and crime*. Policy Press.

Transform Drug Policy Foundation (2022) *After the war on drugs: Blueprint for regulation*. Retrieved May 7, 2025, from https://transformdrugs.org/publications/blueprint-for-regulation

UK Drug Policy Commission (UKDPC). (2010). *Representations of drug use and drug users in the British Press*. UKDPC. Retrieved May 1, 2025, from https://www.ukdpc.org.uk/wp-content/uploads/Policy%20report%20-%20Media%20-%20full%20report.pdf

CHAPTER 6

# Between Evidence, Ethics, and Enforcement

**Abstract** This chapter offers a critical examination of UK drug policy through the specific lens of drug-driving legislation, positioning it as a revealing case study in how moral and political imperatives often outweigh empirical evidence in the formation of law. It argues that, far from being guided by science or public health priorities, UK drug policy remains shaped by punitive logic, symbolic politics, and long-standing ideological narratives around drug use and criminality. The chapter begins by tracing the historical shift in British drug policy from a public health orientation to a predominantly criminal justice model. Drawing on key works such as Edwards (1989), McKeganey (2007), and Taylor (2008), it demonstrates how successive governments have responded more to moral panics than to empirical trends, with drug users repeatedly constructed as "folk devils" to justify repressive legal responses. This ideological foundation is maintained through what Monaghan (2008) terms the "new rules of engagement," where scientific evidence is selectively employed to reinforce predetermined policy goals, rather than to inform rational debate. The chapter uses the example of Section 5A of the Road Traffic Act 1988 (amended in 2013) to explore how drug-driving legislation epitomises this trend. Despite limited evidence on its prevalence or comparative danger relative to alcohol, drug driving became a political and media priority. Drawing on the work of Wolff et al. (2013), Hasan et al. (2022), and Allsop (2020), the chapter critiques the zero-tolerance thresholds, the questionable scientific basis for per se limits, and the disproportionate



E. Peatfield, *Drugs Disorder by Design*,
https://doi.org/10.1007/978-3-032-07814-8_6

focus on illicit substances, particularly cannabis and cocaine. It also examines how roadside testing technology and enforcement practices raise concerns around fairness, particularly for young and minority drivers. From an ethical standpoint, the chapter, building on Holland (2020), argues that the UK's criminal justice approach to drug use—particularly when applied to drug driving—fails to meet principles of proportionality, care, and justice. The policy contributes to social exclusion, reinforces stigma, and does little to prevent harm. The ethical critique is bolstered by David Nutt's (2009, 2012) work, which highlights the inconsistent application of harm assessments in drug policy and the marginalisation of scientific voices. In its final section, the chapter proposes a new policy direction grounded in evidence, ethics, and equity. It explores the potential of reformist models including harm reduction, scientific reclassification, and participatory policymaking, drawing on examples such as Portugal's decriminalisation model. Using Stevens' (2025) concept of "policy constellations," it underscores the need to dismantle entrenched narratives and include lived experience in the formation of future drug laws. Ultimately, the chapter argues that drug-driving legislation is not an isolated case but a microcosm of broader failures in UK drug policy. Reform must go beyond technical fixes to address the ideological and moral underpinnings that continue to prioritise punishment over protection, and symbolism over substance.

**Keywords** Drug policy, Drug driving, Criminal justice, Harm reduction, Moral panic, Public health, Evidence-based policy, David Nutt, Policy constellations, Ethics

## Introduction

This chapter explores the complex tensions and contradictions embedded in the UK's current drug policy framework. While official narratives often frame drug laws as grounded in public health and safety, closer scrutiny reveals that they are frequently shaped by political expedience, moral anxieties, and media influence rather than robust empirical evidence. This chapter critically interrogates how evidence is used—and more often misused—within this policy landscape, with a particular focus on the selective targeting of behaviours such as drug driving, while comparatively neglecting more pervasive issues like alcohol misuse.

Drug driving provides a revealing case study of these dynamics. A significant legislative shift occurred with the introduction of Section 5A of the Road Traffic Act 1988, as amended by the Crime and Courts Act 2013. This law, which came into force in March 2015, criminalised driving with certain controlled substances in the body above legally defined limits, regardless of whether impairment could be demonstrated. This marked a departure from previous practice by removing the requirement to prove impairment and instead relying on the presence of drugs in the bloodstream above predetermined thresholds (Wolff & Johnston, 2014, p. 5). The law covers 17 substances, including both illicit drugs (e.g. cannabis, cocaine, MDMA) and prescribed medications (e.g. morphine, diazepam), with thresholds set in micrograms per litre of blood.

Many of these thresholds are set at extremely low levels, effectively creating a zero-tolerance regime for illegal substances. For example, the legal limit for THC, the psychoactive component in cannabis, is set at just 2 μg/L—an amount that may not correspond to any meaningful impairment (Allsop, 2020, p. 212). This approach stands in stark contrast to alcohol legislation, which requires either proven impairment or a blood alcohol concentration above a defined level. Such inconsistencies point to a drug policy framework that is shaped more by cultural stigma and political considerations than scientific understanding.

This concern has been most prominently articulated by Professor David Nutt, former chair of the Advisory Council on the Misuse of Drugs (ACMD), who was famously dismissed in 2009 for criticising the government's refusal to base drug policy on scientific evidence. Nutt (2009) has consistently argued that the UK's drug classification system, including its approach to drug driving, lacks internal logic and often exaggerates the dangers of illicit substances while minimising the harms of legal drugs like alcohol and tobacco. In his comparison of drug harms published in *The Lancet*, Nutt et al. (2010) placed alcohol as the most harmful drug overall—both to users and to society—yet alcohol remains comparatively under-regulated in driving law. Nutt argues that the government's refusal to rationalise policy based on harm reflects the dominance of political ideology over evidence-based reform.

The government's justification for the 2015 legislation focused on improving road safety and simplifying prosecution by removing the need for field impairment testing (Department for Transport, 2012). Yet, as Wolff et al. (2013, p. 10) and Hasan et al. (2022, p. 287) demonstrate, the scientific basis for these thresholds is weak, particularly given the variability in how individuals metabolise substances like cannabis and benzodiazepines. Roadside enforcement tools also detect only a limited range of substances (HMICFRS, 2019), and growing evidence suggests that younger and minority drivers are more frequently targeted for roadside testing, raising broader ethical concerns about discrimination and unequal treatment (Allsop, 2020, p. 214).

In sum, the UK's approach to drug driving exemplifies a broader pattern: privileging symbolic deterrence and moral reassurance over coherent, scientifically-informed regulation. This chapter will build on the work of Nutt and others to interrogate whether UK drug policy is primarily driven by ideology rather than evidence. It will reflect on the ethical implications of these inconsistencies and explore alternative frameworks—such as harm reduction, critical realism, and international public health models—that could guide more just and effective reform.

### *Historical and Political Context of UK Drug Policy*

The evolution of British drug policy reflects a shift from early public health approaches to a predominantly criminal justice model. In the early twentieth century, drug use was largely treated as a medical issue, with legislation such as the Dangerous Drugs Act 1920 placing regulatory power in the hands of doctors, pharmacists, and medical professionals (Edwards, 1989). This framework was rooted in a pragmatic desire to control substance use through prescription, reflecting the socio-medical context of the time. However, by the mid-twentieth century, increasing anxieties over heroin and cannabis use—particularly among working-class youth and immigrants—prompted a shift towards prohibitionist and punitive strategies.

The 1971 Misuse of Drugs Act (MDA) marked a decisive move towards criminalisation. This legislation categorised drugs into Classes A, B, and C based on their perceived harm and established a punitive framework for possession, trafficking, and production. The classification system, however, was not derived from empirical evidence but was a product of political and cultural considerations. As David Nutt (2009) and others have argued, the Act was less about reducing harm and more about asserting political control over the moral panic surrounding drugs. Over time, the public health framing of substance use was overshadowed by a criminal justice logic, which continues to dominate UK drug policy today.

Successive UK governments have routinely responded to drugs not through long-term planning or public health investment, but through reactive policymaking driven by media pressure and moral panics. Cohen's (1972) seminal work on moral panics remains relevant here: he noted how "folk devils" are constructed by the media and political elites to justify social control. Drug users—particularly those framed as "junkies," "ravers," or "gang members"—have long been cast in this role. Political responses have therefore been performative as much as pragmatic. For instance, the reclassification of cannabis from Class B to Class C in 2004 (under a Labour government) was reversed in 2009 after a campaign by tabloid newspapers and police unions, despite evidence showing cannabis posed comparatively low harm (Stevens, 2011). The policy reversal directly contradicted advice from the Advisory Council on the Misuse of Drugs (ACMD), which had argued that Class C was more proportionate.

### *Drug Politicisation*

This politicisation of drug policy is most clearly illustrated in the dismissal of Professor David Nutt as Chair of the ACMD in 2009. Nutt had publicly criticised the government for ignoring scientific evidence in its drug classifications, pointing out that substances like alcohol and tobacco were more harmful than some illegal drugs. In a landmark paper published in The Lancet, Nutt et al. (2010) used a multi-criteria decision analysis to assess drug harms. The findings were striking: alcohol was ranked the most harmful drug overall when considering harm to both users and society, while drugs such as LSD and ecstasy ranked much lower. Nutt's dismissal for "crossing the line between science and policy" exemplified how government drug policy operates more as a moral enterprise than an evidence-led strategy (Monaghan, 2011).

Drug policy in the UK has consistently reflected the anxieties, ideologies, and symbolic needs of the political establishment, rather than empirical trends or health outcomes. Monaghan (2008) argues that policymaking in this area follows "new rules of engagement" where evidence is filtered through ideological lenses. Scientific findings are accepted only when they support the existing policy direction; dissenting views are marginalised or dismissed. The case of Nutt shows how the "neutral expert" is tolerated only insofar as they reinforce governmental objectives. Once that boundary is crossed, expertise is sacrificed for political expediency.

Understanding drug policy as a "moral enterprise" (Becker, 1963) provides a critical framework for analysing these developments. Policies are constructed and legitimised not on the basis of scientific neutrality but through narratives that reinforce dominant cultural values. In the UK, these narratives have long relied on binaries between "respectable citizens" and "deviant drug users." This framing legitimises coercive measures—such as stop and search, incarceration, and surveillance—as necessary tools of moral correction. The fact that drug enforcement disproportionately targets poor and minority communities further reveals the ideological underpinnings of drug law. Stevens (2025) notes that such policies function as a form of symbolic reassurance: they provide the public with a sense that "something is being done," even if the actual public health impact is negligible or counterproductive.

The war on drugs in the UK thus serves political and moral functions more than practical or health-oriented ones. The use of punitive measures is not just about deterrence, but about reasserting social norms and delineating moral boundaries. Garland (2001) argues that modern criminal justice policies often operate through the "politics of reassurance"—providing visible responses to public fears, regardless of their effectiveness. Drug policy, especially in high-profile areas like drug driving or county lines policing, follows this logic closely.

Moreover, this emphasis on public reassurance over public health outcomes has serious consequences. Despite the overwhelming evidence of the harms of alcohol, successive governments have failed to implement effective restrictions—such as minimum unit pricing or advertising bans—due to lobbying pressure and cultural acceptability. Conversely, the government has imposed increasingly harsh penalties for possession of relatively low-harm drugs like cannabis and MDMA. This selective moralism undermines the credibility of drug policy and reinforces health inequalities.

David Nutt's work has been central in exposing these contradictions. In Drugs Without the Hot Air (2012), Nutt calls for a system where drugs are regulated based on actual harm, not historical stigma or political calculations. He advocates for a rational framework that includes regulated access, harm reduction, and education—echoing international best practices such as Portugal's decriminalisation model. Importantly, Nutt and colleagues argue that transparency, accountability, and independence in advisory bodies are essential to break the cycle of ideology-driven policy.

One could argue that the development of UK drug policy has been shaped less by public health priorities and more by political ideologies, moral panics, and reactive governance. From its early medical origins to the entrenched criminal justice model that we see today, British drug policy has functioned as a tool of symbolic reassurance and social control. Evidence—when it challenges dominant narratives—is frequently ignored or suppressed, as demonstrated by the treatment of experts like David Nutt. Recognising this historical and political context is crucial for imagining more ethical, evidence-informed alternatives. As this chapter will argue, reforming UK drug policy requires not just technical adjustments, but a fundamental rethinking of the moral and ideological narratives that sustain it.

UK drug policy is frequently framed by politicians as evidence-led and rational, yet a close inspection reveals a very different reality. As scholars have argued, while evidence plays a role in the policymaking process, it is rarely neutral or determinative. Instead, evidence is selectively mobilised to support pre-existing ideological positions, often subordinated to moral discourse, media narratives, and political expediency. This section explores how power operates through the production and deployment of knowledge in the UK's drug policy landscape, focusing on the mechanisms by which scientific voices are either co-opted or marginalised depending on their alignment with dominant agendas.

Monaghan's (2008) analysis of drug policy provides a crucial starting point. He challenges the common-sense assumption that drug policy is guided by impartial research and instead outlines a set of what he terms "new rules of engagement," where evidence is filtered through an ideological lens. In this framework, research is not used to explore new policy directions but to bolster predetermined objectives. Monaghan documents how Home Office publications and select research commissions give an appearance of scientific legitimacy while marginalising dissenting or inconvenient findings. He argues that policymakers increasingly rely on what he calls "policy-based evidence" rather than "evidence-based policy" (Monaghan, 2008, p. 431).

This dynamic is particularly evident in how governments have responded to expert recommendations regarding drug classifications. A notable example is the classification of ecstasy (MDMA). Despite the ACMD's advice that the harms of MDMA were significantly lower than those of alcohol or heroin, the government refused to downgrade its classification from Class A to Class B, citing public concern and political optics (Stevens, 2025). In such instances, science becomes a secondary consideration to perceived public morality and electoral calculations.

### *Flaws in the Misuse of Drugs Act and the Classification System*

McKeganey (2007) similarly critiques the UK's classification system under the Misuse of Drugs Act 1971, arguing that it lacks any coherent or consistent basis in scientific assessments of harm. The tripartite classification system (Classes A, B, and C) purports to reflect levels of danger to users and society, but McKeganey contends that the criteria underpinning these categories are opaque, historically contingent, and often politically driven. As he notes, "the location of a drug within a particular classification appears to be as much about the political salience of the issue as it is about the pharmacological properties of the substance" (McKeganey, 2007, p. 315).

The example of cannabis is instructive. The drug has oscillated between Class B and Class C over the past two decades, with changes driven not by significant new scientific findings but by media campaigns and shifts in political leadership. McKeganey points out that public and political perceptions of risk frequently outweigh the advice of expert panels and that such volatility undermines the legitimacy of the entire framework. Rather than offering a stable, evidence-informed regulatory system, the Act serves as a tool for symbolic politics—a point echoed by Taylor (2008), who argues that British drug policy is more about "managing deviance" than managing harm.

### *The Power of Moral Narratives-Punishment Versus Care the False Moral Economy*

Stevens (2025) adds a crucial dimension to this analysis by introducing the concept of "policy constellations"—a term that captures the enduring networks of political, bureaucratic, and media actors who shape drug policy over time. These constellations operate not simply through formal institutions but through shared beliefs, cultural assumptions, and power alliances that persist across electoral cycles. Within these constellations, empirical evidence must be framed in ways that align with dominant moral discourses if it is to influence policy.

According to Stevens, these constellations often fuse concerns about public order, morality, and national identity, constructing drug users—especially those from racialised or lower-class backgrounds—as threats to the moral fabric of society. As such, policy debates become less about harm reduction or scientific rigour and more about reaffirming social norms. This helps explain why punitive responses remain politically popular despite their limited effectiveness in reducing drug-related harm.

The durability of these constellations ensures that even progressive recommendations—such as the decriminalisation of drugs or the implementation of regulated markets—struggle to gain traction. Evidence is not absent, but its meaning is negotiated within power-laden discursive and institutional environments. In Stevens' words, "drug policy is not simply a site of scientific debate but a terrain of ideological struggle" (Stevens, 2025, p. 113).

As we have already mentioned in previous chapters one of the most emblematic examples of this ideological filtering of evidence is the dismissal of Professor David Nutt from his role as Chair of the Advisory Council on the Misuse of Drugs (ACMD) in 2009. Nutt had published a paper comparing the harms of legal and illegal substances, ranking alcohol and tobacco as more harmful than ecstasy, cannabis, and LSD. He argued that drug classifications should reflect actual harm data and accused the government of distorting science for political ends (Nutt, 2009).

In response, the then-Home Secretary Alan Johnson removed Nutt from his position, claiming that he had blurred the line between science and politics. Yet Nutt's work—later elaborated in *Drugs Without the Hot Air* (2012) and *The Lancet* (Nutt et al., 2010)—was grounded in rigorous empirical analysis using a multi-criteria decision analysis (MCDA) model. This model assessed both personal and societal harms, providing a more comprehensive picture of risk than the blunt categories of the Misuse of Drugs Act.

Nutt's removal was widely criticised by the scientific community as evidence of the government's unwillingness to engage with inconvenient truths. For Ian Taylor (2008), this episode illustrated the "paradox of technocracy": experts are brought into policy advisory roles but are expected to remain politically compliant. Once they challenge the prevailing narratives, they are expelled from the policymaking arena. This politicisation of scientific advice undermines the credibility of drug policy institutions. It also sends a chilling message to other experts: align with government policy or risk professional marginalisation. The net effect is a narrowing of the policy conversation and the continued dominance of punitive, morally-charged approaches.

At a broader level, these dynamics reveal that evidence in UK drug policy functions more as a symbolic resource than a foundation for rational decision-making. As Lancaster et al. (2015) have argued, evidence can be deployed to legitimise policy choices, but it rarely drives them. Instead, political actors often engage in "evidence work," selectively citing research that supports their position while ignoring contradictory findings.

This symbolic use of evidence is particularly apparent in high-profile initiatives like drug-driving laws, which claim to enhance public safety but rest on contested science and technological limitations (Nutt, 2012; Wolff & Johnston, 2014). The deployment of roadside drug testing technology, for instance, creates a powerful image of modern, science-led enforcement. Yet the thresholds used in these tests are often based on political compromise rather than pharmacological validity.

This section has shown that evidence is neither absent nor irrelevant in UK drug policy—it is ever-present, but highly politicised. Through the work of Monaghan, McKeganey, Stevens, and Nutt, we see that policy is not shaped by a rational appraisal of harm but by an ideological framework in which certain substances, behaviours, and populations are constructed as morally problematic. The classification system under the Misuse of Drugs Act 1971 lacks scientific coherence, and dissenting expert voices are often silenced or ignored when they challenge dominant narratives. Ultimately, evidence is mediated through political and moral filters that determine what knowledge counts and whose voices are heard. Reforming UK drug policy, therefore, requires not only better data but a transformation in the political and cultural frameworks within which evidence is interpreted.

The UK's drug policy has long relied on a criminal justice framework to address drug use and dependency. This approach is ethically fraught, particularly given its sustained failure to reduce drug-related harm or death. As Holland (2020) argues, a punitive model that prioritises deterrence over care raises serious moral concerns—not only because it fails in its stated aims, but also because it inflicts disproportionate harm on some of the most vulnerable individuals in society. This section critically explores the ethical dimensions of UK drug policy by examining the moral implications of punishment versus care, the role of stigma in perpetuating harm, and the structural injustices embedded in the criminalisation of drug users.

At the heart of the ethical critique lies a fundamental tension between punishment and care. The criminal justice model assumes that drug use is a moral failing or a choice that can be deterred through punitive sanctions. In practice, this model obscures the complex socio-economic, psychological, and physiological dimensions of substance use and dependency. Holland (2020, p. 93) challenges the assumption that punishment is ethically justifiable when applied to individuals whose drug use is driven by trauma, poverty, mental ill-health, or childhood adversity. He argues that rather than acting as a deterrent, criminalisation entrenches cycles of marginalisation and makes access to healthcare and recovery support more difficult.

This punitive logic also stands in stark contrast to the approach taken with other public health issues. Alcoholism and tobacco dependence, for instance, are typically framed as health concerns deserving of compassion and treatment, rather than criminal prosecution. The ethical inconsistency in treating illegal drug users as criminals while offering support to legal substance users undermines any claim that drug policy in the UK is rooted in harm reduction or public health objectives. It reflects instead a moral economy in which some forms of substance use are medicalised and others are moralised—a distinction often rooted in class and race.

### *The Failure of Deterrence and the Persistence of Drug-Related Deaths*

A central rationale for criminalisation is the deterrence of drug use. Yet, as Holland and others argue, this deterrent model has failed. The UK continues to experience some of the highest rates of drug-related deaths in Europe, with 4907 deaths related to drug poisoning recorded in England and Wales in 2022—the highest figure since records began (ONS, 2023). These deaths are not evenly distributed: they are concentrated in areas of high deprivation and disproportionately affect marginalised populations.

The failure of deterrence is not just an empirical problem—it is an ethical one. A policy that persists despite overwhelming evidence of its ineffectiveness and harmful consequences fails a basic moral test. As

Holland (2020) observes, ethical policymaking requires that interventions are both proportionate to the problem and supported by evidence that they will do more good than harm. On both counts, UK drug policy fails. The persistence of drug-related deaths despite decades of punitive measures calls into question the moral legitimacy of the criminal justice approach.

### *Stigma, Criminalisation, and Structural Injustice*

Criminalisation does more than punish individual behaviour—it reproduces and legitimises stigma. Drug users are not only punished by the legal system but also marked socially as deviant, unreliable, and undeserving. This stigma has material effects. It creates barriers to employment, housing, healthcare, and family life. It deters people from seeking help for fear of legal consequences or social judgement. As Taylor (2008) notes, criminalisation functions as a mechanism of social exclusion, reinforcing a "hierarchy of worth" that positions drug users as morally inferior.

This dynamic is especially pronounced for people who are already socially marginalised. Numerous studies have shown that drug policing in the UK disproportionately targets people from working-class and racialised communities (Stevens, 2025). Black people are nine times more likely than white people to be stopped and searched for drugs, yet they are less likely to use drugs overall (Shiner et al., 2018). This racialised enforcement not only undermines public trust in the justice system but also compounds existing inequalities in health, education, and economic opportunity.

From an ethical standpoint, this constitutes structural injustice—a term used by political philosophers such as Iris Marion Young to describe harms that result from entrenched social arrangements rather than individual wrongdoing. UK drug policy, by criminalising a health issue and enforcing it through discriminatory policing practices, actively contributes to the reproduction of inequality. This stands in direct opposition to principles of justice, fairness, and human dignity.

The use of custodial sentences for drug offences raises further ethical concerns. Incarceration is a blunt instrument that offers little in the way of rehabilitation or support. Instead, it exposes individuals to environments where drug use often continues and mental health deteriorates. According to the Prison Reform Trust (2022), over 60% of people entering prison with a history of drug use continue to use drugs inside. Rather than acting as a site of recovery, prison frequently becomes a revolving door that deepens cycles of addiction and criminalisation.

Ethically, this raises serious questions about proportionality and efficacy. If the goal is to reduce harm and support recovery, then the use of imprisonment for non-violent drug offences is not only ineffective but morally indefensible. It diverts resources from treatment services, imposes long-term social penalties (such as criminal records), and exacerbates health inequalities. As Holland (2020, p. 101) puts it, "punishment does not cure addiction, nor does it redress social injustice—it compounds them."

Moreover, drug policy often relies on forms of coerced treatment—for example, offering treatment as an alternative to custody under Drug Rehabilitation Requirements (DRRs). While this may appear more humane, it raises complex ethical issues around consent and autonomy. True rehabilitation requires voluntary engagement, not compliance under threat of incarceration. Coercive treatment may reduce short-term offending but risks undermining the therapeutic relationship and obscuring the structural conditions that sustain drug dependency.

### *Ethical Alternatives: Harm Reduction and Human Rights*

If the criminal justice model is ethically indefensible, what would a more ethical approach look like? Holland (2020) and other reform advocates point to harm reduction as a morally sound alternative. Rather than seeking to eliminate drug use, harm reduction aims to minimise its negative consequences through practical interventions—such as needle exchange programmes, supervised consumption facilities, and heroin-assisted treatment.

Harm reduction operates on the principle of respect for persons—acknowledging the autonomy and dignity of people who use drugs. It avoids moral judgement and instead focuses on evidence-based strategies that reduce overdose, infection, and social harm. It also aligns more closely with public health ethics, which prioritise interventions that are proportionate, effective, and equitable.

A further ethical foundation for reform lies in human rights. The United Nations Special Rapporteur on the right to health has repeatedly criticised punitive drug laws as violations of the right to health, housing, and freedom from cruel or degrading treatment (UNODC, 2020). The decriminalisation of drug possession for personal use—adopted in countries such as Portugal, Uruguay, and Switzerland—has been associated with reductions in drug-related deaths, HIV transmission, and incarceration rates. These models suggest that ethically informed, rights-based approaches are both possible and effective.

The UK's criminal justice approach to drug use is ethically unsustainable. It fails to meet basic standards of proportionality, effectiveness, and justice. It perpetuates social marginalisation, contributes to preventable deaths, and ignores the structural causes of drug-related harm. Holland's (2020) critique makes clear that what is needed is not more punishment, but a radical ethical shift—one that centres care over condemnation, evidence over ideology, and rights over repression.

To achieve this, drug policy must be reimagined not as a tool of control but as a domain of public health, social justice, and human dignity. Ethical reform is not simply about doing less harm—it is about recognising the humanity of people who use drugs and building systems that support their well-being, not their criminalisation.

### *Drug Driving—A Case Study in Selective Policy Focus*

In recent years, drug driving has become an increasingly prominent feature of UK drug policy, culminating in the introduction of Section 5A of the Road Traffic Act 1988, amended by the Crime and Courts Act 2013. This legislation, which came into effect in March 2015, introduced a "zero-tolerance" framework whereby it became an offence to drive with certain controlled substances in the body above predefined thresholds, regardless of whether actual impairment could be demonstrated. While framed as a road safety measure, this section contends that the political and moral drivers behind the policy far outweighed its scientific justification. In this sense, drug-driving legislation offers a textbook case of how UK drug policy is shaped by ideological imperatives, public reassurance, and moral panic rather than consistent evidence.

### *The Rise of Drug Driving on the Policy Agenda*

The prominence of drug driving in UK policy debates has grown rapidly, particularly in the 2010s. Media narratives of reckless, intoxicated drivers and tragic road fatalities involving drugs have helped generate public concern and policy urgency. However, as Wolff and Johnston (2014, p. 5) note, the empirical evidence on the prevalence of drug driving in the UK has historically been sparse and inconsistent. Prior to 2015, few reliable data sets existed, and estimates of prevalence varied significantly due to differences in testing procedures, definitions of impairment, and sample populations.

Despite this, political momentum surged. Public consultations, such as the Department for Transport's 2011 review, emphasised the danger posed by drug-impaired driving, particularly in comparison with the more established regime around drink driving. Yet, as critics have argued, the moral weight of "drugs" as a category—particularly illicit ones—allowed the policy to proceed despite a weak evidential foundation (Allsop, 2020, p. 211). This highlights a key theme of this chapter: drug policy in the UK often prioritises visibility and reassurance over scientific consistency or measured harm assessments.

### *The Flawed Scientific Basis for Thresholds*

One of the most problematic aspects of the drug-driving law is its reliance on fixed per se limits—blood concentration thresholds that criminalise drivers if exceeded, regardless of actual impairment. Wolff et al. (2013) provided the scientific framework that informed the list of 17 substances included in the legislation. While their contribution brought technical rigour to the discussion, even they acknowledged the limitations of applying uniform thresholds across diverse substances with highly variable pharmacokinetics. For many illicit drugs, such as cannabis, impairment does not correlate neatly with blood levels due to the drug's long half-life and lipophilic nature.

Wolff and Johnston (2014) further warned that a zero-tolerance approach—especially where limits are set at levels close to detection thresholds—runs the risk of criminalising individuals who pose no actual safety risk. For instance, the limit for THC (tetrahydrocannabinol), the psychoactive component in cannabis, is set at just 2 μg/L of blood. However, frequent cannabis users may test above this level long after any impairing effects have subsided (Allsop, 2020, p. 212). Such inconsistencies cast doubt on whether the policy is truly oriented towards reducing road traffic harm or if it reflects broader symbolic concerns about illicit drug use.

### *Comparing Risks: Drug Driving Versus Alcohol*

The scientific literature offers a more nuanced view of drug-related impairment than the legislation suggests. Rudram (1999) undertook one of the earliest comparative studies of drug and alcohol impairment in the UK, concluding that while certain drugs could impair driving, alcohol remained the most consistently dangerous substance in terms of road safety. More recently, Hasan et al. (2022) conducted a meta-analysis of road traffic studies and reinforced this conclusion, finding that alcohol significantly increased crash risk at all consumption levels, whereas the risk from drugs was more variable and often context-specific.

Hasan et al. (2022, p. 287) argue that the evidence base does not support the idea that drug driving presents a greater or equivalent public safety risk than drink driving. Yet the political response has been asymmetrical: the development of sophisticated enforcement mechanisms, public awareness campaigns, and legislative reform has focused heavily on drugs—particularly illicit ones—while alcohol, a legal and culturally embedded substance, continues to be under-policed by comparison. As Allsop (2020, p. 213) notes, this reflects a broader cultural bias in which certain substances are treated as inherently deviant and dangerous, irrespective of actual risk profiles.

### *The Role of Moral Panic and Media Amplification*

The framing of drug driving within public discourse reveals the enduring influence of moral panic on UK drug policy. Drawing on Cohen's (1972) model, we can see how drug-driving offences have been constructed as a social threat requiring immediate and visible intervention. Media coverage often sensationalises rare but tragic incidents involving young drivers and drugs, fuelling public anxiety, and legitimising harsh policy responses. This framing rarely extends to alcohol, despite its far more prevalent and statistically significant role in road traffic deaths.

Moreover, the focus on "illicit" substances reinforces broader moral narratives about deviance and irresponsibility. Drivers who use cannabis or cocaine are symbolically cast as threats to the social order, while alcohol users retain a veneer of normality and acceptability. This selective concern is politically expedient: it allows governments to demonstrate a tough stance on drugs without challenging powerful alcohol lobbies or confronting widespread cultural habits.

### *Technological Enforcement and Disproportionate Impacts*

Another area of ethical concern involves the technology used to enforce drug-driving laws. Roadside screening devices, such as the DrugWipe system, are limited in scope and primarily detect only a handful of substances, mainly cannabis and cocaine. This raises questions about fairness: drivers impaired by other drugs—prescription or otherwise—may go undetected, while others may be penalised simply for the presence of residual metabolites (Wolff & Johnston, 2014, p. 6).

There are also social justice implications. Allsop (2020, p. 214) notes that young and minority ethnic drivers are more likely to be stopped and tested for drug driving. This reflects wider patterns of disproportionality in UK policing, particularly the over-surveillance of racialised communities. In effect, drug-driving enforcement functions not only as a road safety initiative but as another vector of punitive drug policing, contributing to the broader criminalisation of marginalised groups.

Furthermore, the consequences of a drug-driving conviction are severe. In addition to fines and driving bans, individuals face long-term impacts on employment, insurance, and mobility. For young people or those already living precariously, these penalties can be life-altering. This raises serious ethical questions about proportionality, particularly when many convictions may not be based on evidence of actual impairment.

### *Symbolism Over Substance*

In sum, the UK's drug-driving legislation exemplifies how drug policy can become untethered from its evidential foundation. While driving under the influence of drugs is a legitimate road safety concern, the legal framework introduced in 2015 prioritises deterrence, visibility, and moral messaging over scientific consistency and proportionality. The legislation's thresholds are often arbitrary, the technology used to enforce them is limited, and the policy disproportionately affects already marginalised populations.

As this case study demonstrates, drug driving has become a symbolically loaded issue that reflects the broader moral and political anxieties underpinning UK drug policy. The real danger—alcohol—remains comparatively under-regulated, revealing a deep inconsistency in the state's approach to risk. Addressing these inconsistencies requires a shift from ideologically driven enforcement to evidence-based, harm-reduction-oriented policymaking. Until then, drug-driving laws will continue to serve more as instruments of moral control than of public safety.

### *Towards a New Policy Direction*

The preceding sections of this chapter have illustrated the deep inconsistencies, scientific weaknesses, and ethical failings embedded in the UK's current drug policy framework. If drug law in Britain is to move beyond moral panic, symbolic reassurance, and punitive control, it must undergo both structural reform and a reimagining of its normative foundations. This final section outlines key reformist proposals drawn from the literature, focusing on scientifically-grounded reclassification, harm reduction, the integration of social justice and lived experience, and the application of international best practices. These ideas represent not just policy tweaks but a fundamental shift in how society conceptualises drug use, users, and state responsibility.

### *Reclassification and the Restoration of Scientific Credibility*

One of the most urgent reforms relates to the classification of drugs under the **Misuse of Drugs Act 1971**. As argued by McKeganey (2007), the current three-tiered classification system (Classes A, B, and C) lacks coherence and is not underpinned by consistent scientific assessments of harm. Drugs are often placed into categories based not on pharmacological evidence, but on political acceptability, media narratives, and electoral risk. Cannabis, for example, has been shifted between Class B and C in recent decades, driven more by shifting public attitudes and political pressure than by new scientific findings.

McKeganey (2007, p. 315) calls for a reclassification system based on objective, evidence-based evaluations of harm—both to the user and to society. Such models have already been proposed and tested. For instance, David Nutt's multi-criteria decision analysis (MCDA) model ranks drugs by physical harm, dependence potential, and social costs, concluding that alcohol and tobacco pose greater overall risks than many currently illicit drugs such as LSD or ecstasy (Nutt et al., 2010). A rational classification system would recalibrate legal responses according to the actual dangers involved, not historical stigma or political palatability.

Implementing this would not only restore scientific integrity to drug policy but would also allow for proportional and tailored interventions—ranging from education and prevention to regulation and therapeutic support—depending on the relative risk posed by different substances.

### *Public Health, Harm Reduction, and Social Justice*

Holland (2020) emphasises that effective and ethical drug policy must be grounded in the principles of public health, harm reduction, and social justice. These principles recognise that drug use is a complex, multifaceted phenomenon—often shaped by trauma, poverty, mental ill-health, and systemic inequality—and not simply a matter of individual moral failure.

Harm reduction offers a suite of pragmatic, evidence-informed interventions that reduce the negative consequences of drug use without requiring abstinence. These include supervised drug consumption rooms, needle exchange programmes, opioid substitution therapies, and take-home naloxone. Countries such as Switzerland, Canada, and Portugal have successfully implemented these measures, resulting in significant declines in overdose deaths, HIV transmission, and drug-related crime (EMCDDA, 2023).

Yet, in the UK, harm reduction services have been progressively underfunded and politically marginalised. Reintegrating harm reduction into mainstream policy would not only reduce mortality and morbidity, but also acknowledge the rights and dignity of people who use drugs. Holland (2020) argues that this is not simply a matter of efficacy but of ethics: a humane society does not punish suffering, it alleviates it.

Moreover, a public health approach would necessitate rebalancing investments—shifting resources away from punitive enforcement towards accessible treatment, housing support, mental health services, and community-based recovery models. This would require a reconfiguration of institutional priorities, underpinned by political courage and cultural change.

### *Challenging the Narrative: Stevens' Policy Constellations*

One of the barriers to reform is not just institutional inertia but the ideological architecture that sustains punitive drug policy. Stevens (2025) introduces the concept of "policy constellations"—networks of political actors, bureaucratic interests, media discourses, and cultural beliefs that stabilise and reproduce dominant narratives about drugs. These constellations explain why evidence alone is insufficient to drive reform: it must contend with deep-seated values and vested interests.

Stevens argues that meaningful change requires both policy entrepreneurship and discursive disruption. Reformers must learn to navigate, challenge, and reconstruct the narratives that link drug use with criminality, deviance, and threat. This includes exposing the inconsistencies of current policy—such as the tolerance of alcohol harms versus the demonisation of cannabis—and reframing drug use as a social and health issue.

Importantly, Stevens also calls for participatory policymaking. Drug policy should not be crafted exclusively by politicians, police, and technocrats, but should include the voices of those most affected by it—namely, people who use drugs, their families, and frontline service providers. This aligns with the growing movement for co-production in social policy, which recognises that legitimate and effective policy must be grounded in lived experience.

### *International Models and the Promise of Decriminalisation*

There is no need to reinvent the wheel. Successful models for humane, effective drug policy already exist and can inform a new direction for the UK. Portugal's 2001 decriminalisation model is often cited as a benchmark. Under this system, the possession of small quantities of drugs for personal use is no longer a criminal offence, but an administrative one. Offenders are referred to dissuasion panels composed of health professionals and social workers rather than courts and police.

The results have been impressive: drug-related deaths and HIV infections have dropped significantly, and drug use rates have remained stable or declined (Hughes & Stevens, 2010). Crucially, decriminalisation has allowed Portugal to redirect resources into prevention, treatment, and harm reduction. It also reduces the stigma associated with drug use, enabling more people to access support.

Other countries—such as the Czech Republic, Uruguay, and parts of Canada and the United States—have also introduced regulated markets or decriminalised possession with similarly positive results. These models show that punitive prohibition is not the only option—and that alternative frameworks can be both more ethical and more effective.

### *Functional Versus Problematic Use: A Needed Distinction*

Another important aspect of reform involves acknowledging the difference between functional and problematic drug use. Current UK policy tends to treat all drug use as inherently deviant, yet research consistently shows that many people use drugs recreationally or medicinally without experiencing harm or dependency. As Nutt (2012) and Taylor (2008) argue, equating all use with misuse creates a false binary and results in over-policing and unnecessary criminalisation.

A new policy direction should therefore differentiate between levels of use, contexts of use, and types of substances. Functional users—those who use drugs in a non-problematic, controlled, and socially integrated way—should not be subject to the same legal sanctions or social stigma as individuals whose use is associated with serious harm or dependency. This distinction would allow for a more proportionate, humane, and targeted policy approach.

### *Lived Experience and Ethical Policymaking*

Finally, embedding lived experience and ethical reasoning into policymaking is essential for sustainable reform. People who use drugs have often been silenced in policy debates, cast as passive objects of control rather than active agents with knowledge, insight, and rights. Including their voices is not just ethically justified—it results in better policy. Peer-led services, co-designed interventions, and community advocacy have all been shown to increase the effectiveness and acceptability of treatment and harm reduction services (Neale et al., 2019).

Ethical policymaking also requires a shift in moral perspective—from viewing drug use as a sin to be punished, to a complex behaviour to be understood and supported. This shift would bring UK drug policy in line with principles of public health ethics, which emphasise proportionality, autonomy, equity, and solidarity. It would also help repair the trust that has been eroded between marginalised communities and the institutions that claim to serve them.

### *Imagining a Different Future*

The case for reforming UK drug policy is not merely pragmatic; it is moral. The evidence is clear: punitive prohibition has failed to reduce harm, while exacerbating inequality, stigma, and death. Scholars like McKeganey, Stevens, and Holland offer a blueprint for change—one that centres science, ethics, and humanity. A new direction in drug policy must reject the politics of fear and punishment in favour of evidence-informed, rights-based, and compassion-led approaches. Only then can the UK begin to build a system that truly serves the public good.

### *Authors Reflection—The Case of the ruined Life*

One of the most upsetting drug-driving cases I encountered during my time on the bench was that of a young woman I'll call *Abby* (not her real name). Abby was 22 years old and had struggled with her mental health since childhood. She had been in and out of social services' care and had made multiple attempts to end her life over the years. Despite all this, she had recently begun to turn her life around.

After leaving home, Abby had managed to stabilise her situation. She'd just been accepted as an apprentice at a company producing music recordings for the record industry—her dream job. She would be travelling, meeting big names in the industry, and working in studios mixing new tracks. It was everything she had hoped for. Her parents were supportive and had bought her a small car so she could drive to the job, which was located some distance away.

The incident occurred after she had worked a set as a DJ at an electronic rave night. Her mum, dad, and boyfriend had all attended the event. Abby, who didn't drink and was working, was the designated driver. Around 5 a.m., as she was driving home with her boyfriend—who was, in colloquial terms, *off his tits*—they were pulled over by police for a random stop.

Her boyfriend was loud and mouthy with the officers, and this may well have influenced what followed. The officers breathalysed Abby—she passed, of course. But seemingly unsatisfied, they proceeded to conduct a drug test.

Abby admitted, honestly, that she had taken a single line of cocaine earlier in the evening. She said she'd been pressured into it by her boyfriend and had taken it several hours before driving. She was open about it, thinking honesty would count for something. But that admission was enough for her to be arrested and taken to the station for further testing.

The legal limit for cocaine in the UK is 10 μg/L of blood. Abby tested at 10.02. Her solicitor argued passionately in court. Abby had never been in trouble before. She had a clean record, had done well at school, had represented her country in martial arts competitions, and was now beginning a new and promising chapter of her life. She was clearly remorseful. She told us how she had said no, how she'd been pressured, how she had drunk multiple energy drinks to stay alert during the night. She wasn't high or impaired when she was driving, and the amount of cocaine in her system was barely over the legal limit—0.02 above.

But the law is strict and clear. The offence of drug driving in the UK is a zero-tolerance one. Presence, not impairment, is enough.

As magistrates, we had no discretion. Abby lost her licence. Her job was now at risk. Because of the conviction, she would no longer be able to travel to countries like the United States—something that had been central to her new role. Her life, which had taken years to stabilise, came crashing down in a matter of hours.

I've sentenced people for all sorts of crimes, but this case still haunts me. I genuinely did not believe that punishing Abby in this way served the interests of justice. Yet my hands were tied. I can only hope her employer saw past the conviction and that she found another path forward. But I've never forgotten her—and I doubt I ever will.

### *Conclusion Beyond Ideology—Reclaiming Evidence, Ethics, and Equity in UK Drug Policy*

In Conclusion, this chapter has traced the contours of a UK drug policy landscape deeply shaped by ideology, moral panic, and political expedience. Using drug-driving legislation as a focal point, the analysis has exposed how policy is often guided less by science than by symbolic politics, cultural anxieties, and institutional inertia. Despite its ostensible concern with public safety, the legal framework around drug driving exemplifies the wider dysfunction of UK drug control: inconsistent scientific standards, ethical contradictions, and a persistent failure to prevent harm—especially among the most vulnerable populations.

At the heart of this critique lies a disjuncture between what drug policy claims to do and what it actually achieves. The introduction of Section 5A of the Road Traffic Act 1988 (as amended) in 2015 created a zero-tolerance model of enforcement that criminalises individuals for the mere presence of specified drugs in the body, irrespective of actual impairment.

As demonstrated in the work of Wolff and Johnston (2014) and Wolff et al. (2013), the scientific foundations of these thresholds are weak, often based on detection capabilities rather than pharmacological correlation with driving risk. In contrast to the relative tolerance of alcohol in road traffic law—despite it being the most dangerous drug in this context—drug-driving laws reflect a symbolic need to be "tough" on drugs, rather than a proportionate response to empirical realities.

This asymmetry is not accidental. As explored in the historical and political context of UK drug legislation, policymaking has long prioritised public reassurance over public health outcomes. The Misuse of Drugs Act 1971, and subsequent legal frameworks, have embedded a punitive logic that treats drug use as criminal deviancy rather than as a complex social and health issue. Monaghan's (2008) concept of the "new rules of engagement" in policy discourse shows how evidence is selectively mobilised to support pre-existing agendas, rather than to challenge or inform them. In such a policy environment, dissenting scientific voices—like that of Professor David Nutt—are not just ignored but actively marginalised when their findings disrupt dominant moral narratives.

This politicisation of evidence is ethically untenable. As Holland (2020) and others have argued, the ethical failings of UK drug policy are clearest in its human costs: rising drug-related deaths, widening health inequalities, and the criminalisation of vulnerable people. The criminal justice approach to drug use does not deter harm but reproduces it. It institutionalises stigma, justifies coercion, and undermines the principle of care that should be central to any ethical public health framework.

The case of drug driving underscores these ethical contradictions. While drink driving is rightly condemned and regulated, the political treatment of drug driving has been shaped by media amplification and selective outrage. As Hasan et al. (2022) show, the relative risk of drug-related impairment varies widely across substances and is often lower than that posed by alcohol. Yet, drug driving receives disproportionate policy attention, fuelled by the enduring spectre of "illicit" drugs as symbols of disorder and danger. This leads to over-policing, particularly of younger and racially marginalised drivers, and the misdirection of legal and financial resources away from more pressing and empirically grounded risks.

This chapter also highlighted the limitations of the classification system under the Misuse of Drugs Act, as critiqued by McKeganey (2007). The tripartite framework lacks a clear scientific basis and has become a political instrument for managing moral panic rather than guiding harm reduction. The drug-driving regime reflects this same dynamic: it does not aim to prevent harm in proportion to its likelihood or severity but to perform political toughness in the face of public concern.

Despite this bleak assessment, a more humane and evidence-informed approach to drug policy is possible—and urgently needed. As outlined in Section 5, reform must begin with the recognition that the criminal justice model has failed in both ethical and practical terms. Reclassification based on empirical harm, as advocated by Nutt et al. (2010) and McKeganey (2007), would restore credibility and consistency to legal responses. Replacing zero-tolerance thresholds with scientifically determined, impairment-based standards would help align enforcement with actual risk and reduce the number of unjust prosecutions.

Equally essential is the integration of public health, harm reduction, and social justice principles into drug policy, as proposed by Holland (2020). This would involve shifting resources from punishment to care—expanding access to evidence-based treatment, de-stigmatising drug use, and addressing the structural conditions (poverty, housing, trauma) that often underpin problematic consumption. The success of international models such as Portugal's decriminalisation system and Switzerland's heroin-assisted treatment scheme demonstrates that non-punitive approaches can achieve better health, safety, and social outcomes without resorting to criminalisation.

Crucially, any new direction in drug policy must confront the discursive and institutional barriers that sustain the current system. Stevens' (2025) theory of "policy constellations" reveals how dominant coalitions of policymakers, media outlets, and cultural assumptions work to stabilise punitive approaches and resist reform. To dismantle these constellations, drug policy must be reconceptualised not merely as a technical problem but as a site of ideological struggle. This entails challenging the narratives that equate drug use with criminality and reshaping public discourse around principles of autonomy, dignity, and equity.

Moreover, future policymaking must centre the voices and experiences of those most affected by drug laws—people who use drugs, their families, and communities. Embedding lived experience into the design and evaluation of policy can ground reform in real-world needs and conditions, making it not only more just but more effective. Co-production, peer-led support services, and community engagement should become standard practices, not optional add-ons.

Finally, it is essential to move beyond the binary framing of drug use as either functional or problematic. Many individuals use drugs in ways that do not lead to harm or dependency, yet the legal framework treats all use as inherently dangerous. Recognising and responding to this diversity of experience would enable more proportionate, respectful, and targeted policies. It would also help reduce the stigma that prevents many from seeking help when needed and that drives punitive overreach.

In conclusion, drug-driving legislation offers a microcosm of the broader failings of UK drug policy: moral panic over evidence, punishment over prevention, and ideology over ethics. Reform will not be easy, but it is both necessary and achievable. The tools already exist: rigorous harm assessment models, proven international alternatives, ethical public health frameworks, and the knowledge of lived experience. What is required is the political will to act—not to reassure, but to repair; not to punish, but to protect.

As long as UK drug policy continues to be driven by moral symbolism and political short-termism, it will fail to reduce harm and perpetuate social injustice. But by grounding future approaches in evidence, ethics, and equity, we can begin to build a system that genuinely serves the goals of public health, social inclusion, and human dignity.

## References

Allsop, S. (2020). *Drugs and driving: Impairment, risk and the law*. Routledge.

Becker, H. S. (1963). *Outsiders: Studies in the sociology of deviance*. Free Press.

Cohen, S. (1972). *Folk devils and moral panics: The creation of the mods and rockers*. MacGibbon and Kee.

Department for Transport. (2012). *Drug driving: Summary of responses to the consultation on specified limits*. DfT.

Edwards, G. (1989). *The treatment of drug problems*. Cambridge University Press.

European Monitoring Centre for Drugs and Drug Addiction (EMCDDA) (2023). European Drug Report 2023: Trends and Developments. Lisbon: EMCDDA.

Garland, D. (2001). *The culture of control: Crime and social order in contemporary society*. Oxford University Press.

Hasan, H., Sinyor, M., & Remington, G. (2022). Drugs and driving: A systematic review of risk and policy. *Journal of Drug Policy, 32*(3), 283–295.

HMICFRS. (2019). *Roads policing: Not optional—An inspection of roads policing in england and wales*. Her Majesty's Inspectorate of Constabulary and Fire & Rescue Services.

Holland, S. (2020). *Public health ethics* (2nd ed.). Polity.

Hughes, C. E., & Stevens, A. (2010). What can we learn from the Portuguese decriminalization of illicit drugs? *British Journal of Criminology, 50*(6), 999–1022.

Lancaster, K., Duke, K., & Ritter, A. (2015). Producing the "Problem of Drugs": A cross national comparison of "Recovery" discourse in two policy documents. *International Journal of Drug Policy, 26*(7), 617–625.

McKeganey, N. (2007). The politics of drugs: Perceptions, power and policies. *Drugs: Education, Prevention and Policy, 14*(4), 313–325.

Monaghan, M. (2008). Tolerance through ignorance: The UK drug policy "Experiment". *British Journal of Politics and International Relations, 10*(3), 409–428.

Monaghan, M. (2011). *Evidence versus politics: Exploiting research in UK drug policy making?* Policy Press.

Neale, J., Tompkins, C. N. E., & Strang, J. (2019). Engaging people with lived experience of drug use in research and policy. *Drugs: Education Prevention and Policy, 26*(1), 1–5.

Nutt, D. (2009). Equasy—An overlooked addiction with implications for the current debate on drug harms. *Journal of Psychopharmacology, 23*(1), 3–5.

Nutt, D. (2012). *Drugs without the hot air*. UIT Cambridge.

Nutt, D., King, L. A., & Phillips, L. D. (2010). Drug harms in the UK: A multicriteria decision analysis. *The Lancet, 376*(9752), 1558–1565.

Office for National Statistics (ONS). (2023). *Deaths related to drug poisoning in England and Wales: 2022 registrations*. Retrieved from July 1, 2025, from https://www.ons.gov.uk

Prison Reform Trust. (2022). *Bromley briefings prison factfile, winter 2022*. Prison Reform Trust.

Rudram, H. (1999). Comparative impairment of driving: Alcohol versus drugs. *Traffic Safety Research Review, 23*(2), 45–59.

Shiner, M., Carre, Z., Delsol, R., & Eastwood, N. (2018). *The colour of injustice: 'Race', drugs and law enforcement in England and Wales*. StopWatch & Release.

Stevens, A. (2011). *Drugs, crime and public health: The political economy of drug policy*. Routledge.

Stevens, A. (2025) Policy constellations: Understanding drug policy in a political context. Forthcoming.

Taylor, S. (2008). *Crime, capitalism and community: Three essays*. Routledge.

United Nations Office on Drugs and Crime (UNODC). (2020). *Report of the special rapporteur on the right to health: Harm reduction policies and programmes*. UN.

Wolff, K., Brimblecombe, R., Forfar, J.C., Forrest, A.R., Gilvarry, E., Johnston, A., Morgan, J., Osselton, M.D., Read, L. & Taylor, D., (2013). *Driving under the influence of drugs—Report from the expert panel on drug driving*. (March 2013).

Wolff, K., & Johnston, A. (2014). *Driving under the influence of drugs—Report from the expert panel on drug driving*. Department for Transport.

CHAPTER 7

# Legal Highs, Loopholes, and the Politics of Panic

**Abstract** This chapter critically examines the UK's response to the rise of Novel Psychoactive Substances (NPS), particularly synthetic cannabinoids like Spice, through the lens of media panic, reactive legislation, and systemic inequality. Tracing the shift from the early emergence of "legal highs" to the sweeping Psychoactive Substances Act 2016, it explores how policy was shaped less by scientific evidence and more by sensationalist narratives and political expediency. Drawing on personal experience working as a nightclub bouncer, the chapter reveals the lived realities of Spice users—many of whom were far from the stereotyped homeless or prison populations portrayed in the media. It critiques the Act's vague definition of "psychoactivity," its failure to target harmful legal substances like alcohol, and its disproportionate impact on marginalised groups. While expert bodies such as the ACMD warned against the law's flaws, their advice was sidelined in favour of tough-on-drugs posturing. By contrasting the UK's approach with international models like Portugal and New Zealand, the chapter argues for a shift towards evidence-based, health-oriented drug policy that prioritises care over control.

**Keywords** Psychoactive Substances Act, Legal highs, Spice, Moral panic, Drug policy, Novel psychoactive substances (NPS), Criminalisation, Media amplification, Harm reduction, Drug law reform


E. Peatfield, *Drugs Disorder by Design*,
https://doi.org/10.1007/978-3-032-07814-8_7

## Introduction

By the early 2000s, the UK's approach to drug policy—still largely anchored in the punitive logic of the Misuse of Drugs Act 1971—was beginning to unravel. While legislation remained fixated on long-established substances like heroin, cocaine, and cannabis, an entirely new category of drugs began to proliferate. Marketed as "legal highs," these novel psychoactive substances (NPS) mimicked the effects of controlled drugs but fell outside existing legal frameworks. They were sold openly in headshops, on the internet, and in some cases even in local convenience stores.

What followed was not a measured policy response, but an escalating moral panic. Between 2008 and 2016, the number of NPS detected in Europe rose dramatically—from 13 in 2008 to over 100 by 2015, according to the European Monitoring Centre for Drugs and Drug Addiction (EMCDDA, 2016). The UK was at the forefront of this trend, becoming one of the largest consumers of NPS in Europe. Government figures revealed that in 2013/14, approximately 280,000 people aged 16 to 59 in England and Wales reported using an NPS in the past year (Home Office, 2014).

Rather than prompting a rethink of prohibitionist frameworks, the emergence of NPS produced a knee-jerk reaction from politicians and tabloid media alike. The press, particularly outlets like *The Sun* and the *Daily Mail*, revelled in lurid headlines warning of "zombie drugs" that turned users into violent, incoherent threats to society. Much of this panic centred on synthetic cannabinoids like Spice, which were described in headlines as "the most dangerous drug in Britain" and blamed for everything from street crime to the decline of urban civility. In 2017, the *Daily Mail* ran a feature titled "The Spice Zombies of Britain's Streets," accompanied by dehumanising images of homeless people slumped and semi-conscious in public places.

Such reporting rarely included nuance or evidence. Little distinction was made between different NPS, despite vast differences in pharmacological profile and harm potential. Nor was there much reflection on why certain populations—particularly the homeless and prisoners—were disproportionately using drugs like Spice. Instead, NPS became a symbolic shorthand for social disorder, their use portrayed not as a symptom of marginalisation, but as a moral failing.

From my own perspective as I was still a bouncer at this point, I witnessed this transformation on the ground. Clubgoers who once described the euphoric clarity of MDMA began talking about mephedrone—or "meow meow"—with similar enthusiasm, often unaware of its chemical origins. Later, I would see a different side of the legal high's phenomenon altogether, as homeless defendants and vulnerable prisoners appeared before the courts dazed, paranoid, or in withdrawal from synthetic cannabinoids. The physical and psychological toll of these substances was obvious, yet the policy response remained primarily punitive.

Perhaps nowhere was this more apparent than in the prison estate. Following the 2007 ban on tobacco advertising and the eventual implementation of smoke-free prisons from 2015 onwards, the use of Spice surged. With tobacco no longer available and traditional drugs like cannabis more easily detected through drug testing, Spice emerged as the substance of choice—cheap, potent, and difficult to trace. The Independent Monitoring Boards (IMBs) repeatedly warned of rising violence, self-harm, and medical emergencies linked to Spice in prisons, yet little was done to address the root causes of this trend. A 2017 report by HM Inspectorate of Prisons described NPS as the "most serious threat to the safety and security of prisons" (HMIP, 2017, p. 5), with incidents of violence, debt, and medical emergencies all rising in tandem with its use.

Rather than seeing this as an indictment of both carceral and drug policy, lawmakers once again turned to criminalisation. The 2016 Psychoactive Substances Act sought to ban the sale of all substances with psychoactive effect, excluding those specifically exempted—such as alcohol, tobacco, and caffeine—thereby revealing the ideological double standards at play. Scientific evidence, including the recommendations of the Advisory Council on the Misuse of Drugs (ACMD), was largely ignored. As Nutt (2015) observed, the Act criminalised substances not on the basis of their relative harm, but on their deviation from the culturally sanctioned drugs protected by commercial interest.

In this chapter, I argue that the rise of legal highs—and the panic they provoked—laid bare the contradictions at the heart of British drug policy. These substances were born from prohibition, shaped by loopholes in the law, and ultimately demonised through media campaigns more interested in spectacle than substance. While the public was told that these drugs posed an existential threat, the deeper truths—about poverty, incarceration, and social alienation—were obscured by a politics of panic.

### *What are Legal Highs?*

The term "legal highs" became common shorthand in the UK media and public discourse during the late 2000s and early 2010s, but it was always a misnomer. These substances were not necessarily safe, regulated, or harmless—they were simply not (yet) illegal. More accurately referred to as *Novel Psychoactive Substances* (NPS), these compounds were designed to mimic the effects of traditional illicit drugs such as cannabis, ecstasy (MDMA), cocaine, or LSD, while staying just outside the reach of existing legislation.

NPS typically involved minor chemical modifications to known psychoactive molecules. These tweaks rendered them structurally distinct from drugs already scheduled under the Misuse of Drugs Act 1971, thus allowing suppliers to market them legally—often with disclaimers like "not for human consumption" or labels such as "plant food," "incense," or "research chemicals." This created a regulatory grey zone where legality was determined less by harm and more by molecular structure.

Between 2009 and 2014, over 400 new psychoactive substances were identified across Europe, with the UK accounting for a significant share of use and distribution. According to the Home Office, by 2014 around 100 headshops operated across Britain, openly selling substances like mephedrone, synthetic cannabinoids, and benzofurans. One survey from the Global Drug Survey (2013) suggested that nearly 20% of UK respondents had tried at least one NPS, a higher figure than most European counterparts.

Among the most well-known early NPS was **mephedrone**, a synthetic stimulant related to cathinone (a compound found in the khat plant). It produced effects similar to MDMA or cocaine—including euphoria, increased sociability, and alertness—but was initially legal and widely available online. Mephedrone's rapid rise in popularity, particularly among young clubbers and students, led to a flurry of media attention. The *Guardian* reported in 2010 that mephedrone could be purchased for as little as £10 a gram online, often shipped in innocuous-looking packaging. Yet the risks were poorly understood. Early reports linked the drug to agitation, paranoia, and several deaths, though causality was often unclear or overstated.

The synthetic cannabinoids—perhaps the most socially damaging group of NPS—were marketed under names like "Spice," "K2," and "Black Mamba." These substances were designed to act on the same cannabinoid receptors as THC, the active component in cannabis, but were often significantly more potent and unpredictable. Unlike plant-based cannabis, synthetic cannabinoids were sprayed onto dried plant material or dissolved in e-liquids, allowing for easy smoking or vaping. The variability in dosage and composition created serious risks, including acute psychosis, seizures, and cardiovascular events.

These risks were compounded by the fact that users—particularly in marginalised groups—often believed synthetic cannabinoids to be a "safer" or less detectable alternative. This was especially true in prisons, where standard drug testing failed to identify new variants of Spice. A 2015 report by the National Offender Management Service noted that synthetic cannabinoid use in prisons had increased "exponentially," contributing to violence, mental health deterioration, and medical emergencies.

Despite their diversity, what united most NPS was their emergence from the gaps—legal, scientific, and ethical—left by Britain's outdated drug laws. Suppliers relied on the slowness of legislative processes, while users often assumed that legality implied safety. But this legal status rarely lasted long. As new substances gained popularity, they were swiftly banned, prompting manufacturers to tweak their formulas again. This game of cat-and-mouse meant that enforcement agencies, clinicians, and users were always one step behind the chemistry.

Critically, many NPS were created not to innovate or improve upon existing drugs, but to *evade prohibition*. In that sense, they were a product of policy failure. As Professor Fiona Measham has argued, "legal highs were born out of a system where prohibition created demand for substances that were unregulated, poorly understood, and often more dangerous than the drugs they replaced." Unlike traditional recreational drugs with decades of accumulated research, many NPS had no toxicological profile, no accepted dosage, and no known long-term effects.

Yet this sharp focus on synthetic highs obscures one of the most glaring contradictions in British drug policy: the status of **alcohol**. If a legal high is defined as a psychoactive substance not subject to criminal prohibition, then alcohol—by far the most widely used and harmful psychoactive substance in the UK—is the archetype. Alcohol is responsible for over

7000 deaths annually in the UK and contributes to a significant proportion of domestic violence, road traffic accidents, and hospital admissions. According to Public Health England (2016), alcohol-related harm costs the NHS an estimated £3.5 billion per year—far more than all illegal drugs combined.

Despite these harms, alcohol remains not only legal but socially embedded and commercially protected. It is advertised during primetime television, consumed in celebratory contexts, and taxed as a revenue-generating commodity. In contrast, NPS—many of which caused less societal harm on aggregate—were portrayed as existential threats. This disparity has not gone unnoticed. David Nutt's now-infamous 2009 ranking of drug harms placed alcohol above heroin, crack cocaine, and methamphetamine in terms of overall social and individual impact. For making this scientifically supported argument, Nutt was sacked as chair of the ACMD—a telling example of how UK drug policy responds to evidence that challenges the status quo.

It is, then, not the pharmacology of a substance that determines its legality, but its cultural and economic position. Alcohol is embedded in British identity and profit structures, while NPS are seen as alien, underground, and disruptive. This creates a situation in which the label "legal high" becomes politically weaponised: it is not a neutral descriptor, but a tool for distinguishing between "acceptable" and "unacceptable" forms of intoxication—often along lines of class, visibility, and compliance.

In the next section, we'll examine how the media capitalised on these fears, constructing a narrative of crisis that further distorted public understanding and paved the way for reactive and repressive legislation.

### *The Media and the Making of a Panic*

If Britain's legal response to Novel Psychoactive Substances (NPS) was reactionary, then the groundwork for that reaction was laid by the media. From the earliest mentions of mephedrone to the widespread sensationalism surrounding Spice, the press did not simply report the rise of legal highs—it actively constructed a social crisis. In doing so, it shaped public perception, intensified political pressure, and arguably fuelled the very harms it claimed to expose. What unfolded was a textbook case of *moral panic*, as theorised by Stanley Cohen in his landmark 1972 work *Folk Devils and Moral Panics*.

Cohen described moral panics as episodes where a person, group, or behaviour is cast as a threat to societal values, often exaggerated or misrepresented through media distortion. These panics follow a familiar trajectory: identification of a deviant "folk devil," sensational coverage, escalating public concern, and then demands for stronger control measures. In the case of NPS, the folk devils were many: the reckless young clubber on mephedrone, the slumped Spice smoker in a city centre doorway, the violent prisoner hallucinating in his cell. Each was portrayed as both victim and villain, stripped of context and turned into a justification for ever-tighter restrictions.

By the early 2010s, headlines about legal highs were ubiquitous. The *Daily Mail*, *Sun*, and *Mirror* all ran frequent stories warning of "zombie drugs" ravaging Britain's streets. In 2010, the *Daily Star* proclaimed "Mephedrone Turns Teens into Raving Psychos," while another article described Spice as "the killer drug turning prisoners into monsters." These reports often included grainy photographs of people unconscious, semi-clothed, or convulsing, designed not to inform but to horrify.

This was not limited to tabloid journalism. Even reputable outlets like the BBC and *The Guardian* adopted emotive language when covering NPS-related deaths, often failing to differentiate between causation and correlation. In the absence of toxicological certainty, the drugs were still blamed. As media narratives snowballed, public concern mounted, prompting politicians to promise immediate action—not because evidence demanded it, but because headlines did.

What this represents is not just moral panic but what Howard Becker called **deviancy amplification**. In his seminal 1963 text *Outsiders*, Becker argued that social reaction to deviance—particularly from moral entrepreneurs such as media figures or politicians—often worsens the problem. The labelling process identifies a behaviour as deviant, which in turn pushes individuals further into marginalisation and drives the behaviour underground. This results in more secrecy, more danger, and more punitive response, in a feedback loop of escalating repression.

Spice provides a particularly stark example. The drug was originally marketed as a legal alternative to cannabis—a synthetic cannabinoid that was cheaper, less detectable, and initially not prohibited. As its use grew among street homeless populations and prisoners, the media began portraying it as not just dangerous, but as socially contaminating. The "Spice zombie" trope—repeated endlessly in headlines—not only dehumanised users but fuelled public calls for crackdowns in city centres. These calls were heeded. Local authorities and police responded with dispersal orders, raids on headshops, and later, enforcement of the Psychoactive Substances Act 2016. Yet none of these measures addressed the reasons why vulnerable people were turning to Spice in the first place: addiction, trauma, displacement, and poverty.

By constructing a simplistic narrative of threat, the media erased complexity. There was little space in the dominant discourse for discussions of harm reduction, social context, or evidence-based policy. Instead, drug users—especially visible, non-normative users—were depicted as a threat to civil order. This drew on older tropes of deviance rooted in class prejudice and urban moralism. The depiction of legal high users differed sharply from media portrayals of middle-class drug consumption. Young professionals using cocaine at the weekend were rarely subject to the same level of scrutiny or vilification.

The selective attention of the media is particularly revealing. During the same period that Spice and mephedrone dominated headlines, the much more damaging effects of alcohol—in terms of hospital admissions, domestic violence, and public disorder—received relatively muted coverage. As discussed in the previous section, alcohol remains Britain's most harmful drug, yet it is framed as a personal choice, a lifestyle issue, or at worst, a medical concern. In contrast, NPS use was framed as criminal, parasitic, and alien.

This disparity reflects not just cultural bias but political utility. The panic around NPS allowed successive governments to signal toughness on drugs without tackling more entrenched and profitable substances like alcohol or prescription opioids. It allowed ministers to deflect from underfunded treatment services, decaying prisons, and worsening homelessness. A 2016 Home Affairs Select Committee report criticised the government for failing to produce coherent, evidence-based drug strategy—noting that media-driven legislation often undermined public health goals. Yet by then, the damage was done.

There is a profound irony in the fact that the more the media spotlight fell on "legal highs," the more dangerous these substances became. Crackdowns on mephedrone led to the emergence of more toxic stimulants. The banning of early Spice compounds led to the circulation of even stronger, less predictable variants. And as enforcement intensified, users moved into more precarious environments—off the radar of services, without harm reduction knowledge, and exposed to unscrupulous suppliers. In short, the media did not just mirror public anxieties—it manufactured and intensified them. In doing so, it gave politicians the mandate to legislate with speed rather than sense, and shifted the public conversation away from treatment and support towards punishment and exclusion. As we will explore in the next section, this climate of moral panic directly influenced the drafting of the Psychoactive Substances Act 2016—a piece of legislation so broad and scientifically illiterate that it banned almost everything that gets people high, except the most dangerous drug of all: alcohol.

### *The Pre-2016 Legal Landscape*

Before the blanket ban imposed by the Psychoactive Substances Act 2016, the UK's legislative response to legal highs was piecemeal, reactive, and frequently outpaced by innovation in drug chemistry. The primary instrument—the Misuse of Drugs Act 1971 (MDA)—was never designed to cope with the speed and sophistication of modern synthetic drug production. Instead, it relied on identifying and naming specific chemical compounds for classification under one of its three Schedules (Class A, B, or C). While this framework had sufficed in the era of traditional drugs like heroin, cocaine, and cannabis, it proved woefully inadequate when confronted with the fast-moving world of novel psychoactive substances (NPS).

One of the most pressing problems was that minor alterations to a molecule's structure could create an entirely new compound that was not covered under existing legislation. Chemists—some working for underground labs, others simply tweaking known substances for online markets—exploited this loophole with astonishing speed. As soon as a compound like mephedrone was classified (it was brought under Class B in 2010), new derivatives would appear: methedrone, methylone, MDPV, and others. These would be chemically distinct enough to avoid automatic classification, yet similar enough in effect to appeal to the same users. This led to what many described as a "cat-and-mouse" game between legislators and chemists, with the law always lagging one step behind.

The Advisory Council on the Misuse of Drugs (ACMD)—the government's expert advisory body—found itself under increasing pressure to rapidly assess a growing number of new compounds, often with little or no toxicological data available. Each assessment required careful evaluation, consultation, and legal drafting before an amendment to the MDA could be passed—a process that could take many months, sometimes over a year. In that time, a drug could rise to national popularity, cause significant harm, and be replaced by the next variant before the ink was dry on the legislation. According to the European Monitoring Centre for Drugs and Drug Addiction (EMCDDA), over 100 new NPS were detected in Europe in 2015 alone, placing unsustainable demands on national authorities.

Recognising the inadequacy of the MDA's reactive framework, the government introduced Temporary Class Drug Orders (TCDOs) in 2011 as a stopgap measure. These allowed the Home Secretary to impose a 12-month temporary ban on any new substance deemed potentially harmful, during which time the ACMD could carry out a full risk assessment. TCDOs were used to control substances such as methoxetamine and 5-IAI, but the measure was limited in scope and effect. It still required government intervention for each individual compound, and it did not prevent manufacturers from releasing new analogues that technically fell outside the defined structure of the banned substance.

The legal and enforcement implications of this situation were profound. Police officers, customs officials, and trading standards bodies found themselves dealing with substances that were perfectly legal one week and criminalised the next—sometimes with no easy way to test or confirm their legal status. Meanwhile, online suppliers adapted swiftly, often offering chemical disclaimers and shifting product lines to stay just ahead of enforcement. Some websites would advertise substances as "compliant with UK law as of [date]"—a knowing wink to users that the window of legality was narrow, but currently open.

From a harm reduction perspective, this instability was disastrous. As soon as users found a compound they trusted or could dose safely, it would be taken off the market and replaced by something newer, stronger, and often more dangerous. In many cases, the replacement substances were less well understood, less tested, and more potent than those that came before. The situation created a revolving door of risk, where the desire to avoid criminal penalties produced more unpredictable and toxic outcomes than if the original substances had remained legal and regulated.

Moreover, the classification process under the MDA made no requirement to weigh relative harm, nor to compare a new substance's risks to those of legal drugs like alcohol or tobacco. As David Nutt famously observed, the system was "not fit for purpose," classifying drugs based on political expediency and public perception rather than scientific evidence.

For example, mephedrone was banned in 2010 largely on the basis of tabloid pressure and unverified claims of fatalities, despite the ACMD warning that evidence of long-term harm was lacking and more data was needed. The government overruled expert caution in favour of headline-chasing legislation.

The deeper issue was structural: the legal apparatus treated each new drug as an isolated threat rather than a symptom of a failing prohibitionist model. In reality, these compounds were emerging precisely *because* of prohibition—manufactured to meet a demand that the law itself had helped create. The more aggressively traditional drugs were policed, the more incentive there was for producers to develop alternatives that evaded classification. This is why, despite dozens of bans and legal amendments between 2008 and 2016, the market for legal highs not only persisted but expanded.

The sheer volume and speed of new substances overwhelmed the system, leading policymakers to conclude that piecemeal scheduling under the MDA could no longer stem the tide. This realisation—combined with media pressure, rising use in prisons and homeless populations, and the public visibility of "Spice zombies"—paved the way for a more sweeping legal approach: the Psychoactive Substances Act 2016. But as the next section will show, that Act brought with it a whole new set of contradictions, confusions, and unintended consequences.

| *Substance* | *Type/Class* | *UK Ban Date* | *Legal Instrument* |
|---|---|---|---|
| Mephedrone | Synthetic Cathinone | April 2010 | Misuse of Drugs Act 1971 (Amendment) |
| Methoxetamine (MXE) | Dissociative (Ketamine analogue) | April 2013 (TCDO), Full ban March 2015 | Temporary Class Drug Order, later MDA |
| NBOMe series (e.g., 25I-NBOMe) | Psychedelic (Phenethylamine) | June 2013 | Misuse of Drugs Act 1971 (Amendment) |
| Synthetic Cannabinoids (initial compounds) | Synthetic Cannabinoid | Various bans from 2009 onwards | Misuse of Drugs Act 1971 (Amendments over time) |
| Benzo Fury (6-APB) | Psychedelic/ Entactogen | June 2013 | Misuse of Drugs Act 1971 (Amendment) |

(continued)

(continued)

| *Substance* | *Type/Class* | *UK Ban Date* | *Legal Instrument* |
|---|---|---|---|
| Ethylphenidate | Stimulant | April 2015 (TCDO), Full ban April 2016 | Temporary Class Drug Order, then MDA |
| Alpha-PVP | Stimulant | Not individually banned—covered under PSA 2016 | Psychoactive Substances Act 2016 |
| Etizolam | Designer Benzodiazepine | Not individually banned—covered under PSA 2016 | Psychoactive Substances Act 2016 |

### *The Psychoactive Substances Act 2016: Politics Over Precision*

By 2016, the UK government had grown tired of playing legislative catch-up. The endless cycle of banning individual compounds under the Misuse of Drugs Act 1971 had proved ineffective, resource-intensive, and ultimately futile. Manufacturers always stayed one chemical step ahead, and enforcement bodies were overwhelmed by the sheer volume and speed of new synthetic substances entering the market. Public pressure, driven by a decade of tabloid moral panic and increasing concern over Spice in prisons and public spaces, demanded a definitive response. The government's answer was the Psychoactive Substances Act 2016 (PSA)—a sweeping piece of legislation that promised to "end the game" once and for all.

The PSA marked a radical shift in British drug law. Rather than banning specific substances, it criminalised any substance capable of producing a psychoactive effect, unless it was explicitly exempted. This meant that, for the first time, the burden of proof was reversed: instead of proving a substance was harmful, prosecutors only had to demonstrate that it affected "mental functioning or emotional state." Theoretically, this made the law future-proof—able to cover any newly emerging compound without needing specific classification.

But from the outset, the PSA was riddled with scientific, legal, and ethical contradictions. The definition of "psychoactive" was vague and legally contentious. How, for instance, would courts determine whether a substance altered a person's "emotional state"? What about products like nutmeg, incense, or even laughing gas—all of which can produce psychoactive effects under certain conditions? The Act attempted to clarify this by listing specific exemptions: alcohol, tobacco, caffeine, medicinal products, and food. But these carve-outs were based not on pharmacology or public health evidence, but on political acceptability and economic interest.

This selective logic did not go unnoticed by critics. Professor David Nutt, who had been sacked from the Advisory Council on the Misuse of Drugs (ACMD) in 2009 for stating that alcohol was more harmful than ecstasy or LSD, was particularly scathing. He argued that the PSA was "scientifically absurd" and "legislatively incoherent"—a law that effectively criminalised safer alternatives while protecting more harmful, culturally accepted substances. "This is prohibition dressed up as progress," Nutt wrote. "It has nothing to do with harm and everything to do with control."

The ACMD itself raised serious concerns during the drafting of the Act. In a letter to the Home Secretary, the council warned that the blanket ban risked criminalising harmless substances, that the psychoactivity test would be difficult to prove in court, and that enforcement would be uneven. They also noted the lack of evidence suggesting that banning NPS would reduce demand—particularly among vulnerable populations such as prisoners and the homeless. These warnings were ignored. The Act passed with cross-party support and came into effect in May 2016.

Despite its bold claims, the PSA has struggled in practice. One of the Act's major flaws is that possession is not a criminal offence, except in "custodial institutions" such as prisons. This means that people caught with Spice on the street cannot be charged with possession—unless they are selling or supplying—but the same person inside a prison can be prosecuted for the same act. The result is legal inconsistency and a disproportionate focus on vulnerable groups. Enforcement has also proven challenging. Proving that a substance is psychoactive—and not covered by an exemption—often requires complex testing and expert testimony. In 2017, a High Court ruling found that nitrous oxide (laughing gas) was not illegal under the PSA when used recreationally, because it could also be considered a "medicinal product" under EU regulations. This exposed a loophole that remains unresolved, with conflicting guidance given to police and prosecutors across the country.

Furthermore, the Act has done little to disrupt the underlying market. While headshops largely disappeared, online sales continued, and synthetic cannabinoids like Spice remained widely available on the street—often in more potent and dangerous forms than before. The government's own 2018 review of the Act acknowledged that Spice use in prisons and among rough sleepers had increased since the law's passage. As with earlier prohibition efforts, the crackdown did not eliminate demand—it simply pushed the trade into less visible and more hazardous channels. Perhaps most tellingly, the PSA stands as a symbolic piece of legislation—less about effective policy and more about political signalling. By targeting the ambiguous category of "psychoactivity," the government appeared decisive and tough on drugs, while sidestepping the uncomfortable truths about legal substances like alcohol and tobacco. The Act reinforced a binary between "licit" and "illicit" highs that has no basis in harm or evidence—only in history, politics, and profit.

From my perspective as a criminal justice researcher, academic and ex magistrate, the law has created unnecessary complications. Defendants caught with Spice are still funnelled into the criminal justice system, particularly in custodial settings, where punishment is prioritised over treatment. As a former bouncer, I've watched the same people cycle in and out of A&E and the courts, their underlying problems—addiction, trauma, homelessness—unaddressed by legislation that claims to protect them. The PSA has not solved the legal highs problem. It has merely buried it beneath layers of legal fiction and political theatre.

In the next section, we'll explore the real-world impact of this shift: who has been criminalised under the PSA, who has escaped scrutiny, and how the law has deepened the divide between "problematic" and "functional" drug users.

### *Who Gets Criminalised and (Who Doesn't)?*

A central irony of the Psychoactive Substances Act 2016 (PSA) lies in the question of who it actually targets. Despite its sweeping language and blanket approach, enforcement of the Act reveals a deeply uneven pattern. Those who are marginalised, visible, and already subject to state surveillance bear the brunt of criminalisation. Those who use psychoactive substances in private, professional, or elite settings, meanwhile, largely escape notice, scrutiny, or consequence.

Within the prison estate, the PSA has had some of its most punitive effects. Possession of psychoactive substances is not generally a criminal offence under the Act, yet an exception is made for "custodial institutions," where possession becomes prosecutable under Section 5. This means that the same act—possessing a spliff of Spice—would not constitute a criminal offence on the street but could lead to punishment, segregation, or additional time if it happens behind bars. Since the Act's introduction, there has been a marked increase in prosecutions for Spice-related incidents in prisons. The National Audit Office and HM Inspectorate of Prisons have repeatedly raised concerns that the policy response—grounded in discipline and punishment—has done little to address the complex reasons why prisoners use these substances in the first place: trauma, boredom, self-medication, or coercion by other inmates.

Outside prison walls, street-level users—particularly those who are homeless—have become the public face of synthetic cannabinoid use. The "Spice zombie" narrative, fuelled by tabloids and even local authorities, has resulted in visible users being disproportionately policed and prosecuted. These individuals are often charged not only under the PSA but also under public order legislation or anti-social behaviour injunctions. Local authorities have increasingly adopted zero-tolerance approaches to open drug use, issuing dispersal orders, fines, and injunctions—all of which exacerbate the instability of people already living on the margins. Yet these highly visible users are only one part of the picture. Behind them lies a vast and largely invisible user base that is rarely subjected to the same scrutiny.

In sharp contrast, certain sectors of society continue to use highly psychoactive substances—including some far more harmful than Spice—with impunity. Nowhere is this clearer than in the corridors of power. In December 2021, an investigation by *The Sunday Times* revealed that traces of cocaine had been found in 11 out of 12 lavatories tested in the Palace of Westminster, including facilities near the offices of the Prime Minister and Home Secretary. The Speaker of the House of Commons referred the matter to the Metropolitan Police, and media reports described the findings as "deeply concerning." Yet no arrests were made, no formal investigation was launched, and the matter quietly disappeared from the headlines.

Reports of a widespread "cocaine culture" in Westminster have circulated for years. Former staffers have spoken anonymously about regular drug use among aides and advisers, while journalists have described cocaine being consumed at political events and late-night parliamentary bars. Yet despite cocaine being a Class A drug—subject to far harsher penalties than any NPS—no prosecutions or disciplinary actions have followed these revelations. The political class, it seems, enjoys not just access but immunity.

The contrast between Spice in the prison cell and cocaine in the Commons could not be more stark. While marginalised users are demonised, surveilled, and criminalised, elite users are shielded by discretion, professional networks, and a culture of silence. The enforcement of the PSA and wider drug laws is thus not about harm reduction or public safety. It is about visibility, class, and control.

This pattern is not limited to Parliament. Middle-class professionals who use drugs recreationally—whether MDMA at a music festival or cocaine at a private party—are unlikely to be arrested, charged, or even judged. Their use is often framed as hedonistic but ultimately harmless, especially when it occurs in private spaces. In contrast, those whose drug use is visible, erratic, or entangled with poverty are cast as dangerous or disorderly. The law, in practice, does not treat substances equally. It does not even treat users equally. Instead, it reproduces existing social inequalities, punishing those least able to defend themselves and sparing those with the greatest access to protection.

This is not a system that fails by accident; it is one that functions precisely as designed. The appearance of legal neutrality cloaks a reality of selective enforcement. Those most likely to face arrest and imprisonment are those already embedded in punitive institutions—people without legal representation, political protection, or the benefit of social invisibility. Middle-class professionals who use drugs recreationally—whether MDMA at a music festival, ketamine at a private party, or cocaine in the office bathroom—are unlikely to face the same risks. Their use is often treated as deviant pleasure, not criminal conduct. Police resources are rarely directed towards their detection. Courts rarely see them as defendants. When they are caught, diversions or cautions are more likely than convictions.

These dynamics are not only classed, but often racialised. Black and working-class communities have long borne the brunt of drug enforcement in the UK, with disproportionate stop-and-search practices and sentencing outcomes well documented across decades. The PSA, though ostensibly neutral, replicates these same patterns by focusing on the most visible and vulnerable.

These contradictions erode public faith in the justice system. When headlines show Spice users being hauled through the courts while the political elite avoids scrutiny despite credible reports of cocaine use, it becomes difficult to argue that drug policy is applied fairly. The PSA, rather than protecting the public or reducing harm, has deepened a two-tier system of enforcement. It criminalises poverty while excusing privilege. It targets dysfunction while turning a blind eye to function. And it does so in the name of control, not care.

In the next section, we'll explore how this enforcement disparity is not only ethically troubling, but was foreseen and warned against by experts—whose advice was ignored in the rush to legislate.

### *Evidence Ignored*

If drug policy were driven by evidence, the Psychoactive Substances Act 2016 (PSA) would never have made it to the statute book. By the time it was introduced, expert bodies had already warned that a blanket ban on psychoactive substances would be unworkable, scientifically incoherent, and unlikely to reduce harm. Yet these warnings were repeatedly ignored. Instead, the UK government prioritised public image over public health, crafting a piece of legislation designed not to improve outcomes, but to appear decisive in the face of a media-fuelled panic. The result was a law that many in the scientific and legal communities viewed as a case study in bad policymaking—a monument to political convenience dressed in the language of protection.

The most high-profile example of this disconnect between evidence and enforcement came in 2009, with the sacking of Professor David Nutt from his role as Chair of the Advisory Council on the Misuse of Drugs (ACMD). Nutt's offence was not scientific misconduct, but candour: he publicly stated that alcohol and tobacco caused more harm to society than many illegal drugs, including ecstasy and LSD. His comments were drawn from peer-reviewed research published in *The Lancet*, and echoed by other academics in the field. Nonetheless, the then-Home Secretary, Alan Johnson, removed him from his post, declaring that he had "lost confidence" in Nutt's judgment. The message was clear: when scientific evidence clashed with political narrative, it was the evidence that would be sacrificed.

This pattern continued into the drafting and implementation of the PSA. The ACMD expressed a series of serious concerns in correspondence with the Home Office. Chief among them was the definitional problem: how would "psychoactivity" be determined in practice? The

Council argued that the government had failed to demonstrate a robust scientific method for testing substances against this standard. There was also concern about enforcement. Would the police be equipped to identify and distinguish psychoactive substances from legal ones? Would forensic laboratories be resourced and prepared for the inevitable deluge of compounds needing analysis?

These were not abstract academic concerns; they were operational and legal realities. And yet, rather than engaging with these questions, the government pressed ahead. When asked to explain how the Act would function in practice, ministers offered vague assurances that the burden of proof would fall on suppliers, not the state. This overlooked the simple fact that psychoactivity is not a binary property but a spectrum, and that many legal products—from nutmeg to incense to herbal remedies—could conceivably fall within its remit. Instead of answering these challenges, the Home Office carved out broad exemptions for alcohol, tobacco, caffeine, and medicinal products—not because they were non-psychoactive, but because they were culturally and economically entrenched.

This exemption regime made a mockery of the law's scientific credibility. Alcohol and tobacco remain two of the most harmful substances in UK society by almost every public health metric. Alcohol alone is responsible for more than 7000 deaths per year in England and a host of secondary harms including domestic abuse, road traffic accidents, and long-term liver disease. Yet it is not only exempted from prohibition—it is promoted, taxed, and integrated into social life. The PSA's failure to even acknowledge this contradiction confirms what many experts already knew: the law was never about harm, it was about optics.

The consequences of this disregard for evidence have been real and measurable. As noted in the government's own post-legislative review of the PSA in 2018, the use of synthetic cannabinoids—particularly among the prison population and homeless communities—had increased, not decreased, following the Act. Emergency services reported a rise in Spice-related incidents, with some areas experiencing a doubling of ambulance callouts for related complications. Police forces struggled to enforce the law due to the challenges of proving psychoactivity, and the courts were left to interpret a vague and complex statute with little guidance or consistency.

Meanwhile, no serious investment was made into harm reduction education, treatment programmes, or community outreach. This omission is particularly glaring given the success of evidence-led models elsewhere. Portugal's decriminalisation approach, for example, is grounded in public health and has led to reductions in problematic drug use, drug-related deaths, and HIV transmission. Similarly, New Zealand's brief experiment with regulating low-harm NPS under a controlled licensing model—although ultimately hindered by political resistance—showed early signs of reducing black-market sales and improving quality control.

The UK, however, chose the opposite path: prohibition without evaluation, control without clarity. This approach has reinforced a punitive cycle that targets the visible and vulnerable, while failing to challenge the underlying drivers of problematic drug use. The ACMD's recommendations for more nuanced scheduling, proportionality in sentencing, and investment in scientific research have largely gone unheeded.

There is a deep irony here. Politicians defending the PSA often claimed that it was necessary because the existing system could not keep up with the pace of innovation. And yet, by ignoring the very experts who could help them develop an adaptive, evidence-based framework, they guaranteed that the law would once again fall behind the market. Far from solving the problem, the PSA simply moved it out of sight—away from headshops and into alleyways, prisons, and psychiatric wards.

In doing so, the UK government didn't just ignore the evidence. It actively undermined it, sending a message to scientists, clinicians, and policy researchers that their expertise counts for little when it contradicts political imperatives. As the next section explores, this has serious ethical implications—particularly when the cost of that wilful ignorance is borne by the most vulnerable members of society.

### *Alternative Approaches*

While the UK doubled down on prohibition through the Psychoactive Substances Act 2016, other countries chose different paths—some cautious, others bold, but all informed to varying degrees by public health evidence, harm reduction principles, and pragmatic realism. The contrast between these models and the UK's zero-tolerance strategy underscores a broader truth: that criminalisation is not the inevitable or most effective response to drug use. It is a political choice, shaped by ideology, institutional inertia, and vested interests.

Portugal's now widely cited approach is a prime example. In 2001, facing one of the worst drug crises in Europe, the Portuguese government decriminalised the personal possession of all drugs, including heroin and cocaine. Rather than arresting users, the state redirected them to dissuasion commissions and treatment services, offering support rather than punishment. The policy was not a free-for-all; trafficking remained illegal, and repeat offenders could still face sanctions. But the philosophical shift was significant: addiction was treated as a health issue, not a criminal one. Over the next two decades, Portugal saw a marked reduction in problematic drug use, drug-related deaths, and HIV transmission rates. Crucially, these changes were accompanied by sustained investment in drug treatment, social reintegration, and housing support—precisely the areas that have been underfunded in the UK.

New Zealand also offers instructive lessons, albeit from a more experimental framework. In 2013, it introduced the Psychoactive Substances Act—a different version from the UK's—that allowed for the regulated sale of low-risk NPS. Products could only be sold if they passed strict safety tests, and only through licensed retailers. Advertising was banned, packaging was standardised, and youth access was restricted. While the scheme faced political resistance and was ultimately paused due to gaps in the testing regime, the concept was fundamentally different from the UK's approach. Rather than banning all psychoactive substances by default, New Zealand attempted to build a regulatory framework that acknowledged demand, assessed risk, and sought to control rather than suppress.

In stark contrast, the UK continues to prioritise criminalisation over care. Despite growing evidence that punitive policies fail to reduce drug use or harm, the UK has invested disproportionately in policing, border enforcement, and the expansion of custodial powers. Between 2010 and 2020, government spending on drug treatment services fell by over £160 million, while the Home Office budget for drug-related enforcement increased. According to a 2021 report by the House of Commons Health and Social Care Committee, this has created a "crisis in addiction services," with rising drug-related deaths and shrinking access to support—particularly for young people and those in areas of high deprivation.

This imbalance is not accidental. Criminalisation is politically expedient; treatment is not. Arrests create headlines. Convictions boost short-term statistics. Investment in community outreach, trauma-informed therapy, and long-term rehabilitation, on the other hand, takes time, coordination, and political will. Moreover, treatment challenges the punitive narrative that underpins much of UK drug policy—a narrative rooted in the belief that drug use is a moral failing, not a social symptom.

Even within the UK, small-scale pilot projects have shown the benefits of alternative models. Diversion schemes such as the Durham Checkpoint or Thames Valley's Drug Diversion programme have redirected low-level drug offenders away from the criminal justice system and into support services. These initiatives have demonstrated reductions in reoffending and improvements in health outcomes. Yet they remain limited in scale, often underfunded, and sometimes politically vulnerable.

Part of the resistance to reform lies in the entrenched interests that benefit from the status quo. The UK's criminal justice system, from policing to probation, is built around a model in which drug offences provide a steady stream of low-hanging fruit. As many researchers have pointed out, drug enforcement disproportionately targets communities that are already over-policed and under-resourced—typically working-class, racialised, or homeless populations. Meanwhile, the more discreet forms of drug use—in professional, middle-class, or elite settings—are rarely subject to the same scrutiny. In this context, criminalisation is not just ineffective; it is structurally discriminatory.

It is also economically incoherent. The cost of policing drug offences far exceeds the cost of funding treatment. A 2022 analysis by the Home Office estimated that every £1 spent on drug treatment yields around £4 in reduced crime and healthcare costs, yet treatment budgets remain fragmented and fragile, dependent on short-term commissioning cycles and vulnerable to local authority cuts.

What the international comparisons show—and what the UK continues to ignore—is that treating drug use as a public health issue is not only more humane, but more effective. Blanket prohibition, as exemplified by the UK's PSA, fails to reduce supply, fails to protect users, and fails to address the root causes of problematic use. In contrast, harm reduction, regulation, and decriminalisation offer pragmatic tools for reducing the harms that prohibition often exacerbates.

The UK stands almost alone in its stubborn adherence to punitive orthodoxy. It is a position that costs lives, entrenches inequality, and squanders public money—not in ignorance, but in defiance of the evidence. In the next and final section, we turn to the ethical implications of this wilful refusal to reform, and ask what kind of drug policy might look like if it were built not on fear or moralism, but on care, justice, and truth.

### *Authors Reflection—On the Doors*

As a bouncer working five or six nights a week across some of the busiest clubs in the city, I got to know a lot of regulars. Many of them I knew by name, which—considering that some of the venues had thousands of customers through the doors each night—I was always quite proud of. You start to notice things over time. Relationships began and ended. People's drinking habits changed. But what stood out most during the 2000s was the shift in drug use—particularly the rise of synthetic cannabinoids.

Neither cannabis nor any drug use was ever allowed inside the clubs I worked, of course, but cannabis users—much like the original pill heads—rarely caused us any trouble. Most of them just wanted to have a mellow night, maybe dance a bit, and go home without incident. But when the so-called "legal highs" arrived, things changed. These substances were far cheaper than actual marijuana, which made them more accessible to younger punters and those on tighter budgets. That's when I started to see the change. These weren't just people getting drunk or stoned—these were people who were gone.

We all started to encounter customers who were virtually unresponsive. They would sit or stand in a trance-like state, their eyes glassy, their movements sluggish or twitchy. It was frightening. We began calling ambulances more frequently, and the paramedics—already stretched thin—were far from thrilled. But we had no choice. As a bouncer, my job was to maintain order and keep people safe, not to act as a paramedic or a social worker. And yet, with the arrival of Spice and other synthetic cannabinoids, I found myself increasingly out of my depth.

Even when we could rouse someone and get them out of the building, it didn't solve the problem. More than once, a customer would collapse on the pavement outside minutes after we'd escorted them from the club. It was terrifying. I'd read the stories in the papers, of course—the headlines about "zombie drugs," about homeless people and prisoners. But this wasn't just happening in back alleys or custody suites. It was happening on the doors of licensed venues, to people in their late teens and early twenties, many of whom looked no different from the students and partygoers I'd seen a hundred times before.

Spice had become, for many, a cheap alternative to booze or cocaine. And just like we're now seeing with ketamine—which has dropped in price and surged in popularity—it wasn't the price that made it dangerous. It was the unpredictability. You never knew what was in it, how strong it was, or what effect it would have. And as someone who spent night after night trying to keep people safe while they were under its influence, I can tell you: it didn't feel like any of the drug trends that had come before. It felt like a rupture—a shift into something darker, cheaper, and far harder to manage.

### *Legal High, Legal Loopholes, Conclusions*

The story of legal highs in the UK is not just about chemistry or legislation—it is a story about political convenience, public fear, and profound social neglect. From the rapid rise of synthetic cannabinoids like Spice to the sweeping provisions of the Psychoactive Substances Act 2016, the state's response to novel drugs has been defined more by panic than by principle. Rather than asking why these substances were being used—who was using them, under what conditions, and with what consequences—the government focused on symbolic crackdowns and legal generalisations, punishing visibility while ignoring vulnerability.

The failure to listen to experts, including the Advisory Council on the Misuse of Drugs, reveals a fundamental flaw in the UK's approach: evidence is only valued when it fits the preordained narrative. Harm reduction, regulation, and decriminalisation—strategies shown to reduce deaths, improve public health, and save money—are dismissed in favour of punitive measures that do neither. Meanwhile, the state continues to pour millions into enforcement and prison expansion, while systematically disinvesting from addiction services, housing support, and mental health care.

My own experience working as a bouncer during the height of the legal highs wave gave me a front-row seat to these failures. I watched as predictable, low-harm behaviours gave way to frightening, chaotic states brought on by unpredictable substances. I dealt with users who weren't criminals, but casualties—of austerity, of exclusion, and of a system more concerned with appearances than outcomes.

The PSA didn't end the game. It simply moved the goalposts, forcing the market deeper underground and the harms further out of sight. It widened the gulf between those who are punished and those who are protected, reinforcing the double standard that runs throughout UK drug policy: control for the poor, impunity for the powerful.

If we are serious about reducing drug harm, we must start by abandoning the myth that prohibition equals protection. We need a policy grounded not in panic or punishment, but in evidence, equity, and care. Until then, the war on legal highs—like the wider war on drugs—will continue to fail those who need help most.

## Bibliography


European Monitoring Centre for Drugs and Drug Addiction (EMCDDA). (2016). *European drug report 2016: Trends and developments*. Publications Office of the European Union.

Global Drug Survey. (2013). *Global Drug Survey 2013 findings*. Retrieved July 2, 2025, from https://www.globaldrugsurvey.com

HM Inspectorate of Prisons (HMIP). 2017. *Annual report 2016–17*. HMIP.

Home Affairs Select Committee. 2016. *Drugs: Breaking the cycle* (HC 103). House of Commons.

Home Office. (2014). *Drug misuse: Findings from the 2013/14 Crime Survey for England and Wales*. Home Office.

House of Commons Health and Social Care Committee. (2021). *Drugs policy: First report of session 2021–22* (HC 117). House of Commons.

Nutt, D. (2015, July 2). The Psychoactive Substances Bill is a ban on common sense. *The Guardian*. Retrieved July 2, 2025, from https://www.theguardian.com/commentisfree/2015/jul/02/psychoactive-substances-bill-ban-common-sense

Public Health England. (2016). *The public health burden of alcohol and the effectiveness and cost-effectiveness of alcohol control policies*. PHE.

The Sunday Times. (2021, December 5). Cocaine traces found in Parliament toilets. *The Times*. Retrieved July 2, 2025, from https://www.thetimes.co.uk/article/cocaine-traces-found-in-parliament-toilets-8dkhvrz2r

CHAPTER 8

# The Real Harm—Why Alcohol is the Most Dangerous Drug

**Abstract** This chapter interrogates the paradox at the heart of UK drug policy: that the most harmful drug in society—alcohol—is not only legal but celebrated, marketed, and protected. Drawing on public health data, criminal justice statistics, and sociocultural analysis, the chapter explores alcohol-related deaths, violence, addiction, and social costs, contrasting these harms with the marginalised treatment of less dangerous illicit drugs. It examines the policy blind spot created by the normalisation of alcohol and critiques the failure to adopt meaningful harm reduction or regulatory interventions. Through personal reflections from frontline experience in nightlife and the courts, this chapter challenges the moral double standards that underpin British drug discourse. It concludes by arguing that a just and coherent drug policy cannot ignore alcohol, and that the legal/illegal divide reflects politics—not pharmacology or risk.

**Keywords** Alcohol harm, Drug policy hypocrisy, Legal drugs, Public health, Criminal justice, Violence and alcohol, Harm reduction, Cultural normalisation, Policy contradiction, Functional substance use


E. Peatfield, *Drugs Disorder by Design*,
https://doi.org/10.1007/978-3-032-07814-8_8

## Introduction: The Legal Drug that Causes the Most Harm

In Britain, we tend to separate alcohol from the word "drugs." Alcohol is something we celebrate, toast with, rely on to socialise, and increasingly, to cope. Drugs, on the other hand, are something we criminalise, moralise over, and condemn. But this separation is arbitrary—cultural, not pharmacological—and it obscures a fundamental truth: alcohol is a drug. Not only that, it is by far the most harmful drug in the UK.

The irony is stark. While vast swathes of public policy, policing, and media discourse are devoted to demonising the use of substances like cannabis or cocaine, alcohol continues to enjoy legal protection, cultural elevation, and government endorsement. From supermarket shelves to football sponsorships, from pub culture to political fundraising dinners, alcohol is everywhere. It is the only drug we have to justify *not* taking. Yet when its impact is assessed empirically, the results are clear and damning.

In 2010, Professor David Nutt and his colleagues published a groundbreaking study in *The Lancet*, which ranked drugs based on their overall harm to individuals and society. Alcohol topped the list, scoring higher than heroin and crack cocaine. Unlike most illicit substances, alcohol combines personal health risks—liver damage, cancer, heart disease, mental health deterioration—with an immense social footprint. It fuels domestic violence, child neglect, sexual assault, street crime, and costly hospital admissions. It ruins lives not only through addiction and long-term health damage, but also through its acute capacity to damage others.

Despite this, alcohol remains a cornerstone of British life. Our economic system benefits from it through taxes and industry profits. Our cultural system romanticises it, from the archetype of the "lovable drunk" to the marketing of prosecco as female empowerment. Our political system avoids confronting it—perhaps out of convenience, perhaps out of cowardice. While billions are spent criminalising drug users and waging a failing war on substances, far less is done to address the far more destructive, socially accepted presence of alcohol. When politicians discuss substance misuse, alcohol is often conspicuously absent—despite costing the NHS upwards of £3.5 billion per year and wider society an estimated £21 billion annually.

I have seen the consequences of this double standard up close. As a magistrate, I watched alcohol ripple through courtrooms in the form of violent offences, broken families, and repeat offenders with little hope of intervention. As a bouncer, I saw the chaos of alcohol-fuelled aggression and vulnerability every weekend—the tears, the bruises, the ambulances. Yet the offenders weren't "junkies" or "druggies"—they were ordinary people under the influence of something legal, encouraged, and profitable.

This chapter will examine the true scale of harm caused by alcohol. We will look at the rising death toll from liver disease and other alcohol-related conditions; the central role alcohol plays in domestic violence and public disorder; the enormous burden placed on emergency services and the NHS; and the sheer accessibility of a drug that ruins lives. We will also follow the money—tracing how alcohol's harmful impact is tolerated, even defended, because of the economic benefits it brings to both industry and government.

Ultimately, the aim is not to demonise those who drink, but to question why our policies target the least harmful substances while leaving the most dangerous ones untouched. If drug policy is truly about reducing harm, then alcohol must be central to the debate. Its absence from most discussions on drugs and justice reveals the political incoherence—and moral cowardice—of our current approach.

## Alcohol-Related Deaths—The Unspoken Crisis

Despite its legal status and cultural acceptability, alcohol is responsible for an escalating public health crisis in the UK. Each year, thousands of people die as a direct result of alcohol consumption, with many more suffering long-term physical and mental harm. Unlike the sudden, headline-grabbing overdose deaths associated with illegal drugs, alcohol kills slowly and quietly, through liver failure, cancers, heart disease, and suicides. It is a killer in plain sight—one that disproportionately affects deprived communities and places immense strain on an already overburdened NHS.

According to the Office for National Statistics (ONS), there were 10,048 alcohol-specific deaths in the UK in 2022—the highest number since records began and a 4.2% increase from the previous year (ONS, 2023). Alcohol-specific deaths are those directly attributable to alcohol, such as alcoholic liver disease and alcohol poisoning, but this figure does not account for the full scale of harm. When broader alcohol-related conditions are included—such as heart disease, stroke, and a range of cancers—the death toll is likely to be significantly higher. Public Health England has previously estimated that alcohol contributes to more than 25,000 deaths per year across England alone (PHE, 2018).

The rise in alcohol-related deaths is not an isolated trend, but a symptom of wider social and political neglect. The COVID-19 pandemic intensified harmful drinking patterns, particularly among high-risk drinkers, many of whom increased consumption due to stress, isolation, or the loss of support services. While middle-class drinking habits were largely shielded by privacy and cultural permissiveness, it was the most vulnerable—those in poverty, with pre-existing mental health issues, or in precarious housing—who suffered the most severe consequences. In this sense, alcohol-related mortality reflects broader patterns of structural inequality, where health outcomes are tied closely to class, geography, and access to care.

Geographical disparities in alcohol-related harm are stark. The North East of England consistently records the highest rates of alcohol-specific deaths, while more affluent areas of the South report significantly lower figures. This is not simply a matter of personal choice, but of availability, affordability, and accumulated disadvantage. Research by Alcohol Change UK has shown that people living in the most deprived areas are 60% more likely to die from alcohol-related causes than those in the least deprived areas (Alcohol Change UK, 2022). The government's continued reluctance to implement meaningful public health interventions—such as minimum unit pricing in England—only exacerbates these inequalities.

The burden of alcohol-related illness also falls heavily on NHS services. In 2022, there were over 980,000 hospital admissions in England where alcohol was the primary or secondary cause—a figure that has risen steadily over the past decade (NHS Digital, 2023). These admissions include conditions such as liver cirrhosis, gastrointestinal bleeding, alcohol-related psychosis, and acute intoxication. The direct cost to the NHS is estimated at £3.5 billion per year (Public Health England, 2018), but this does not capture the full impact, such as A&E pressures, ambulance callouts, and long-term social care costs.

Despite this growing crisis, treatment services for alcohol misuse have been systematically underfunded and fragmented. Local authority spending on alcohol treatment in England fell by over 17% between 2015 and 2020, following the devolution of responsibility for addiction services from the NHS to cash-strapped councils (Alcohol Health Alliance, 2021). Many areas have seen closures or privatisation of alcohol services, with service users reporting long waiting times, inconsistent care, and limited access to mental health support. This is particularly troubling given that alcohol dependency is often co-morbid with depression, anxiety, and trauma-related disorders—all of which require sustained and holistic treatment models.

What makes this all the more galling is the sheer invisibility of these deaths in public discourse. When a young person dies from an ecstasy overdose at a music festival, it dominates news cycles. Politicians call for tougher enforcement, and tabloid papers decry the moral decline of youth. But when someone dies slowly from alcoholic liver disease in a council flat, there is no media outcry. No war on alcohol. No calls to criminalise the industry that sold them the poison. Instead, these deaths are framed as individual failings, disconnected from the structural and political choices that shaped their circumstances.

This silence is political. Alcohol is deeply embedded in British identity, from binge-drinking culture to the sentimentalism of the local pub. It is also economically significant: the alcohol industry contributes an estimated £46 billion to the UK economy annually, with the Treasury collecting over £12 billion in alcohol duties in 2023 (HMRC, 2023). The state, therefore, finds itself in a deeply compromised position—tasked with protecting public health, yet dependent on a substance that both drives illness and funds public services. It is little wonder that policy responses remain timid.

The refusal to treat alcohol as a serious drug of harm reflects a broader incoherence in the UK's substance misuse policy. If drug laws were truly based on evidence, alcohol would be at the top of the list of substances requiring public education, regulation, and harm reduction. Instead, it remains the outlier—dangerous but socially accepted, deadly but commercially protected.

It is important to stress that the victims of alcohol-related harm are not confined to those who drink. Alcohol tears through families, workplaces, and communities. Children growing up in alcohol-dependent households suffer long-term psychological effects. Partners experience abuse and trauma. Public services strain under the weight of invisible harm, with paramedics, social workers, and healthcare staff left to pick up the pieces.

In this context, the idea that UK drug policy is about *protecting the public* begins to fall apart. The reality is that some drugs are criminalised not because they are more harmful, but because they are associated with stigmatised groups. Meanwhile, the most dangerous drug of all flows freely through our shops, schools, and homes—its victims largely unseen, its cost externalised to the most vulnerable, and its profits quietly collected by those in power.

## Alcohol and Crime—Violence Behind Closed Doors

Alcohol is a key driver of violent crime in the UK, yet it is rarely acknowledged as such in mainstream discourse. Unlike illicit drugs, which are often stigmatised as inherently dangerous and criminogenic, alcohol retains a veneer of acceptability—even when it is central to acts of aggression, injury, and trauma. The data leaves little doubt: alcohol is implicated in 39% of all violent incidents in England and Wales, according to the Crime Survey (ONS, 2022), and in a staggering 48% of domestic abuse cases recorded by the police (Home Office, 2021). These are not minor scuffles between consenting adults—they are the ruptures of families, communities, and lives.

As someone who has worked the doors of nightclubs and pubs for over two decades, I've witnessed the reality of alcohol-related violence up close. For all the warnings about dangerous drug users, I've never been hurt by one. But alcohol? That's another story.

When I was working the doors, I was very lucky (and good at my job), so I didn't get injured too badly over the two decades. But I did get stabbed—right in the back —during a fight that broke out after I refused entry to a clearly intoxicated customer.

According to the law, we can't legally allow someone into a licensed venue if they're obviously drunk. This particular group of lads could barely stand, and one of them was especially nasty—slurring abuse and calling me, among other things, "some f*cking dumb bitch." We turned them away and thought they'd gone. A few minutes later, with my back to the street, I felt a sudden sharp pain. That same man had come back, fuming about being refused, and stabbed me in the back to get his revenge. Fortunately, my colleagues restrained him—forcefully—and he was later prosecuted.

In court, you wouldn't have thought it was the same man. He apologised profusely to me and to the court, admitted guilt straight away, and seemed genuinely remorseful. But the fact that he was drunk didn't help his case. As the judge rightly said, alcohol is an aggravating factor in sentencing—not a mitigating one.

What that incident laid bare for me is how quickly alcohol can transform someone from obnoxious to violent. And yet, unlike drug users, alcohol-fuelled offenders are rarely pathologised or demonised in the same way. Their violence is excused as out-of-character, a "one-off," a result of stress or "too much to drink." But those of us who deal with it know better. Alcohol emboldens, disinhibits, and fuels male aggression in ways that are both terrifying and entirely predictable.

This tendency is even more disturbing in the context of domestic abuse, where alcohol plays a prominent and often under-recognised role. According to Women's Aid, up to 50% of intimate partner violence incidents involve alcohol (Women's Aid, 2022). The link is not about causation—abuse is always rooted in power and control—but alcohol often escalates the severity, frequency, and lethality of violence. The Institute of Alcohol Studies (2020) found that in domestic incidents involving alcohol, violence was more likely to be repeated, severe, and result in physical injury. Alcohol also acts as a mask: abusers use it as an excuse, victims are more likely to blame themselves, and professionals can be misled by the chaotic circumstances. Services are rarely coordinated—domestic abuse support workers may lack training in substance misuse, while alcohol services often fail to screen for abuse, especially in female clients.

In cases I've seen in court, and from what survivor's report, alcohol can make it harder for women to seek help. If the victim is also drinking—whether to cope or as part of the household dynamic—they may be seen as "unreliable" or undeserving. Alcohol doesn't just escalate the violence; it complicates the response to it.

## A System Strained by the Consequences

Beyond the home, alcohol violence places a massive burden on police, healthcare staff, and emergency services. The Association of Chief Police Officers estimated that up to 70% of weekend policing time is spent dealing with alcohol-related incidents (ACPO, 2012). Paramedics, already under strain, face threats and assaults from intoxicated individuals. A&E departments are flooded with alcohol-related injuries, often involving aggression, falls, and alcohol poisoning. Unlike illegal drugs—often policed proactively—alcohol-related crimes are reactive and resource-intensive. From street fights and vandalism to domestic assaults, officers respond after the damage is done. These are not niche occurrences—they're routine. The policing of alcohol harms is embedded in everyday operations. And yet there is little public appetite to discuss the source of that harm.

In the courtroom, alcohol-related offending is often viewed through a strange lens. The Sentencing Council makes it clear: voluntary intoxication is an aggravating factor in sentencing, not an excuse. But this principle is inconsistently applied. When the offender is from a respectable background, a first-time offender, or otherwise seen as "redeemable," intoxication is often reframed as an explanation. "He's not a bad man—he was just drunk."

In my experience as a magistrate, I saw these dynamics play out repeatedly. Men or women who assaulted their partners while drunk were presented as remorseful, responsible citizens. Drink was framed as the problem—not the pattern of violence. Some were sent on anger management or alcohol awareness courses, while others received suspended sentences. The victim's trauma was rarely central. Contrast this with how drug-related offences are treated. A young man with heroin possession—even if he committed no violent offence—would be met with suspicion, stigma, and often, custodial sentencing. In the eyes of the court, he was a risk to society. But a drunk man who punches his girlfriend? That, too often, was seen as a momentary lapse.

This unequal framing reflects a deep hypocrisy in how British institutions view harm. Alcohol is understood, at least culturally. It is familiar, woven into the fabric of British life. Drug use, on the other hand, is associated with "otherness"—with deviance, urban decline, and moral panic.

## Who We Excuse

There is no question that alcohol makes people dangerous. It fuels over 40% of all violent crimes, often with devastating, long-term consequences for victims. And yet, as a society, we continue to protect its image, minimise its harms, and refuse to confront its true impact. This reluctance has roots in economy and culture. The alcohol industry is worth billions. Its products are promoted on television, in sports, and across social media. Alcohol is marketed as relaxation, celebration, even femininity ("wine o'clock"), despite the carnage it causes. Politicians toast with champagne in public; pubs are praised as community hubs even as they serve as launchpads for weekend mayhem.

Because alcohol is legal, it's assumed to be manageable. But legality does not equal safety. Tobacco is legal, yet highly regulated because of its health impact. Cars are legal, but heavily licensed and subject to strict rules. Alcohol, by contrast, enjoys far more latitude—even as it destroys lives. What makes this more galling is that it is preventable. Policy could address alcohol's role in violence: through pricing, availability, advertising restrictions, and robust support services. But these measures are politically risky. Challenging the status of alcohol means challenging powerful industries, cultural traditions, and voter habits.

Alcohol is not just another drug—it is the *most* dangerous drug when judged by its combined harms to individuals and society. It fuels violence in homes and on streets, places massive strain on policing and healthcare, and distorts justice in the courtroom. Yet it is allowed to flourish because of its legal status, economic value, and cultural familiarity. The consequence is a system that punishes less harmful drug users while excusing violent, often privileged drinkers. It is a system that fails to protect women, burdens emergency services, and leaves communities traumatised—all while generating billions in profit. If we are serious about reducing harm, then alcohol cannot be treated as the exception. It must be named for what it is: a dangerous, addictive drug with a body count to match. Anything less is not just inconsistent—it's unjust.

## Accessibility and Normalisation—The Everyday Drug

One of the most striking differences between alcohol and illegal drugs is not just legal status, but *proximity*. Alcohol is everywhere. It is accessible, affordable, and, crucially, normalised. For many people in Britain, the first exposure to a drug is not cannabis or cocaine, but a sip of alcohol offered by a parent or relative. Drinking is a rite of passage—part of turning eighteen, part of going to university, part of grieving, celebrating, relaxing, dating, and working. We drink to bond and to forget, to socialise and to survive. And we rarely question the risks until it's too late.

The availability of alcohol is astounding when viewed objectively. Supermarkets sell spirits next to soft drinks. Petrol stations stock beer.

Discount retailers push cider multipacks and cheap vodka. Pubs and bars are ubiquitous in town centres, villages, train stations—even airports. In England and Wales, there are over 250,000 licensed premises, and laws introduced in 2003 permit 24-hour alcohol sales. There is no equivalent for any other drug, not even caffeine or tobacco.

This saturation is by design, not accident. The alcohol industry, worth over £46 billion to the UK economy, spends vast sums on marketing—crafting an image of alcohol that is desirable, stylish, and aspirational. From champagne to craft beer, alcohol is sold as identity. It is aligned with success, class, relaxation, and rebellion, depending on the audience. Women are targeted with fruity gins and slogans like "mummy's little helper," while men are offered rugged lager campaigns steeped in masculinity. Young people are bombarded with imagery that links drinking to freedom and fun.

This level of commercial and cultural saturation creates what public health experts call an "alcogenic environment"—a society that promotes, rewards, and sustains alcohol consumption. It also distorts our sense of risk. Because alcohol is omnipresent, we perceive it as inherently safe, manageable, or at worst, indulgent. The harms—liver disease, violence, addiction—are treated as exceptions, not expected outcomes. Meanwhile, substances that are far less harmful (like cannabis or ecstasy, in measured doses) are framed as reckless and criminal.

## Marketing, Manipulation, and Mixed Messages

Alcohol advertising goes beyond product promotion—it creates social norms. Unlike drug education, which tends to be rooted in avoidance, alcohol messaging often centres around moderation and control: "drink responsibly," "know your limits." These slogans subtly imply that the problem lies not with alcohol, but with the individual's inability to handle it. Responsibility is shifted onto the user, while producers and promoters escape scrutiny. This strategy mirrors that of the tobacco industry in its heyday: admit just enough harm to deflect criticism, fund research that minimises risks, and place the burden on consumers to regulate their own behaviour. Yet while tobacco marketing is now tightly controlled—banned from TV, stripped of glamour—alcohol continues to enjoy unregulated access to sports sponsorship, social media, and festivals. Even health charities are not immune. Organisations like Drinkaware, which present themselves as independent providers of alcohol education, have well-documented ties to the alcohol industry. This raises serious concerns about conflicts of interest. When those profiting from a product are also shaping the public conversation about its risks, it becomes almost impossible to generate coherent, unbiased public health messaging.

## Class, Identity, and Respectability

Alcohol use and its acceptability are also deeply shaped by class. Middle-class drinking—whether a nightly bottle of wine or gin-and-tonic brunches—is often framed as cultured, moderate, and harmless. The same level of consumption in working-class communities is more likely to be described as problematic. This cultural framing affects who gets judged, who gets treatment, and who gets punished. Public health campaigns rarely focus on middle-class drinking habits, despite the fact that liver disease rates are rising across social strata. Meanwhile, alcohol dependency in working-class communities is pathologised—seen not just as an individual weakness, but as evidence of wider social decay. These narratives influence policy, funding, and public sympathy. The result is a two-tier system: silent tolerance for the respectable drinker, and suspicion or condemnation for everyone else.

This links back to a broader theme in UK drug policy—*respectability politics*. Just as certain drug users are demonised based on race, class, and lifestyle, so too are certain drinkers. Who is drinking, how they present, where they do it, and what they can afford all shape how their behaviour is interpreted. A lawyer drinking alone in a wine bar is a professional under stress. A homeless man drinking White Lightning in a doorway is a public nuisance.

Perhaps the most insidious aspect of alcohol's normalisation is how deeply it has infiltrated the very institutions charged with promoting well-being. Alcohol is served in hospitals and universities, poured at political fundraisers, and sold at charity events. Staff rooms have bottles of wine raffled off. Graduation ceremonies are toasted with champagne. Police officers, judges, and MPs all drink socially—and often heavily—but this consumption is rarely scrutinised.

This contradiction creates a situation where the harms of alcohol are addressed only at the point of crisis—when someone ends up in A&E, in court, or in a coffin. Until then, problematic use is ignored, minimised, or even celebrated. Dry January and Sober October are treated not as public health interventions but as quirky lifestyle challenges—temporary abstinence rather than long-term change.

The cumulative effect is that alcohol retains a privileged place in British society. It is exempt from the usual rules of risk. It is a known danger that we pretend can be managed through personal discipline alone, even as it causes mass harm. Policymakers hesitate to touch it because to do so would mean confronting not just an industry, but a national identity.

## De-normalisation: A Missed Opportunity

There are examples of what could be done. Scotland's introduction of minimum unit pricing in 2018 led to a drop in alcohol sales and has shown early signs of reducing hospital admissions and alcohol-specific deaths. But England has resisted similar moves, citing concerns about consumer freedom and industry disruption. Meanwhile, labelling on alcohol products remains weak. Unlike cigarettes, alcohol bottles are not required to display prominent health warnings, calorie content, or cancer risk. These missed opportunities show where priorities lie. Politicians may speak of "tackling alcohol harm," but few are willing to confront the structural forces that maintain that harm. A public health approach to alcohol would mean rethinking advertising, access, pricing, and education—policies that work for tobacco but remain taboo when it comes to Britain's favourite drug.

## Profits Over Public Health—Follow the Money

If drug policy in the UK were genuinely driven by a desire to protect public health, then alcohol would be its central focus. But it isn't. Despite its well-documented harms, alcohol remains legal, accessible, and largely unregulated compared to its illicit counterparts. This is not an oversight—it is a choice. And like many political choices, it follows the money.

The UK government collects over £12 billion a year in alcohol duty, making alcohol one of the most lucrative commodities in the country. That figure doesn't include VAT, business rates, or the wider economic activity generated by alcohol sales—hospitality, logistics, entertainment, tourism. The alcohol industry as a whole contributes an estimated £46 billion annually to the economy and supports over 900,000 jobs, according to the Office for National Statistics. In economic terms, alcohol is a heavyweight player. And when public finances are stretched, few governments want to risk alienating such a powerful sector.

This economic dependency creates a clear conflict of interest. The same government departments responsible for reducing alcohol-related harm are also under pressure to support business growth and tax revenue. Health ministers may campaign for stronger labelling or reduced availability, but treasury officials and business secretaries are often pushing in the opposite direction. The result is policy paralysis—years of consultations, timid reform, and voluntary codes of conduct that lack teeth.

One example is the failure to introduce mandatory labelling of alcohol products. Despite strong public health evidence and repeated calls from the Chief Medical Officer, alcohol producers are still not legally required to display full nutritional information, alcohol units, or cancer risks on packaging. Contrast this with the tobacco industry, which must plaster cigarette packets with graphic health warnings and standardised designs. The difference is not scientific—it is political. Tobacco has been de-normalised; alcohol, for now, remains sacred.

What little regulation does exist often takes the form of voluntary codes, asking the producers of alcohol to effectively regulate themselves. Through initiatives like the Portman Group's marketing code and Drinkaware's public education work, the industry projects an image of responsibility and self-restraint—while continuing to aggressively promote products that fuel harm. But this is akin to asking Big Tobacco to write its own advertising rules, or asking fast-food giants to lead the fight against obesity. It is a clear conflict of interest. No commercial enterprise built on consumption can be trusted to meaningfully reduce that consumption. The illusion of self-regulation buys time, silences critics, and deflects calls for stronger legislative control.

The same pattern holds for minimum unit pricing (MUP). Introduced in Scotland in 2018, MUP sets a legal floor price per unit of alcohol, targeting cheap, high-strength drinks disproportionately consumed by those at highest risk. Early evaluations have shown reductions in alcohol sales and hospital admissions. Wales followed suit in 2020. But England, despite being home to the largest population and highest overall alcohol burden, has refused to implement it. Industry lobbying played a key role in this decision, warning of impacts on consumers, small businesses, and "responsible drinkers."

Behind this resistance lies a well-funded, well-connected network of alcohol producers, distributors, and trade associations. Bodies like the

Portman Group and the Alcohol Industry Partnership present themselves as promoters of responsible drinking, but their real function is to protect the interests of producers. They resist regulation under the guise of defending consumer freedom, yet privately lobby against evidence-based policies that might reduce harm. Their influence is felt in parliamentary debates, health strategy papers, and even the framing of government-funded education campaigns.

This influence extends into public-facing charities and research bodies. As mentioned earlier, Drinkaware—a major source of alcohol education materials—is funded largely by industry contributions. While it provides helpful resources, it rarely challenges the commercial structures that promote excessive drinking. This is not surprising. No sector voluntarily supports its own dismantling. But it does mean that much of the alcohol "education" in the UK is subtly shaped by those with the most to lose from a drop in consumption.

What we're left with is a policy environment built on contradiction. The NHS spends around £3.5 billion annually dealing with alcohol-related illness and injury, and wider societal costs—including policing, social care, and lost productivity—are estimated at over £21 billion. Yet this public cost is consistently outweighed in political discourse by private profit. The externalities of alcohol harm—broken families, overwhelmed A&Es, court backlogs—are absorbed by society, while the profits flow to private shareholders and Treasury coffers.

This is not unique to the UK. Across Western democracies, alcohol policy is shaped by a blend of cultural exceptionalism and economic expediency. But Britain's case is especially stark because of how systematically alcohol is embedded in its national identity. From "Downing Street drinks" to televised beer ads during football matches, the message is clear: alcohol is not just tolerated, it is celebrated.

And yet, in the very same breath, the government positions itself as tough on drugs. Young people caught with cannabis are criminalised. Partygoers found with ecstasy are vilified. People dependent on heroin are treated as moral failures. Functional drug users are forced into secrecy. But alcohol users—however chaotic, violent, or dependent—are rarely scrutinised. The state's moralising stance on drugs collapses under the weight of its financial reliance on alcohol. Perhaps most galling is that this system creates a two-tier approach to harm. Middle-class drinking is ignored. Working-class dependence is punished. Alcohol's harms are medicalised only once they become unmanageable, while drug harms—many far less severe—are pre-emptively criminalised. What binds these decisions is not evidence, but vested interest.

## Comparative Framing—Alcohol vs Other Drugs

If the UK's approach to substance regulation were genuinely rooted in evidence, logic, or public health, alcohol would be classified as one of the most dangerous drugs in circulation. But it isn't. Instead, we criminalise users of far less harmful substances while enabling, excusing, and even encouraging widespread alcohol use. The contrast between how alcohol is treated and how other drugs are policed exposes a deep incoherence in UK drug policy—one that cannot be explained by harm alone.

In 2010, Professor David Nutt and colleagues published a landmark study in *The Lancet* that sought to compare the harms of 20 different substances using a comprehensive multi-criteria analysis. The study assessed not only the *personal* harm caused to the user—through toxicity, dependency, or physical damage—but also the *social* harm inflicted on others, such as violence, crime, family breakdown, and economic cost. When all factors were combined, alcohol topped the list. Not heroin. Not crack cocaine. Alcohol.

As Nutt explained, "Overall, alcohol was the most harmful drug because it is so widely used and has such devastating consequences both to individuals and to society" (Nutt, 2020, p. 35). Its harm is not just pharmacological but social and structural, amplified by its legal status and widespread cultural acceptance. This finding shocked the political class, but it didn't shift policy. Instead, Nutt was sacked from his role as Chair of the Advisory Council on the Misuse of Drugs the year before, after asserting that ecstasy and cannabis were less harmful than alcohol and tobacco. His dismissal was a watershed moment—not just in drug policy, but in the wider relationship between science and politics. "You cannot have a rational debate about drugs policy in this country," he later wrote, "because the facts are often seen as inconvenient" (Nutt, 2020, p. 14).

The harm scale Nutt developed showed that alcohol scored high across nearly every domain: physical harm to the user, risk of addiction, mental health deterioration, and above all, social harm to others. Heroin and crack ranked high in individual harm but far lower in social impact due to their lower prevalence. Cannabis, LSD, and ecstasy scored far lower in both personal and social harm. Yet these are the substances most criminalised, policed, and stigmatised. Why? Because harm is not the true yardstick of UK drug classification—public perception is.

This becomes clearer when we separate *personal harm* from *societal harm*. Many illicit substances, particularly psychedelics and MDMA, carry relatively low risks when used in controlled settings. Their dangers are largely physiological and individual. But alcohol's social footprint is massive: it fuels interpersonal violence, domestic abuse, sexual assault, drink driving, workplace absenteeism, and criminal damage. Its use by one person can harm dozens of others—physically, emotionally, and economically. And because it is so widely used, these harms are not rare or marginal—they are systemic.

Despite this, alcohol retains cultural legitimacy. When someone drinks to excess, we often ask, "What's going on in their life?" When someone uses heroin, the question becomes, "What's wrong with them?" Drug users are pathologised. Alcohol users are empathised with—until their behaviour becomes unmanageable, by which time the system is already too late to intervene.

This moral framing runs deep. Consider cannabis: possession can still lead to arrest, fines, and criminal records—especially for young, Black, or working-class users. Yet alcohol, which causes more deaths and costs the NHS far more, is available in every corner shop and advertised on national television. A person who uses ecstasy occasionally at festivals risks losing their job or being branded a danger, while a wine-drinking executive with liver damage may be seen as simply stressed.

As Nutt bluntly put it, "The legal status of a drug is a very poor guide to the harms it causes" (*Nutt* 2020, p. 3). And nowhere is that more evident than in the UK's refusal to confront alcohol's true impact.

We speak of "functional alcoholics" as if they're a separate species—those who still hold jobs, raise families, or maintain appearances. Yet we rarely speak of "functional drug users" even though they exist in large numbers. Many professionals use stimulants, painkillers, or cannabis without any visible collapse. But their use must be hidden, for fear of reputational ruin or legal consequence. Functioning drinkers are pitied. Functioning drug users are invisible.

This asymmetry is especially cruel in the context of addiction. People dependent on alcohol are often referred to treatment services, framed as patients. People dependent on heroin or crack are routed through the criminal justice system, framed as offenders. In both cases, the issue is complex, rooted in trauma, poverty, and mental health. But only one group is consistently criminalised, and it's not the group causing the most harm.

There's also a gendered and racialised edge to this hypocrisy. Alcohol violence is overwhelmingly committed by men, yet male drinking is often celebrated as macho, humorous, or simply part of life. Black and Brown drug users, however, are demonised as gang-affiliated or dangerous—regardless of actual behaviour. The state's tolerance for harm, then, is not just about the drug itself, but who is using it, how they are perceived, and what political capital can be extracted from punishing them.

The public health costs of this double standard are enormous. Resources are poured into drug enforcement, while alcohol-related harm continues to rise. Lives are lost not only to substance misuse, but to bad policy: to the decision to prioritise stigma over support, punishment over prevention, and economic gain over evidence. There is no logic to it—only a set of interests that protect alcohol from scrutiny and direct fear elsewhere.

## Conclusion—Time to Reframe the Debate

Alcohol is not just a drug—it is the most dangerous drug in the UK, both in terms of individual health outcomes and its widespread, corrosive impact on society. It contributes to more deaths than all illicit drugs combined, drives violent crime and domestic abuse, burdens the NHS and emergency services, and yet remains legal, promoted, and deeply woven into the fabric of British life. This is not the result of scientific oversight or cultural accident. It is a deliberate, institutionalised contradiction—one that reveals the true priorities of the UK's drug and public health policies.

Throughout this chapter, we've seen how alcohol kills quietly but consistently, disproportionately affecting the poor, the vulnerable, and the socially marginalised. It fuels not only personal tragedy but social harm: hospitalisations, assaults, road deaths, trauma in children, the degradation of public services. These harms are vast, predictable, and preventable. And yet, the state's response is muted—not because the evidence is unclear, but because alcohol is protected by profit, politics, and culture.

We've also seen that alcohol-related violence, especially in domestic settings, is treated differently—often more leniently—than drug-related offending. The courts may recognise that alcohol is an aggravating factor, but society still treats it as a source of individual lapses rather than a structural enabler of violence. Meanwhile, those using criminalised drugs—even ones with far lower harm profiles—face stigma, exclusion, and punishment, regardless of whether they've caused harm to others.

There is no justice in this system. The respectable drinker who causes damage is forgiven; the marginalised drug user who harms no one is criminalised. Public health funding is diverted to managing chaos rather than preventing it. Policy is driven by lobbyists and vested interests, not by harm reduction or compassion. And the most dangerous drug continues to flow freely through supermarkets, sports stadiums, and school staff rooms, shielded from scrutiny by its cultural familiarity and economic utility.

The government's failure to regulate alcohol meaningfully—whether through minimum pricing, advertising bans, or mandatory health warnings—shows how little appetite there is to upset powerful commercial actors or challenge public behaviours that have become normalised. The illusion of "responsible drinking" allows industry to self-regulate, education to stay toothless, and the public to remain misinformed about the true costs of our drinking culture.

This chapter does not argue for prohibition—history has taught us that criminalising widely used substances without addressing underlying social needs creates its own harms. But what we must demand is consistency. If drug policy is to have any credibility, it must be based on actual harm, not historical habit or political convenience. The first step towards that is to be honest: alcohol is a drug. It is addictive. It is destructive. And it is allowed to flourish not because it is safe, but because it is profitable.

Reframing the debate means pulling alcohol out from behind the curtain of respectability and examining it under the same lens we apply to other substances. It means holding producers to account, challenging cultural myths, and ensuring that public health comes before corporate gain. It also means acknowledging that drug users—whether legal or illegal, functional or dependent—deserve support, not stigma, and certainly not policies built on hypocrisy.

In short, the war on drugs has always been a war on *some* drugs—and some people. Alcohol's protected status exposes that war for what it really is: a political tool, not a public health strategy. If we are to move towards a more just and effective approach to substance use, then confronting the real harm caused by alcohol is not optional—it's essential.

## References

Alcohol Change UK. (2022). *Alcohol and health statistics*. Retrieved September 2025, from https://alcoholchange.org.uk/alcohol-facts/fact-sheets/alcohol-statistics

Alcohol Health Alliance. (2021). Commission on Alcohol Harm: Report of Findings. : AHA UK. Retrieved September 2025, from https://ahauk.org/news/commission-on-alcohol-harm-report-published/

Association of Chief Police Officers (ACPO). (2012). *Alcohol and the Night-Time Economy: Key Findings*. ACPO.

HM Revenue & Customs (HMRC). (2023). *Alcohol Bulletin: July 2023*. HMRC. Retrieved September 2025, from https://www.gov.uk/government/statistics/alcohol-bulletin

Home Office. (2021). *Domestic Abuse, England and Wales: Year Ending March 2021*. Office for National Statistics. Retrieved September 2025, from https://www.ons.gov.uk

Institute of Alcohol Studies. (2020). Alcohol and domestic abuse: policy and practice in England. IAS. Retrieved September 2025, from https://www.ias.org.uk

NHS Digital. (2023). *Statistics on Alcohol, England 2023*. NHS Digital. Retrieved September 2025, from https://digital.nhs.uk

Nutt, D. J. (2020). *Drugs Without the Hot Air: Making Sense of Legal and Illegal Drugs* (2nd ed.). UIT Cambridge.

Nutt, D. J., King, L.A. & Phillips, L.D. (2010). Drug harms in the UK: a multicriteria decision analysis. *The Lancet, 376*(9752), 1558–1565. https://doi.org/10.1016/S0140-6736(10)61462-6

Office for National Statistics (ONS). (2022). Crime survey for England and Wales: Drug and alcohol data tables. ONS. Retrieved September 2025, from https://www.ons.gov.uk

Office for National Statistics (ONS). (2023). Alcohol-specific deaths in the UK: 2022 registrations. ONS. Retrieved September 2025, from https://www.ons.gov.uk

Portman Group. (2023). Code of practice on the naming, packaging and promotion of alcoholic drinks. London: Portman Group.

Public Health England. (2018). *The public health burden of alcohol and the effectiveness and cost-effectiveness of alcohol control policies: An evidence review*. PHE.

Women's Aid. (2022). *Domestic abuse and substance use: guidance for professionals*. Women's Aid Federation of England.

CHAPTER 9

# Beyond Prohibition—What a Just, Drug Policy, Could Look Like from Punishment to Possibility: Building a Fair Drug Policy

**Abstract** Chapter Nine explores what a fair, humane, and effective drug policy could look like in the UK by examining international models and outlining seven core principles of reform. Drawing lessons from Portugal's decriminalisation, Israel's state-led medical cannabis programme, and decentralised reforms in the United States, the chapter assesses how other nations have shifted from punishment to public health—and the limitations they still face. In contrast, the UK remains rooted in outdated prohibitionist frameworks, despite rising drug-related deaths, scientific evidence, and growing public support for change. Through critical analysis and grounded policy recommendations, the chapter proposes a blueprint for a just drug policy centred on decriminalisation, harm reduction, scientific credibility, structural equity, and democratic accountability. This is not an abstract vision, but a practical and ethical imperative for saving lives and restoring dignity.

**Keywords** Decriminalisation · Harm reduction · International comparisons · Portugal model medical cannabis · Drug policy reform · Public health · Equity and justice · Policy design · Evidence-based policy



E. Peatfield, *Drugs Disorder by Design*,
https://doi.org/10.1007/978-3-032-07814-8_9

## Introduction

The UK's drug policy has long been shaped not by compassion, evidence, or justice, but by a tangle of political expediency, moral panic, and systemic inequality. As explored in earlier chapters, the current framework punishes the poor and marginalised while turning a blind eye to the drug use of the powerful. Functional users in corporate boardrooms and political circles are rarely scrutinised, while problematic users—often visibly struggling with poverty, trauma, or homelessness—are criminalised and stigmatised. Meanwhile, the far more harmful effects of alcohol are normalised and even celebrated, exposing a glaring contradiction at the heart of British drug legislation.

This chapter turns from critique to possibility. If the system we have is riddled with injustice, what might a just drug policy actually look like? What would it mean to reimagine our approach to drugs—not as a matter of criminal law and punishment, but as a question of public health, human dignity, and social justice?

To answer this, we will examine international examples that offer meaningful alternatives. Portugal's decriminalisation model has gained global recognition for its public health focus, while Israel's state-led innovation around medical cannabis provides a compelling case of science-informed reform. In contrast, the United States reveals the dangers of punitive enforcement and racialised mass incarceration, but also the potential for progressive change at the state level. These models—with all their strengths and shortcomings—offer valuable insights into what is possible, and what should be avoided.

As we explore these comparisons, the question at the core of this chapter is not simply "what works?" but "what is just?" A just drug policy should be grounded in principles of harm reduction, equity, proportionality, and evidence. It must address the root causes of drug-related harm, not just the symptoms. And it must challenge the enduring legacies of stigma, hypocrisy, and structural discrimination that have shaped our current laws.

Crucially, any reform must go beyond the theoretical. Justice in drug policy also demands practicality: policies must be designed with implementation in mind, taking into account real-world constraints and political realities. Support services—from addiction treatment to housing and mental health care—must not only be promised, but *funded*. Without ring-fenced resources and long-term investment, even the most enlightened reforms risk becoming empty gestures. As we will see, the countries that have made real progress have done so by backing policy with infrastructure, investment, and public education.

This chapter aims to draw lessons from abroad not for wholesale adoption, but to provoke a rethink of what justice in drug policy could mean in the UK. At its heart lies a simple truth: criminalisation has failed. The time has come to build something better—and to make sure it actually works.

Having examined the failures and contradictions of current UK drug policy in previous chapters, it becomes clear that reform must be more than symbolic or reactive—it must be principled, purposeful, and anchored in justice. Through my research, policy analysis, and experience on the frontlines of the criminal justice system, six key themes emerge as critical to the creation of a drug policy that is not only effective, but fair. These principles are not abstract ideals; they are practical necessities if we are to shift from a culture of punishment and neglect to one of care, prevention, and proportionality.

First, evidence-based decision-making must replace political gamesmanship. For too long, policy has been driven by newspaper headlines rather than public health data, and by ideological rigidity rather than scientific advice. Second, a commitment to harm reduction should form the moral core of any just system. This means recognising that drug use exists on a spectrum, and that reducing harm—not eliminating use entirely—is both more humane and more realistic. Third, equity and non-discrimination must guide every aspect of reform. The current system disproportionately targets Black and working-class communities, while wealthier, whiter, or more functional users are largely ignored. A just policy must be intentionally anti-racist and class-conscious.

Fourth, proportionality demands that we stop criminalising low-level possession and begin treating drug use—especially non-problematic use—as a matter of health and personal agency, not as a criminal offence. Decriminalisation, where implemented carefully, has proven to reduce incarceration without increasing drug use, and allows for better allocation of law enforcement resources. Fifth, any policy shift must be supported by ring-fenced investment and infrastructure. As the failures of austerity have shown, warm words and white papers mean little if frontline services are underfunded and overstretched. Without sustained and protected funding, especially in treatment, housing, and mental health services, reform risks becoming little more than a paper exercise.

Finally, a just policy must be shaped and sustained through transparency, accountability, and public engagement. People who use drugs, their families, service providers, and affected communities must have a seat at the table. Policy should not be done *to* people but *with* them. This also means that outcomes—whether reduced harm, lower deaths, or improved well-being—must be measurable, public, and open to scrutiny.

These six themes form the backbone of what a just drug policy must entail. In the sections that follow, I will explore how different nations have approached drug policy reform—with varying degrees of success—and assess how these principles have been applied, resisted, or distorted in practice. From Portugal's bold decriminalisation experiment, to Israel's medical innovation, to the fragmented and contradictory landscape of the United States, these international examples offer both inspiration and caution. They remind us that justice is not only a matter of what we do, but how we do it—and whether we are prepared to fund, deliver, and sustain the change we claim to believe in.

## Portugal: Decriminalisation and Harm Reduction in Practice

In 2001, facing one of the highest rates of problematic heroin use in Europe and a spiralling HIV epidemic, Portugal introduced a bold and unprecedented reform: the decriminalisation of all drugs for personal use. This reform, passed under Law 30/2000, did not legalise drugs, but instead reclassified possession of small quantities (up to a 10-day supply) as an administrative offence rather than a criminal one (Hughes & Stevens, 2010, p. 1004). Individuals caught with drugs are no longer prosecuted but referred to Commissions for the Dissuasion of Drug Addiction, which comprise a legal expert, a social worker, and a medical professional. These bodies can recommend treatment, issue fines, or take no action, depending on individual circumstances.

This approach was revolutionary not only in legal terms, but in how it reframed drug use as a public health issue rather than a criminal act. Resources previously directed towards punitive enforcement were reallocated to prevention, treatment, harm reduction, and social reintegration (Greenwald, 2009, p. 17). The reform was part of a broader national drug strategy, grounded in the recognition that punitive drug policy had failed to address addiction, stigma, or the social harms surrounding drug use.

The evidence for Portugal's success is compelling. Between 2001 and 2012, drug-related deaths fell from 80 to 16 per year, one of the lowest rates in the European Union (EMCDDA, 2017, p. 5). New HIV infections among people who inject drugs dropped from 1016 cases in 2001 to just 56 by 2012 (EMCDDA, 2017, p. 6). Meanwhile, drug use did not significantly increase, particularly among young people—a key concern of critics prior to reform. Lifetime drug use among 15–24-year-olds actually declined slightly from 14.1% in 2001 to 12.3% in 2007 (Hughes & Stevens, 2010, p. 1015).

Moreover, treatment uptake increased dramatically. The number of people receiving opioid substitution treatment rose from 6040 in 1999 to over 14,800 by 2008 (Laqueur, 2015, p. 784), and the stigma attached to seeking help was significantly reduced. Portugal's integrated approach—combining decriminalisation with investment in treatment and social services—has since become a model of best practice in global harm reduction circles.

Despite its successes, Portugal's model is not without limitations. Critics have pointed out that while criminal sanctions were removed, stigma persists, particularly towards users of harder drugs (Santos, 2016, p. 108). Moreover, although funding for services increased in the early years, subsequent austerity measures eroded support infrastructure, raising concerns about the sustainability of the model without ring-fenced investment (Quintas, 2019, p. 92). The Dissuasion Commissions themselves vary in their approach, with some adopting a more therapeutic orientation and others leaning towards discipline and control.

Portugal's policy has also not addressed broader social determinants of drug use, such as poverty and housing insecurity, with some users continuing to cycle through informal support networks or remaining in marginalised conditions (Pinto, 2020, p. 66). This reinforces the argument—central to this book—that decriminalisation alone is insufficient without structural support and policy coherence.

For the UK, Portugal offers both a blueprint and a cautionary tale. It demonstrates that decriminalisation, when combined with well-funded public health infrastructure, can reduce harm, improve treatment access, and shift public attitudes. However, it also shows that token reforms without systemic support will fail to deliver long-term justice. The UK's punitive stance continues to criminalise vulnerable people for low-level possession, while treatment services have been gutted by funding cuts and fragmented commissioning (ACMD, 2021, p. 14).

Portugal's model suggests that a proportionate, health-centred, and non-punitive approach is both possible and effective—but only when backed by political will, cross-sector collaboration, and a sustained financial commitment.

## Israel: Medicalisation and State-Led Reform

While Portugal is known for its sweeping decriminalisation of all drugs, Israel has taken a different, but equally instructive, path: one grounded in medicalisation, scientific research, and controlled innovation. Although Israel has not decriminalised all drug use, it is widely recognised as a global leader in medical cannabis research and regulation, offering a unique case of evidence-driven policy in an otherwise conservative drug landscape.

### *From Prohibition to Regulation: The Rise of Medical Cannabis*

Israel's government began formally regulating medical cannabis in the early 1990s, and by 2007, the Ministry of Health had established a dedicated unit—the Medical Cannabis Unit (Yakar)—to oversee approvals, cultivation, and patient access (Zolotov et al., 2018, p. 75). Unlike many countries where cannabis reform has emerged from grassroots activism or court rulings, Israel's policy has been state-led and centrally managed, with a strong emphasis on scientific legitimacy.

The country now supports over 100,000 registered patients, with medical cannabis approved for conditions ranging from chronic pain and cancer to PTSD and epilepsy (Sznitman & Lewis, 2015, p. 450). Cannabis is distributed through licensed growers and pharmacies, and Israeli research institutions receive state backing to conduct clinical trials and pharmacological studies—a level of investment unmatched in the UK.

Israel's approach is characterised by tight regulatory control, clinical oversight, and a clear separation between medical and recreational use, which remains criminalised for the general population. However, in 2019, the government introduced reforms that decriminalised first-time cannabis possession offences through administrative fines rather than prosecution—a modest but symbolic shift towards a less punitive stance (Ben-Zion, 2019, p. 4). Israel's influence in the field of cannabinoid science is profound. The pioneering work of Professor Raphael Mechoulam—who first identified THC in the 1960s—laid the foundation for a national culture of scientific curiosity and legitimacy around cannabis. Today, Israeli universities and biotech firms are at the forefront of cannabis-based medicine, with international collaborations spanning Europe, North America, and Australia (Zohar et al., 2021, p. 113).

This focus on medical innovation has helped normalise cannabis in public discourse, reduce stigma for patients, and build political consensus across ideological lines. While countries like the UK continue to frame cannabis through a law-and-order lens, Israel has increasingly treated it as a pharmaceutical challenge, subject to state regulation rather than moral judgment.

Despite these advances, Israel's drug policy is far from fully progressive. Recreational cannabis remains illegal, and access to medical cannabis is highly stratified, often requiring persistent advocacy from patients and physicians (Golan et al., 2020, p. 28). Critics argue that the system privileges certain medical conditions while excluding vulnerable populations, such as Palestinians living under occupation, who face harsher policing and limited access to care (Cohen & Shalev, 2021, p. 99).

Moreover, Israel's harm reduction strategies are selectively applied. While opioid substitution therapy and methadone maintenance are available, there is less emphasis on decriminalisation for substances beyond cannabis, and no national equivalent to Portugal's holistic support model. In some sectors, especially among religious and conservative populations, stigma remains strong, and drug use continues to be moralised rather than medicalised (Sznitman, 2017, p. 517).

Israel offers a compelling case of how the state can drive reform through scientific leadership and regulatory clarity, particularly in the medical space. For the UK, this raises key questions: Why is medical cannabis access still limited, bureaucratic, and inconsistent, despite legalisation in 2018? Why is so little public investment directed towards cannabinoid research? Israel's model shows that state infrastructure, investment, and legitimacy matter—and that medical reform need not be at odds with public safety or social values.

However, Israel also reminds us that medicalisation is not a panacea. Without broader reforms to policing, public health, and social equity, medical cannabis policies can entrench existing inequalities or serve only a narrow population. A truly just UK drug policy must combine the evidence-led ethos of Israel's medical system with the inclusive, decriminalising impulse seen in Portugal.

## The United States: Contradictions, Criminalisation, and Corporate Reform

Few countries illustrate the contradictions of modern drug policy more starkly than the United States. On one hand, the United States remains the epicentre of the punitive "War on Drugs," responsible for some of the world's highest incarceration rates and deeply racialised enforcement. On the other, it is also a laboratory for state-level experimentation, with dozens of jurisdictions legalising cannabis, adopting decriminalisation measures, or expanding harm reduction services. The result is a fragmented policy landscape marked by both innovation and enduring injustice.

The punitive foundations of modern drug control cannot be understood without recognising the US's formative role in shaping international law. The United States was a primary architect of the United Nations Single Convention on Narcotic Drugs (1961), which enshrined prohibitionist frameworks into global treaty obligations (Bewley-Taylor, 2012, p. 38). American pressure ensured that the treaty emphasised criminal sanctions and eradication strategies over harm reduction or cultural nuance. Successive US administrations—particularly during the Cold War—exported a moralised, zero-tolerance model of drug control, tying foreign aid and diplomatic relations to compliance with US-backed enforcement strategies (Crick et al., 2013, p. 3).

This has had lasting consequences: many countries, including the UK, adopted legislation and enforcement patterns that mirrored the US' focus on criminalisation, even when domestic evidence pointed in other directions. The Misuse of Drugs Act 1971 was deeply influenced by these international norms, despite its lack of a clear public health foundation.

## The War on Drugs at Home: Inequality and Incarceration

Domestically, US drug policy has been devastating. The Controlled Substances Act (1970) established a rigid classification system that continues to underpin federal prohibition, often at odds with scientific evidence (Nutt et al., 2007, p. 1047). Enforcement escalated dramatically in the 1980s and 1990s, particularly under Reagan and Clinton, leading to the incarceration of millions for non-violent drug offences.

By 2020, over 1.15 million arrests were made for drug violations, the vast majority for simple possession (ACLU, 2021, p. 12). Despite similar drug use rates across racial groups, Black Americans are nearly four times more likely to be arrested for cannabis possession than white Americans (Alexander, 2012, p. 96). Michelle Alexander's seminal work, *The New Jim Crow*, argues that the War on Drugs has functioned as a system of racial and social control, entrenching disadvantage through criminal records, voting restrictions, and economic exclusion (Alexander, 2012, pp. 158–161).

## Reform from Below: State-Level Legalisation and Decriminalisation

Despite federal intransigence, reform has emerged at the state level. California legalised medical cannabis in 1996, and since then, over 23 states have legalised recreational cannabis, with others pursuing decriminalisation or harm reduction reforms (Kilmer, 2022, p. 13). Oregon decriminalised possession of all drugs in 2020, redirecting users to treatment via administrative citations rather than arrest—a bold move inspired in part by the Portuguese model (Drug Policy Alliance, 2021, p. 7).

Some states, like New York and Illinois, have explicitly sought to embed racial justice provisions in their cannabis laws, aiming to reverse the damage of previous enforcement by prioritising licences and reinvestment in historically criminalised communities (McVey & Nadelmann, 2021, p. 22). However, progress has been uneven. Many new cannabis markets are dominated by large private companies, raising concerns about the commodification of reform and the exclusion of grassroots actors from the legal industry.

The US example is both a warning and an opportunity. It shows the devastating impact of punitive policy on marginalised communities and how politics, not science, has driven the global prohibitionist agenda. It also demonstrates how decentralised, bottom-up reform can drive meaningful change—though not without risks. The UK should take note of both: the dangers of market capture, the limits of decriminalisation without structural repair, and the need to explicitly address the racial and class-based harms of past enforcement.

Moreover, the US's influence on global drug law reminds us that policy is never neutral. The systems we inherit often reflect historical power dynamics, not ethical or scientific coherence. To move forward, the UK must not only consider domestic reform but also advocate for a rethinking of the international frameworks that continue to pressure countries into prohibition.

## Comparative Analysis: Where the UK Stands

Across Portugal, Israel, and the United States, we see divergent responses to drug use—from public health-centred decriminalisation to state-led medical innovation and decentralised reform. Each model reflects unique cultural, political, and economic contexts, but they share a willingness to experiment, to reassess punitive norms, and to embrace pragmatism. The UK, by contrast, has remained largely resistant to meaningful reform, clinging to outdated legislation and rhetorical gestures while failing to address structural injustices or deliver consistent public health outcomes.

## Criminalisation as the Default Setting

The UK continues to criminalise people for low-level possession, with over 100,000 drug offences recorded annually, the majority relating to personal use (Home Office, 2023). Unlike Portugal, which treats possession as an administrative matter, or many US' states where possession is no longer an offence, UK law frames even non-problematic use as criminal conduct, with life-changing consequences. A criminal record for a minor drug offence can restrict employment, housing, education, and international travel—a disproportionate penalty for behaviour that is often harmless or functional. While some police forces have introduced diversion schemes, these remain patchy, unregulated, and easily reversed. In the absence of national guidance or legal reform, postcode justice prevails, where one's treatment depends more on geography than behaviour. This inconsistency contradicts the principle of equal treatment under the law, undermining both legitimacy and effectiveness (Release, 2022, p. 8).

Though harm reduction is now referenced in official strategies, in practice it is undervalued and underfunded. The 2021 *From Harm to Hope* strategy made welcome commitments to increase treatment funding, but only after a decade of austerity that devastated local services (Black, 2020, p. 11). Funding remains time-limited and politically precarious, with no legal requirement for ring-fenced spending by local authorities. Many areas still lack access to core interventions like naloxone distribution, heroin-assisted treatment, or trauma-informed care.

The UK also lags behind international peers in establishing evidence-based innovations. While Canada and Switzerland operate supervised consumption facilities, and Portugal integrates health, housing, and social work through dissuasion commissions, UK efforts remain siloed and often blocked by central government. In Scotland, proposals for safe drug consumption rooms have been stalled for years by Westminster's refusal to adjust legal barriers (UK Parliament, 2023). This institutional inertia costs lives: the UK continues to have Europe's highest drug-related death rate, a fact rarely addressed with the urgency it deserves (ONS, 2023).

## Scientific Hypocrisy and Political Avoidance

Scientific input into drug policy remains marginalised. As noted earlier in this book, the sacking of Professor David Nutt in 2009 after he stated that alcohol and tobacco were more harmful than cannabis or ecstasy (Nutt et al., 2007) illustrates the UK's resistance to evidence that challenges moralistic or populist narratives. Successive governments have maintained the classification of cannabis as a Class B drug, despite substantial evidence to the contrary and widespread public support for reform.

The limited rollout of medical cannabis following its legalisation in 2018 is another example of political performance without delivery. Although technically legal, access via the NHS remains virtually nonexistent, with just a handful of prescriptions issued due to bureaucratic and clinical obstacles (Sumnall, 2023, p. 3). Patients are left either to suffer without care or turn to costly private providers. Meanwhile, the UK remains one of the world's largest exporters of medical cannabis, creating a perverse situation in which British patients are denied access to drugs cultivated domestically for profit (Hawkins, 2021, p. 14).

One of the most persistent failures of UK drug policy is its disproportionate impact on marginalised communities. Stop-and-search powers, still widely used under Section 23 of the Misuse of Drugs Act, are applied overwhelmingly to Black and working-class individuals. Shiner et al. (2018, p. 22) found that Black people are nine times more likely to be stopped and searched for drugs, despite no significant difference in usage rates. These patterns are not accidental; they reflect a system designed to police visibility and social vulnerability, while leaving functional use by professionals, students, and politicians largely untouched.

The result is a system that criminalises the symptoms of poverty, trauma, and exclusion, while ignoring the structural causes. Drug use in itself is not always the problem—it is the unequal way in which it is perceived, policed, and punished that produces injustice.

## A Cautious State in a Changing World

While other nations move, however imperfectly, towards evidence-informed, compassionate drug policy, the UK remains stuck in a reactive, risk-averse posture, unwilling to lead or even follow. It clings to outdated laws, underfunds its services, and targets the vulnerable, all while claiming to act in the name of public safety. The result is a policy landscape defined more by inertia than intention, where symbolic crackdowns take the place of structural reform, and the loudest voices often come from tabloids, not treatment centres.

This refusal to engage seriously with the evidence has real and devastating consequences. Drug-related deaths continue to rise, communities most in need of support face criminalisation rather than care, and vital services are left to compete for shrinking pots of funding. The broader costs—to the NHS, to the criminal justice system, to families and social cohesion—are immense. Yet despite this, reform is repeatedly portrayed as a political risk rather than a moral imperative. The stigma surrounding drug use remains a powerful barrier, not just for users but for policy-makers, many of whom fear backlash more than they fear the loss of life caused by the current system.

If the UK is to create a fair, functional, and just drug policy, it must learn from the countries examined here—not by copying wholesale, but by adapting proven principles to its own unique social and institutional landscape. Decriminalisation, harm reduction, scientific integrity, and long-term investment are not radical demands—they are the minimum standards of a civilised, coherent, and ethical approach to drug use. These principles are not simply about reducing harm; they are about recognising the full humanity of those who use drugs, and the collective responsibility we share to build a system that supports, rather than punishes, those in need.

The final section of this chapter outlines what such a policy could look like in practice—and what it would take to move from words to meaningful action.

## The 7 Key Features of a Just UK Drug Policy

If the UK is to move beyond punitive tradition and towards a drug policy grounded in justice, public health, and evidence, then it must be willing to reimagine not just how drugs are classified or policed, but how drug use is understood and addressed in society. This reimagining requires structural change, cultural shifts, and political will—but above all, it requires a commitment to treating people who use drugs not as problems to be managed, but as citizens with rights, needs, and dignity.

The following are the core features of a just and workable drug policy for the UK, informed by the lessons of Portugal, Israel, and the United States, and shaped by the failings of the current system.

Decriminalisation of personal possession of all drugs—following the Portuguese model—would allow the UK to divert individuals away from the criminal justice system and into health and support services. This shift should be embedded in statute, not left to police discretion, to ensure consistency and fairness. Evidence from Portugal and Oregon shows that decriminalisation does not increase drug use, but it does reduce incarceration, stigma, and harm (Drug Policy Alliance, 2021; Hughes & Stevens, 2010).

Rather than facing arrest, people found in possession should be referred to multi-disciplinary assessment panels, similar to Portugal's Dissuasion Commissions, where the focus is on need, not punishment.

Ring-Fenced Investment in Health and Social Support—No reform will succeed without a parallel investment in services. The UK must ring-fence funding for treatment, harm reduction, housing support, and mental health care—with dedicated national minimum standards. Funding should be protected in law and allocated based on local need, ensuring that services are not vulnerable to political cycles or austerity cuts.

Public Health England (now replaced by OHID) previously reported that every £1 spent on drug treatment saves £4 in social costs (PHE, 2017). Long-term investment is both economically prudent and morally essential.

Evidence-Led Drug Classification and Policy Reform—The Misuse of Drugs Act 1971 and its scheduling system should be replaced or radically overhauled, with an independent scientific body tasked with drug classification based on relative harm—physical, psychological, and social—as initially proposed by Nutt et al. (2007). This body must be free from political interference and accountable to Parliament, not individual ministers.

Policy decisions should be based on transparent, peer-reviewed evidence and regularly updated in line with emerging research and health data. This includes removing cannabis from Class B and reclassifying substances like psilocybin to enable research into their medical applications.

A National Harm Reduction Strategy—A just drug policy must have harm reduction at its core—not as an optional add-on but as an integrated national strategy, supported by law. I would suggest that this should include: Supervised drug consumption rooms, Widespread naloxone distribution. Needle and syringe programmes. Heroin-assisted treatment (HAT). Testing services at festivals and community sites.

These interventions are cost-effective, life-saving, and backed by decades of global evidence (ACMD, 2016; EMCDDA, 2023).

Addressing Structural Inequalities and Reparative Justice—The UK must confront the disproportionate impact of drug laws on racialised and marginalised communities. This includes: A formal review of discriminatory policing and prosecution patterns. The expungement of low-level drug convictions. Reinvestment of funds from any future legal cannabis market into communities most harmed by the drug war, as seen in New York's equity-focused legalisation (McVey & Nadelmann, 2021).

### *Drug Policy Must Actively Contribute to Social Repair, not Reinforce Inequality.*

Improved Access to Medical Cannabis and Controlled Innovation—The current medical cannabis framework is functionally broken. A just system would: Remove unnecessary barriers to NHS prescribing, Expand practitioner training and public guidance. Create a regulated domestic supply chain for medicinal use. Promote state-supported research and innovation, similar to Israel's model.

This would de-stigmatise treatment, lower costs, and improve patient outcomes while safeguarding against irresponsible commercial expansion.

Ongoing Public Engagement and Accountability—Finally, drug policy reform must be grounded in public consultation, lived experience, and ongoing transparency. This includes:

Regular national drug summits involving service users, clinicians, academics, and community groups. A statutory obligation for government to report on drug policy outcomes, including treatment access, deaths, and equity metrics. Public education campaigns to reduce stigma and raise awareness of safer use practices. Justice is not a one-time policy event—it is a sustained process of inclusion, evaluation, and correction.

## References


ACLU. (2021). *A tale of two countries: Racially targeted arrests in the era of marijuana reform*. ACLU.

Advisory Council on the Misuse of Drugs (ACMD). (2016). *Reducing opioid-related deaths in the UK*. Home Office.

Advisory Council on the Misuse of Drugs (ACMD). (2021). *Review of drug treatment funding in england*. Home Office.

Alexander, M. (2012). *The new jim crow: Mass incarceration in the age of colorblindness*. The New Press.

Ben-Zion, R. (2019). Israel's cannabis decriminalisation: Balancing reform and public order. *Drugs and Society, 34*(1), 1–7.

Bewley-Taylor, D. (2012). *International drug control: Consensus fractured*. Cambridge University Press.

Black, C. (2020). *Review of drugs: Phase one report*. Home Office.

Cohen, H., & Shalev, N. (2021). Drug policy in Israel/Palestine: Disparities, access, and control. In *Drugs, politics and power in the Middle East* (pp. 85–104). Zed Books.

Crick, E., Mclean, S., & Bewley-Taylor, D. (2013). *Legislating for health and human rights: Model drug laws*. Global Drug Policy Observatory.

Drug Policy Alliance. (2021). *Oregon decriminalization report: One year later*. DPA.

EMCDDA. (2017). *Portugal: Drug policy profile*. European Monitoring Centre for Drugs and Drug Addiction.

EMCDDA. (2023). *European drug report 2023: Trends and developments*. European Monitoring Centre for Drugs and Drug Addiction.

Golan, M., Weiss, D., & Elkayam, O. (2020). Barriers to medical cannabis access in Israel: Patients' perspectives'. *Israel Medical Journal, 22*(3), 25–33.

Greenwald, G. (2009). *Drug decriminalization in Portugal: Lessons for creating fair and successful drug policies*. Cato Institute.

Hawkins, A. (2021). *The UK cannabis market: Profits, patients and prohibition*. Transform Drug Policy Foundation.

Hughes, C., & Stevens, A. (2010). What can we learn from the portuguese decriminalization of illicit drugs? *British Journal of Criminology, 50*(6), 999–1022.

Kilmer, B. (2022). Navigating cannabis legalization: Research gaps and policy choices. *Annual Review of Criminology, 5*, 1–20.

Laqueur, H. (2015). Uses and abuses of drug decriminalization in Portugal. *Law and Social Inquiry, 40*(3), 746–781.

McVey, J., & Nadelmann, E. (2021). Equity in legalisation: Correcting the harms of the drug war. *Journal of Drug Policy Analysis, 14*(2), 17–25.

Nutt, D., King, L., Saulsbury, W., & Blakemore, C. (2007). Development of a rational scale to assess the harm of drugs of potential misuse. *The Lancet, 369*(9566), 1047–1053.

Office for National Statistics (ONS). (2023). *Deaths related to drug poisoning in England and Wales: 2022 registrations*. ONS.

Home Office. (2023). *Crime outcomes in england and Wales: Data tables*. UK Government.

Pinto, M. (2020). Beyond decriminalisation: Challenges of social integration in Portugal's drug policy. *Drugs and Alcohol Today, 20*(1), 63–70.

Public Health England (PHE). (2017). *An evidence review of the outcomes that can be expected of drug misuse treatment in England*. PHE.

Quintas, A. (2019). Resisting austerity: The shrinking of Portugal's harm reduction infrastructure. *International Journal of Drug Policy, 69*, 90–95.

Release. (2022). *Policing and diversion: A national picture*. Release.

Santos, M. (2016). Stigma and the dissuasion commissions in Portugal: A mixed bag. *Drugs: Education, Prevention and Policy, 23*(2), 105–112.

Shiner, M., Carre, Z., Delsol, R., & Eastwood, N. (2018). *The colour of injustice: 'Race', drugs and law enforcement in England and Wales*. Release.

Sumnall, H. (2023). Why is NHS medical cannabis access still so difficult? *Addiction Today, 38*(1), 2–4.

Sznitman, S. (2017). The politics of cannabis policy in Israel: Between prohibition and reform. *Contemporary Drug Problems, 44*(4), 506–521.

Sznitman, S., & Lewis, N. (2015). Is cannabis being normalised in Israel? Medicalisation and stigma. *International Journal of Drug Policy, 26*(5), 446–453.

UK Parliament. (2023, June 6). *Debate on safe drug consumption facilities*. Hansard, House of Commons.

Zohar, A., Meiri, D., & Lahav, E. (2021). Medical cannabis innovation in israel: Scientific culture and policy outcomes. *Journal of Cannabis Research, 3*(1), 110–120.

Zolotov, Y., Vulfsons, S., & Sznitman, S. (2018). Medical cannabis in Israel: The politics of research, regulation and access. *Israel Journal of Health Policy Research, 7*(1), 72–81.

CHAPTER 10

# Disorder by Design—What Now?

**Abstract** This final chapter argues that the failures of UK drug policy are not accidental but structurally produced—a disorder by design. It synthesises the book's central findings to show how political interests, media narratives, and moral panics consistently override scientific evidence, resulting in a system that perpetuates harm rather than reducing it. The chapter demonstrates how the selective criminalisation of certain drugs, and of the people who use them, reinforces class and racial inequalities while protecting functional users, corporate interests, and the alcohol industry. It highlights how evidence-based reforms have repeatedly been sidelined, from the dismissal of scientific advisors to the marginalisation of harm-reduction models. Ultimately, the chapter contends that meaningful reform requires acknowledging that the current system operates exactly as intended: to regulate morality, maintain social hierarchies, and obscure the state's complicity in producing drug-related harm. Only by exposing this design can a just, health-focused, and evidence-led drug policy emerge.

**Keywords** Drug policy reform · State-produced harm · Moral panic · Evidence suppression · Criminalisation · Structural inequality · Harm reduction · Political ideology · Social justice · Policy design


E. Peatfield, *Drugs Disorder by Design*,
https://doi.org/10.1007/978-3-032-07814-8_10

Having experienced drugs, drug use, and drug abuse firsthand—personally, as a bouncer, criminologist, and magistrate—it has always confounded me why UK drug policy remains so unscientific and so invested in distorted visions of morality. Decades of criminalisation have done little to reduce harm, support users, or promote public safety. Instead, they have produced a system that punishes the poor, excuses the privileged, and consistently ignores the evidence.

Across this book, we have traced how drug policy in the UK has evolved not as a response to harm or risk, but as a mechanism of social control. From the colonial foundations of early drug laws to the punitive architecture of the Misuse of Drugs Act 1971, the UK has chosen a path of prohibition, criminalisation, and denial. At every turn, policy has been shaped by media pressure, political gain, and moral panic—not by science, not by health outcomes, and certainly not by justice.

We have seen how the criminalisation of drug users sustains inequality and compounds trauma. The law is applied selectively, targeting those who are most visible and vulnerable, while shielding those whose use is hidden by privilege. Functional drug use is normalised—even celebrated—in certain circles, while problematic use is met with punishment and stigma. This double standard is not incidental; it is built into the very logic of UK drug enforcement.

The consequences are devastating. We have some of the highest drug-related death rates in Europe. Drug-related harm continues to rise. Services are underfunded, fragmented, and overwhelmed. Meanwhile, alcohol—a drug responsible for the most significant levels of harm—remains not just legal, but glorified, protected by commercial interests and cultural traditions. This policy landscape is incoherent, unjust, and unsustainable.

And yet, change is possible.

As explored in Chapter Nine, international examples provide clear evidence that a different approach can work. Portugal's decriminalisation strategy, Israel's state-backed medical cannabis system, and progressive reforms in parts of the United States show what can be achieved when policy is rooted in public health, equity, and evidence. These models are not perfect, but they offer practical alternatives to punishment-based systems. More importantly, they demonstrate political courage—a quality sorely lacking in the UK drug policy debate.

A just UK drug policy would begin with the decriminalisation of personal possession, backed by guaranteed investment in treatment, housing, and mental health support. It would overhaul the drug classification system to reflect actual risk and scientific consensus. It would embed harm reduction as a national strategy, treat users with dignity, and repair the deep social inequalities perpetuated by decades of disproportionate enforcement. It would also require public transparency, democratic accountability, and ongoing engagement with people who use drugs and those who support them.

None of this is revolutionary. It is, in fact, the bare minimum for a policy that claims to serve the public good. The UK's continued reliance on criminalisation is not only ineffective—it is unethical. It wastes resources, destroys lives, and erodes trust in the very systems meant to protect us.

This book has sought to expose not just the outcomes of failed policy, but the design behind it—how our laws and institutions have created and sustained a drug regime that is neither rational nor fair. It is a system that works precisely as intended: to manage disorder, maintain hierarchy, and offer the illusion of control.

But illusions only last so long.

It is time to stop punishing people for drug use and start building systems that support health, dignity, and truth. The evidence is clear. The models exist. The harm is measurable.

What's missing is the will to change.

# Index





E. Peatfield, *Drugs Disorder by Design*,
https://doi.org/10.1007/978-3-032-07814-8

FSC
www.fsc.org
MIX
Papier | Fördert gute Waldnutzung
FSC® C083411

Kolibri 360 GmbH
Ferdinand-Jühlke-Straße 7
99095 Erfurt, Deutschland
produktsicherheit@kolibri360.de